STEPPE DREAMS

CENTRAL EURASIA IN CONTEXT SERIES

Douglas Northrop, Editor

STEPPE DREAMS

Time, Mediation, *and* Postsocialist Celebrations
in Kazakhstan

MARGARETHE ADAMS

University of Pittsburgh Press

Published by the University of Pittsburgh Press, Pittsburgh, Pa., 15260
Copyright © 2020, University of Pittsburgh Press
Manufactured in the United States of America
Printed on acid-free paper
10 9 8 7 6 5 4 3 2 1

Cataloging-in-Publication data is available from the Library of Congress

ISBN 13: 978-0-8229-4614-4
ISBN 10: 0-8229-4614-9

Cover image: Opera and Ballet Theater in Astana, Kazakhstan.
Cover design: Melissa Dias-Mandoly

I wish to dedicate this book to Dina Intysheva, lovely friend, who taught me so much about love, and life, and Kazakhstan. I still miss you and think of you so often.

CONTENTS

ACKNOWLEDGMENTS

I am most grateful to my Kazakh friends and to all those whose "deep hanging out" allowed me to gain an understanding of so many aspects of life in Kazakhstan. I especially wish to thank Bagila Bukharbaeva, Zaure Batayeva, Alessandro Frigerio (honorary Kazakh), Nargis Kassenova, Aliya Kuryshzhanova, Margarita Madanova, Bakhytgul Niyazgul, Bakhytgul Salykhova, Auken and Maira Tungatarova, and Zhar Zardykhan. I have left many others in Kazakhstan unnamed—but wish to thank all the acquaintances and interviewees who so richly contributed to this ethnography.

I am thankful to my friends and colleagues who offered support and friendship through the years of study and fieldwork: Stefan Fiol, Angela Glaros, Sarah Long, Tony Perman, Jennifer Fraser, and Sarah Phillips.

I would like to express my gratitude to all the wonderful writers and scholars who offered invaluable advice and guidance in various stages of this project. I especially thank Donna Buchanan, Sarah Fuller, Deborah Heckert, Erika Honisch, Judith Lochhead, Lilia Kaganovsky, Stephen Decatur Smith, August Sheehy, Ronald Grigor Suny, Benjamin Tausig, and Tom Turino.

To my wonderful Central Asianist, anthro, and ethnomusicology colleagues with whom I have collaborated, argued, and intensely *thought* in one way or another—Alessandra Ciucci, Heejin Kim, Svetlana Peshkova, Megan Rancier, Evan Rapport, and Jane Sugarman—I have learned so much from our discussions and am very grateful for your insights and brilliant theorizations.

Several people ushered me into the wonderful world of ethnomusicology through music—Donna Buchanan, Daphne Hanning, Kevin Moss, Dmitrii Pokrovsky, and Tamara Smyslova—as well as my two Kazakh qobyz teachers, Sayan Akmolda and Sersengali Zhumazbaev, who helped me understand this beautiful instrument. To you I can only express my gratitude through song—so I will have to do it in person.

This book would not have been possible without generous financial support through Fulbright; the Social Science Research Council; the Eurasia Program; and Stony Brook University.

I am especially grateful to Douglas Northrop, editor of the Central Eurasia in Context series, and Peter Kracht, director of the University of Pittsburgh Press, for seeing the value in my work, and to the anonymous readers for their careful and encouraging appraisal of *Steppe Dreams*.

Finally, I wish to acknowledge my wonderful parents, Judith Adams and Arlon Adams, as well as Tatiana Stremlin, and Yelena and Joseph Stremlin, for always encouraging and loving me; my sister, Kate, for always being there to listen; my brothers for being the best uncles ever; and finally, Boris, for always being there, with patience and warm hands. And most especially, I thank my darling girls, Sofie and Sara, who survived it all with such strength and humor, and who always cheered me on.

STEPPE DREAMS

INTRODUCTION

Saturday morning just before show time, on a little side street off Panfilov Park, children line up with their parents in front of the kiosk of the Kazakh State Puppet Theater. A printed placard outside the theater announces today's show, "Prazdnik Prodalzhaetsya"—"The Holiday Continues." It is 2005, but this show is a remnant of the Soviet era, its colorful cast of character—one from each former republic—still popular with the young theater-goers. This central area of Almaty is beautiful, the gingerbread trimming on the nineteenth-century pastel colored buildings mingling with the grey concrete fixedness of Soviet-era structures. The ragged, imposing stateliness of the state puppet theater seems to borrow its grandeur from disparate eras, as if theater has just arrived, hobbling but upright, into the present.

Time is often described as marching inexorably forward—or flooding in like the tide, mighty and unstoppable, washing over the landscape. This book is rather an exploration of the way that time meanders and eddies, lingering here and there in pools, collecting in the present in unexpected forms. We perceive time unevenly, piecemeal, in flashes and fragments. Emotional or whimsical engagements with the past and the future—memories, regrets, projections, and hopeful reveries—crowd into our present, framing our histories and our predictions for future happiness. This book concerns the political significance of temporality in Kazakhstan and its reverberating effects in the personal lives of Kazakhstanis. I am particularly interested in what we can learn from temporal juxtapositions, instabilities, and contradictions. Kazakhstan's political, religious, and secular celebrations in Almaty, the focus of this book, provide a particularly rich source for examining temporality. Like political holidays in many countries, whether newly established or with a long history, public celebrations in Kazakhstan often present utopic visions of the future while staking claims to the past. Like dreams, such images and music continually refract and echo, carrying temporal meanings about nationhood, about our possible or promised futures. Public holidays are further complicated temporally by the fact that they may mark events through refractions of radically different historical and political views. In Kazakhstani holiday concerts, films, and interviews, these unstable and contradictory temporal framings can help illuminate social and political instabilities and uncertainties in post-Soviet Kazakhstan.

I first came to Kazakhstan as a student of the Kazakh language in the summer of 2003, my toddler daughter in tow, in anticipation of future ethnographic research there. Since that time I have spent nearly four years in Kazakhstan and neighboring regions in Xinjiang, China, and western Mongolia, in numerous research trips from 2004 to 2015. My initial plan, to cover a calendar year's worth of celebration, gradually expanded to an exploration of how temporality and political ideology intertwine in Kazakhstani culture, particularly in music, film, and television. What began as an ethnography of live holiday concerts on the square, children's puppet shows, and school plays, grew to include televised programming, seasonal music videos, advertising, and habits of holiday viewing. As much as possible, I have worked with a wide swath of interlocutors, preferring not to privilege performers, but rather to draw from interviews and conversations with Kazakhstanis of disparate professions and economic status. At the same time, my work with musicians, including interviews, music lessons, and research trips to various music schools around Kazakhstan, has helped to provide a fuller picture of Kazakhstani music history, pedagogy, and cultural import and reception. In addition to working with many Kazakhs and ethnic Russians, I have also spent a good deal of time with Korean, Jewish, and Uighur communities in Almaty, in an attempt to convey a sense of the astounding diversity of Kazakhstan's population. To research cross-border ties and differences, I spent several months in the fall of 2005 and the winter and spring of 2006 conducting research with Kazakhs in western Mongolia and Xinjiang.

THEORETICAL ENGAGEMENTS

In theorizing political, conceptual, and experiential aspects of time in twenty-first-century Kazakhstan, I draw on theories of temporality from cultural anthropology, philosophy, and archaeology. I am interested in the ways scholars from different fields contemplate the nonlinearity of time, variously describing it as layered, folded, pointillistic, and "percolating," as the past bubbles up to the surface to meet the present. Taken together, these descriptions paint a picture of a turbulence and disorder—a chaotic multiplicity of temporal experiences. Scholars have also examined how power and time are intertwined, as imperial pasts continually press on the present—a powerful imprint, affecting the social and political shape of the present. *Steppe Dreams* examines the political, public aspects of temporality, particularly during state holidays, while simultaneously investigating the personal, interior, and emotional aspects of the way time is experienced.

Among the temporal aspects I examine are the political and economic facets of temporality (the "precarious present"), and the affective outcomes of failed or unstable socioeconomic systems. Anna Tsing theorizes the social, environmental, and economic conditions of the precarious present. "Modernization was supposed to fill the world—both communist and capitalist—with jobs," Tsing writes (2015, 3), but what remains is this state of precarity, in which "survivors" face both the ideological void of broken promises and expectations, and the harsh reality of "much more irregular livelihoods" (Tsing 2015, 3). In considering Tsing's ethnographic study, which examines the ways in which the marginalized imaginatively survive in the "ruins" of late capitalism, I suggest that postsocialist and postsecular societies represent a particular strain of precarity growing out of the turbulence of the post-Soviet transition and its aftermath. I find Tsing's theorization of precarity particularly useful in discussing Kazakhstanis' ways of coping with crises of faith and survival, particularly in my investigations of evangelical conversions, missionizing and worship in postsocialist Kazakhstan (chapter 5) and the reinvigoration of older practices like faith healing and shrine pilgrimage (chapter 7).

Steppe Dreams examines the way in which the Soviet past continues to press on the present in Kazakhstan, and the ways that this affects Kazakhstani citizens. In considering the enduring Soviet legacy in Kazakhstan, I have found Ann Laura Stoler's theorization of *duress* relevant. Stoler's *duress*—the continued durability of imperial formations—aptly describes how Soviet ideologies and institutions continue to influence Kazakhstani culture (Stoler 2016, 1). While Stoler's concept of *duress* is concerned with how the press of the imperial past exerts influence in the present to create and maintain social, political, and ecological dynamics, I consider its cultural applications to help elucidate how post-Soviet societies are shaped in part by their Soviet pasts. In Kazakhstan, as I will discuss, both institutional and ideological structural remains endure through Kazakhstani society, influencing both social and political arenas (such as demographic policy)—as well as cultural spheres such as the teaching and patronage of music and the arts. Stoler argues that some of the most pressing issues of the present—social inequalities, economic and ecological disasters—"are features of our current global landscape whose etiologies are steeped in the colonial histories of which they have been, and in some cases continue to be, a part" (Stoler 2016, 3). If many of the present conditions of inequality, precarity, and economic instability, are "tied to . . . imperial formations" (3), I am interested in how Soviet social and political structures continue to exert influence in Kazakhstan. My examination of enduring modes of habit, celebration, place-naming, and the persistence of Soviet ideologies (such as "Friendship of the Peoples") expands on Stoler's concept of duress, as I consider the durability of ideological and temporal structures from the Soviet era.

Another central concern of this book is the way that the state—and its citizens—envision the future. In this, I have been inspired by the work of Sara Ahmed, who theorizes the political and economic aspects of temporality, stressing futurity and expectation rather than the influence of regimes past. In my work on pilgrimage (chapter 7), I examine how hopes for the future intersect with economic and social precarity among my interlocutors. In other words, I am interested in how changing government policy, economics, and social structure affect individual lives on a personal level. In this way, Ahmed's discussion connecting happiness to capitalism intersects with my interest in studying the effects of the transition to market economy in the postsocialist world. In examining the expectations and the work of pursuing happiness in a capitalist context, Ahmed takes up an aspect of modern precarity (2010; 2011). Her examination stresses the sense of contingency involved with happiness—the "hap" of happiness, that considers the thwarted expectations of stability and bounty in an uneasy market economy. Ahmed's theorization of happiness in a capitalist society is inherently connected to this struggle with precarity; happiness for some is not an attainable goal, but rather an endless pursuit.

Along with Ahmed's work on affect and happiness, scholarship on the affective aspects of time includes Edward Casey's theorization of *perdura-*

nce, emotion and commemoration (Casey 2000); and Vincent Crapanzano on imaginative horizons (Crapanzano 2004). Casey's theorization of perdurance, a lastingness of the past in the present, is particularly useful in thinking about the continued relevance of past historical events, and their commemorations in the present. Elaborating on the concept of perdurance in my study of the May 9 commemorations of Victory Day in Kazakhstan (chapter 6), I show how reframings of central tropes of the Great Patriotic War (World War II) help to maintain the relevance of the past in the present. Crapanzano attends to the intersections of affect and temporality, but focuses on the anticipations of the future. I engage with Crapanzano's theories of horizon in my examinations of the utopic imaginings of Kazakhstan's future, particularly as a mediator between East and West (chapter 7). I also consider the role of futurity in shrine pilgrimage, especially in the ways that pilgrims try to enact their own futures, to imagine their desires into being through pilgrimage.

To elucidate how temporality becomes entangled with place, *Steppe Dreams* explores how multiple temporalities adhere to particular places and objects. In the varied theorizations of scholars such as Erika Doss and Shannon Dawdy, time swirls around monuments and structures anchored in place, their temporally inflected meanings gathering on the surface, as palimpsests and patinas, and in the layers of earth from eras past. Erika Doss in her *Memorial Mania* (2010) theorizes time by considering historical monuments as palimpsests, revealing layers of different times and multiple meanings. I am interested in how places (and emplaced objects) from both the recent and ancient pasts—such as the public square, memorial statues, and Kazakhstan's petroglyphs—accumulate significance, and how these meanings resonate in the present. The anthropologist Shannon Dawdy advocates thinking in terms of archaeological time in her study of post-Katrina New Orleans (2010) and uses the concept of *patina* (2016) to describe how the past collects in meaningful ways on objects and places. I use similar ideas in my description of Independence Day in Kazakhstan, in looking at how the public square and its memorials have accumulated clashing meanings from the commemorations of disparate events in the center of Almaty.

In my discussion of Nauryz in chapter 4, I take up archaeological conceptions of time in examining how symbols from Central Asia's ancient past— and the histories of the ancient steppe peoples who carved them—have been

"unearthed" and brought to bear in the present in significant ways. The archaeologist Christopher Witmore, working with a conceptualization of archaeological time, describes time as "folded, chiasmic, entangled" (Witmore
2006, 269). He submits the concept of *percolation*, which describes the past
as bubbling up in unexpected, uneven ways, creating disorder in temporal
layers. Witmore argues that we should be thinking about even distant temporalities as proximate precisely because of this tendency for the past to become entangled in the present, particularly in ways that are linked to place.
"The fabric of the Roman road and the contemporary infrastructure of Paris
are proximate," Witmore explains, in that place, function, and a continuity
of transport infrastructure link these two temporalities (281). Witmore therefore advocates attending to "a non-modernist notion of time where entities
and events quite distant in a linear temporality are proximate through their
simultaneous entanglement and percolation" (267). I build on Witmore's concept of percolation to examine how images of ancient petroglyphs and stone
sculptures found in Kazakhstan are used in the service of nation-building,
particularly around the Central Asian New Year, Nauryz.

In ethnomusicology, there is a growing body of scholarship on temporality (Berger 2010; Born 2010; Friedson 2009; Hawkins 2016; McGraw 2013; Porcello 1998; Savage 2009; Slominski 2015; Stone 2008, 2010), which varies from
phenomenological approaches to time in music performance (Berger, Friedson, Porcello, Stone) to studies of time perception on a larger scale, notably
Jonathan Shannon (2007) on temporality and emotion, and ethnographies of
popular music and queer temporality (Hawkins 2016; Slominski 2015), which
build on Halberstam's theories of queer time (Halberstam 2005). This book
contributes to this body of work by focusing on ethnographic treatments of
temporality, with a focus on conceptual, ideological, affective, and experiential aspects of temporality in popular culture, rather than focusing specifically on time in music performance.

As an ethnography of Central Asia, this book owes a debt to anthropologists and cultural historians of Central and Inner Asia such as Laura Adams, Alexia Bloch, Bruce Grant, Caroline Humphrey, Paula Michaels, and
Douglas Northrop whose work first inspired my interest in this region (Adams 2010; Bloch 2003; Grant 1995; Humphrey 1999, 2002; Michaels 2003;
Northrop 2004). It is also in dialogue with recent scholarship, particularly
the rapidly growing body of work on Islam in Central Asia, which contrib-

utes to a fuller, more variegated picture of Muslim belief and practices in this region (Dubuisson, 2017; Féaux de la Croix 2016; Liu 2012; McBrien 2017; Montgomery 2016; Schwab 2012). This book contributes to a growing body of ethnomusicological scholarship of Central Asia (Adams 2010; Daukeyeva 2016; Elemanova 2001; Harris 2008; Koen 2011; Levin 1996; Merchant 2015; Muhambetova 1995; Post 2007; Rancier 2014; Rapport 2014; Sultanova 2014; C. Wong 2012), which not only examines issues specific to music performance but also illuminates topics such as migration (Rapport 2014), gender (Merchant 2015), the environment (Post 2007), and belief (Amanov and Mukhambetova 2002; Sultanova 2014).

A BRIEF HISTORICAL OVERVIEW OF KAZAKHSTAN

Sparsely populated and expansive, Kazakhstan's arid steppes and mountain ranges contain plentiful pasturelands but relatively little arable land.[1] Until the twentieth century, Kazakhs were mainly nomadic herders (of horses, sheep, camels, and other livestock), moving seasonally among several pasturelands. Though few Kazakhs in Kazakhstan now live in this way (it is more common among Kazakhs in Mongolia and northwest China), the nomadic past and the connection to the land looms large in the Kazakh imaginary.

Kazakhs originated from a group of Turkic peoples in the Chagatai *ulus* (polity) during the Mongol Empire (thirteenth and fourteenth centuries). Around 1465, a separatist group of some 200,000 subjects, led by Zhanibek and Kirai, considered the founders of the Kazakh nation, left Transoxania to push north beyond the Syr Darya River into what is now southern Kazakhstan (Olcott 1995, 4).[2] This separatist group, then indistinguishable from Uzbeks in their language and Turkic-Mongol ethnic makeup, became known as Kazakhs. The soil in Transoxania was fertile enough to support the settled oasis communities that came to typify Uzbek lifeways, but aridity increased farther to the north. The separatist group that became known as Kazakhs adopted more nomadic lifeways than their southern relations and relied on herding rather than agriculture. Eventually, it was this key difference that came to typify Uzbek and Kazakh lifeways. Mobile pastoralism became central to Kazakh identity, whereas Uzbeks identified with settled oasis culture. Indeed, although the origin of the word *Kazakh* remains in dispute, some claim that Kazakh actually means a "vagabond" or "rogue" people, in reference to their separatist, nomadic roots. Other scholars believe the term *Ka-*

zakh to be related to the Turkish verb *qaz*, which means "to wander" (Olcott 1995, 4).

Several natural borders partially enclose Kazakhstan: the Caspian Sea to the west, the Syr Darya River and the Qyzylqum Desert to the south-southwest, the Tian Shan Mountains to the south and east, and the Altai Mountains in the northeast. The northern border, however, is free from any natural barrier, a crucial feature in the history of Russian encroachment into the Kazakh steppe. This fertile northern Kazakh land (which supports wheat and other grains) was populated by Russian settlers in the late nineteenth and early twentieth centuries and remains an area with heavy concentrations of ethnic Russians. On the eastern border with China, a break in the Tian Shan system of mountain ranges functioned as a crucial escape route at numerous tumultuous points in Chinese and Soviet history, when Kazakhs fled across the mountainous borderland (in both directions) to safer pasturelands.[3]

KAZAKH CLAN GOVERNANCE AND IMPERIAL RUSSIA

While the designation *Kazakh* appears as early as the sixteenth century, it was not used as a term of self-identification until much later; rather, clan and horde allegiances were of primary concern in early Kazakh history. Kazakhs are organized in three hordes (kz. *zhuz*), each headed by a leader, or khan, and composed of many smaller kinship groups called *clans*.[4] Indeed, clan and horde identities still hold great relevance for Kazakhs and continue to significantly influence political power in Kazakhstan.[5]

Early in the eighteenth century, imperial Russia first made inroads into Kazakhstan to control trade caravans, and during the nineteenth century, Russia built a series of forts across the Kazakh steppe (Svanberg 1999, 135). Though initially Russian involvement in Kazakh territory was largely economic and military in nature, Russian and later Soviet involvement in Kazakhstan became more invasive and influential in Kazakh cultural life. At first, Kazakh Muslim practices and religious schools were allowed to continue largely without interference. At the end of the nineteenth century, however, in response to the rise of a nascent Kazakh nationalist movement, Russia began to establish more control in cultural and educational spheres. Russian literacy schools were given primacy over Islamic schools, and pilgrimages to Mecca were made more difficult. In addition, Russian rulers began to encourage the settlement of Russians in Kazakhstan by granting them tracts of land for cultivation.[6] The continued settlement of Russian farmers in Kazakhstan would have disastrous consequences for Kazakh mobile pastoralists while strengthening Russian control in the region.

The early twentieth century was a time of great upheaval on the Russian-controlled Kazakh steppe. Russian agricultural policies led to waves of Kazakh emigration into China and the Fergana Valley. Revolutionary fervor sweeping Russia spread to Kazakhstan, as fledgling socialist movements, Kazakh elite national movements, and Kazakh peasant rebellions intertwined in the early twentieth century (Anderson 1997). Among Kazakh elites the popular trend of sending their sons to Moscow to receive "enlightened" education—and thereby gaining exposure to Western European and Russian nationalist ideas—also contributed to the rise of Kazakh nationalism. One such effort, the Alash movement, would resurface after the fall of the Soviet Union in newly independent Kazakhstan.

THE SOVIET ERA

After the establishment of the Soviet Union in 1917, the Soviet push to collectivize land and livestock in Central Asia through the 1930s and 1940s (a process mirrored throughout the Soviet Union) met with disastrous consequences and massive loss of life among Soviet Kazakhs. Although the devastation wrought by collectivization was not unique to Kazakhs (the centralized governing mechanism made state-run agriculture highly inefficient; inadequate harvesting, storage facilities, and distribution systems led to the monumental waste of foodstuffs and widespread famine), Kazakhs' experience under collectivization differed from that of their European counterparts, due to the eradication of nomadic lifeways. In 1929 the Soviets launched a twin campaign aimed at forced sedentarization (settlement) and collectivization of Kazakh herds and land. As Kazakhs were forced to settle on pastureland that could not accommodate their livestock, great numbers of their herds starved. This, combined with the agricultural disaster wrought by land collectivization, led to the unparalleled Kazakh famine (ашаршылық) in the 1930s. Soviet records from this time are sketchy, but most scholars agree that at least 1.5 million Kazakhs, or nearly 40 percent of the total Kazakh population, died as a direct result of collectivization (Cameron 2018). Thousands more fled to Afghanistan and across the Tian Shan Mountains to Xinjiang to escape Soviet control and starvation. The Kazakh Soviet Socialist Republic, the second largest in the Soviet Union, after Russia, was formally established in 1936 with Alma Ata as its capital.

The Soviet era left an indelible mark on Kazakh culture, education, language, and religion—indeed, in all areas of life. Collectivization, sedentarization, deportations of whole communities of ethnic Koreans, Germans, Poles, and Chechens into Kazakhstan before and during World War II, and the widespread persecution of indigenous religious leaders wrought large-scale destructive change to Kazakh lifeways, and decimated the Kazakh population.[7] Added to the devastating population depletion, the changes brought to Kazakh lifeways by forced settlement and collectivization were profound, as migratory life had been central to Kazakh experience. The historians Nurlat Amrekulov and Nurbulat Masanov argue that "along with a nomadic way of life and culture, Kazakhs lost their pride, basic values and worldview orientations" (Amrekulov and Masanov 1994, 137; as quoted in Rorlich 2000, 263). Practitioners of older belief systems of shamanism and Tengrism (nature worship specific to Central and Inner Asia) were persecuted, eroding the core of Kazakh pastoralist life. Further changes wrought by the influence of Soviet ideology left a lasting imprint on Kazakhstani arts, media, and habits of celebrations.

ALMATY IN THE SOVIET ERA

During much of the Soviet period, Kazakhstan's capital, Almaty or Alma-Ata, as it was formerly known, was a small, provincial city. Nevertheless, arts and music flourished in Almaty, and an opera house, several theaters, and a conservatory were established (late 1930s–1940s). During World War II, Mosfilm, the monumental Soviet film industry, was moved to Almaty (1941–1943), marking the beginning of the Kazakhstani film industry. Many Almatyites fondly view the 1960s and 1970s in Almaty, under the leadership of Dinmukhamed Konaev, as a golden period when theater, opera, ballet, and the Kazakh film industry flourished, as the Almaty conservatory and the Academy of Sciences supported a new generation of scholars, writers, and musicians. The fall of the Soviet Union brought an influx of foreign capital, and by the beginning of the twenty-first century, Almaty had replaced Tashkent as the cultural center of Central Asia, and a new generation of wealthy entrepreneurs and oil companies had transformed the capital into a cosmopolitan city, with soaring rents and a steeply growing gap between the wealthy and the working class.

INDEPENDENT KAZAKHSTAN

Among the important problems faced by newly independent Kazakhstan were the low numbers of ethnic Kazakhs in Kazakhstan. In January 1995 Kazakhs constituted 44 percent of Kazakhstan's total population (Olcott 1995). Following independence in 1991, The Kazakhstani government encouraged the repopulation of Kazakhs from the diaspora, partly through the implementation of new immigration policies. After independence new presidential edicts issued quotas for repatriated Kazakhs—designated "returnees" [Kz. *oralman*, pl. *oralmandar*], and new immigration laws concerning these returnees were established. These laws specifically indicated that those returning to Kazakhstan must be ethnic Kazakhs, and excluded groups like Uighurs who had fled Kazakhstan along with their Kazakh compatriots in the 1930s (Cummings 1998, 142).

Another development around Kazakhstani independence was the second-wave mobilization of the Kazakh elite, echoing that of the late nineteenth to early twentieth centuries. In the late 1980s, just before Kazakh independence, several Kazakh political organizations and movements were formed, including Azat (Freedom), Alash (a re-formation of the older movement), and Qazaq Tili (Kazakh language) (Zardykhan 2004). These groups protested Russian cultural, linguistic, and political hegemony, culminating in a 1986 demonstration that came to be known as Zheltoksan (December). It took place on December 16, the same day that would become Kazakhstan's Independence Day five years later, in 1991.

CHAPTER 1

SETTING THE SCENE

A Musical Map of Almaty

Almaty is a leafy green city of extreme continental climate, perched on the slope of the Trans-Ili Alatau Mountains, a range of the Tian Shan mountain system that runs along the southeast border of Kazakhstan. Smog from industry, car exhaust, and coal drifting from outlying areas in the winter is mitigated in the summer by the high green canopy of trees lining the streets and by numerous parks bursting with the dazzling colors and heady scent of roses. Dry, hot, and achingly bright in the summer, Almaty comes alive on summer evenings, when couples and families escape from the heat of apartments to stroll through parks and along boulevards. Grandmothers gather in groups to catch up on news while keeping an eye on their young grandchildren running around the fountains and through the pine, birch, and apple trees nearby. Winter brings icy cold down from the mountains, and people on their way to work and shop can be seen gingerly treading expansive sections of black ice covering the sidewalk, trying to avoid the inevitable falls and broken bones so common during this season. Almaty is a city of extremes, whether of climate or wealth. Residents speak nostalgically of the old (Soviet) Almaty, lined with bountiful apple trees, with ample housing and slow but easy life and work for its citizens. Almaty today represents for many a grinding life—a city where low wages do not begin to cover the rent for even the simplest of apartments. And at the other end of the spectrum, luxury apartments and individual houses are being built higher and higher up the mountain slope, where clean air and breathtaking views are available to a privileged few.

The musical landscape of Almaty is similarly varied. This chapter examines the institutions, pedagogies, and venues that feature Kazakh traditional music as well as European art music in Almaty. At the Kazakh Concert Hall, across from the Kurmangazy National Conservatory, you can hear a Kazakh *khalyq an* (folk song), or a Kazakh *küi* (pl. *küiler*), performed on solo *dombra* (plucked two-stringed lute) or more rarely *qobyz* (two-stringed horsehair fiddle). Traditional Kazakh music is now played onstage by professional musicians, but the instruments and music have older connections to everyday life before the advent of the Soviet era and before Kazakhs were sedentarized. As powerful bearers of cultural history, musicians occupy an important place in Kazakh history, mythology, cosmology, folklore, and the local practice of Islam. Indeed, on learning of my field of study, many Kazakhstanis offered comments about music's important role in Kazakh society. Clearly part of local discourse and a point of national pride, the discussion of Kazakh music places a particular emphasis on verbal art forms, specifically, the epic and the improvised song.

The historically important epic singer or *zhyrau* (pl. *zhyraular*) and the poet-bard or *aqyn* (pl. *aqyndar*), a master of verbal improvisation and social commentary, are much revered in Kazakhstan. As the great scholars and philosophers of Bukhara and Samarkand are to Uzbekistan, prominent *zhyraular* and *aqyndar* are held up as the gems of Kazakh cultural heritage. The zhyrau is believed to possess an almost superhuman ability for memory, and the aqyndar are valued for their razor-sharp wit, knowledge of current events, clan dynamics, and political commentary. Nomadic lifeways made these figures important repositories of history and genealogy as well as vehicles for dispersing news and politics. Along with the khan's other advisers, such as the court astronomer, the zhyrau and aqyn were both considered holders of special knowledge. Along with other kinds of musicians, these figures were generally part of the patronage system, and consequently, some of their performances contained references to their patron(s), including relevant local history and genealogy of the family in question.

Verbal arts have their areas of social prominence, but the qobyz, a two-stringed upright fiddle, maintains a place of cosmological significance: up to the early twentieth century qobyz players were strongly associated with shamanism. Today it is played as any other musical instrument, although often with some reference to its supernatural past. Historically, however, the qobyz was the primary instrument used by Kazakh shamans to enter a trance state. Like Siberian and Mongolian shamans, Kazakh shamans were consulted in matters of illness, madness, and magic, and could place a curse or charm on individuals as well as heal the sick and tell the future. The primary (pre-

Islamic) belief system of Kazakh shamans was animism, or nature worship, which stretched across much of inner Eurasia from Central Asia to Mongolia and Siberia. The qobyz repertoire and playing style still bear traces of its animist roots, most prominent in pieces titled "Qasqyr" (Wolf) and "Aqqu" (White Swan), which include sections of animal imitations. In one such example, Ykhylas Dukenuly's "Qasqyr" begins with a rising tritone, falling off after a long held note, in imitation of a lone wolf's howl. This is followed by a parallel melody, in imitation of two wolves. After several repetitions, a rapid figure is played close to the bridge in the lower register, its scratchy timbre and violent motion uncannily resembling a dogfight. Much like the Tuvan sonic offerings to the nature spirits, these animal imitations in qobyz pieces are largely attributed to the shamanic activities of early qobyz players and composers.

The shrines of famous qobyz players are often visited as places of healing, perhaps because of the regional connections between music and shamanism or due to the heightened powers attributed to qobyz players in previous centuries. These gravesites or shrines of qobyz players are included in local pilgrimage circuits as part of the Muslim practice of shrine pilgrimage (i.e., visiting shrines of powerful or spiritually blessed people), which I discuss in greater detail in chapter 7. One such pilgrimage is located just on the outskirts of Almaty. Driving west from Almaty through the beautiful grasslands and occasional towns, you will see the mountains rising on your left to the south. The Almaty pilgrimage circuit includes (among the shrines of a war hero, a composer, and a number of shrines connected to the family of President Nazarbaev) the shrine of Toktybai, the qobyz player who was said to have "healed by playing his qobyz." His shrine, once a mound of grass, marked only by a grillwork metal enclosure, is now enclosed under a tinted glass dome. Toktybai's shrine receives frequent visitors, who believe that the place has healing properties.

Professional and amateur dombra and qobyz performers play both folk tunes and an instrumental genre called küi. A küi is a programmatic, sometimes virtuosic piece often associated with a specific narrative, and seen as encapsulating Kazakh philosophy. A solo genre prior to the nineteenth century, küiler have been adapted and composed for orchestra. Such performances largely revolve around the conservatory, which draws talent from disparate parts of the country and feeds into the main performance venues for Kazakh music: the Kazakh State Kurmangazy Orchestra of Folk Instruments, the concerts of the top solo performers of Kazakh music (singers, dombrists, and qobyz players), and those few performers who become successful recording artists. The conservatory requires standardized instruments and classically trained musicians and often polishes away the exquisite timbral nuances of Kazakh solo music as it was played sixty years ago and is still played in other parts of the country and in less cosmopolitan settings. The conservatory is also home to a large and very important archive of old recordings of great Kazakh performers and composers. Arguably the most recognized, centralized institution of Kazakh music anywhere, the conservatory holds the golden key of access between Kazakh musicians and those producers, recording industries, and festival organizers making inquiries from abroad. The favored conservatory students and alumni put forward by the faculty are those who gain access to the international stage.

Just up the slope from the conservatory (Almatyites describe locations using "up" and "down" rather than the cardinal directions) is the Zhambyl National Philharmonic Hall, which presents orchestral performances of Western art music. The nearby Abay National Ballet and Opera Theater features ballets and operas by Kazakh, Russian, Italian, and French composers, among others. The opera house, a beautifully refurbished building with plush blue-velvet seats and gilded domed ceilings, continues to feature new Kazakh compositions for opera and ballet. One beautiful and innovative modern ballet, *Zheztyrnak*, premiered at the opera on November 12, 2004. A ballet in two acts with music by Beibit Akoshev and Arman Mukatai and a libretto by Galym Dosken, *Zheztyrnak* is based on Kazakh folklore, which describes bloodthirsty humanlike creatures with long, razor-sharp nails who lure and attack unwary travelers. Despite some complaints of plummeting funding and quality,[1] opera, ballet, and symphony performances continue to pack the house and remain a point of pride for Almatyites. Just as the establishment of the opera house was once viewed as a mark of modernization for Kazakhs in the early Soviet era, the recent flourishing of new composers and new works of art, like *Zheztyrnak*, which showcase new Kazakh talent and draw from Kazakh history, literature, and mythology, are hailed by many as essential for bringing independent Kazakhstan into the post-Soviet era.

The building of the opera house, philharmonic, and conservatory was considered a necessary step in the early days of the Soviet Union (1930s–

1940s) in establishing a national music for each ethnic group. By the end of the 1930s "each national republic was required to build a national opera house and to create a repertory for it" (Frolova-Walker 1998, 335). To this end, local composers were trained, sometimes with the cooperation of Russian composers and musicologists, to construct "Classical" Kazakh music using Western compositional techniques and functional harmony with the stylistic "flavor" of Kazakh songs.

Ahmet Zhubanov, who established the Orchestra of Folk Instruments, used similar principles to meld indigenous solo traditions with Western art music. Zhubanov modeled his ensemble after the Andreev Orchestra of Russian Folk Instruments, which adapted and altered indigenous instruments and instrumentation to accommodate Western harmony, timbre, and multisectional orchestration. As Andreev had done with the balalaika in the Russian orchestra, Zhubanov created different sizes of dombra and qobyz to mimic the high, middle, and low ranges of the western string section. The traditional hair strings of the qobyz were replaced with violin strings to approximate a timbre more closely related to the violin.

One of the foundations of the Kazakh folk orchestra's repertoire was the küi. Because of the virtuosic demands of the küi, it was well suited to Western art traditions of orchestration. Set to an orchestral accompaniment, the lead dombra could play expressive, showy passages, much like the concerto setting in Western art music. Several other factors went into this very conscious distancing from the "simplistic" folk music and "advancement" to art music. One was the change from relative diatonic tuning (not based on a particular pitch) to chromatic tuning based on equal temperament. In addition, the adjustments made to instruments often allowed for greater technical virtuosity (i.e., speed, agility, precision) than had the older folk instruments. As Asiya Muhambetova points out, the "'improvements' of the *qobyz* went so far that they led to the creation of a new instrument on which the traditional repertoire could not be performed" (Amanov and Muhambetova 1995, 74). Further, the drive for virtuosity in the new folk orchestra overshadowed the attention to timbral subtleties emphasized in the older Kazakh solo traditions. This attention to timbre endures in the Kazakh solo qobyz tradition, however, in which the pre-Soviet form of the instrument is still quite commonly played.

The Kökil Music College, founded by Abdulhamid Raimbergenov, arguably represents the antithesis of conservatory training. The students are not taught to read music but rather learn to play and sing by ear. They also do not represent an elite group of special talent. Raimbergenov's aim is to recover the ability and appreciation of preconservatory musicianship that was, if not erased, appreciably reduced during the Soviet era. "Our task isn't to train young virtuosos," Raimbergenov explained in a 2003 BBC interview. "For them, there are specialist music schools. Our aim is to let ordinary children hear our own Kazakh music so that they understand and love their musical tradition" (Abdulhamid Raimbergenov, BBC).[2]

When I visited the school in 2004, I was struck by the seriousness of the young students and of Raimbergenov's endeavor to reclaim Kazakh music from the homogenizing machine of conservatory training. He was insistent that Kazakh music was not meant to be written down, and that the very act of transcribing and learning from that written transcription changes the nature of both the learning process and the music itself. He spoke of the narrative and dramatic aspect of Kazakh instrumental music and demonstrated how gesture and physical expression are used to convey the narrative and philosophical meaning of the piece. As he played a küi on dombra, he indicated extramusical hand gestures that ornament the musical performance and help to weave in the story behind it.

Kökil was sponsored by the Aga Khan Foundation, an Ismaili organization supporting cultural and civic development programs in many countries throughout Central and Western Asia.[3] Aga Khan stresses the importance of supporting cultural heritage, particularly in developing nations such as those in post-Soviet Central Asia, in which support for the arts is foundering. Support through Aga Khan's Tradition-Bearers Program is intended to forge a link between artists and performers of older musical traditions (particularly those not included in Soviet-era conservatory training) and a new generation of music students. Happily for Raimbergenov his goal of training a new generation of Kazakhs who will love and understand Kazakh oral traditions fit well with the goals of the Aga Khan Foundation, which has provided both support and exposure for this small school and its lofty ambitions.

One of Raimbergenov's teachers is the epic singer Ulzhan Baibussyno-va. Singing with the throaty "epic voice" reminiscent of Siberian throat singers, Ulzhan believes strongly in the supernatural powers and moral responsibility of a zhyrau. Featured on Theodore Levin's Smithsonian DVD *Bardic Divas*, Ulzhan, shown at the shrine of the legendary qobyz player, Qorqyt

(approximately tenth century), in southern Kazakhstan, speaks about the supernatural gifts of a zhyrau. In my interview with her, Ulzhan explained that
these gifts are innate, the birthright of Kazakhs alone (and then only a few),
and cannot be learned (personal communication, November 12, 2004). In my
interviews with musicians, they frequently confirmed this view that talent,
particularly for zhyraular and aqynlar, is a gift that can neither be taught
nor denied, once bestowed on the receiver. Like shamanism, musicianship
is seen as fated and unavoidable, an unexpected blessing and an unwanted
curse.

Another vibrant hub of musical and ideological activity is the Museum of
Kazakh Folk Instruments, housed in a quaint wooden building at the edge of
Panfilov Park. The museum is at the center of the push to expand the modest
assortment of Kazakh instruments and to create small folk ensembles featuring a greater variety of sounds. The dombra, *shangqobyz* (Jew's harp), *sybyzgy*
(end-blown flute), and qobyz are generally considered core Kazakh music instruments, but other instruments long out of use in the region, like the small
clay flute and the *zhetigen* (a seven-stringed plucked zither), are being "reconstructed" based on instruments found in local archaeological digs. Several
other percussion instruments have been creatively added to the ensembles.

Ensemble music is not native to Kazakhstan—the dombra, qobyz, sybyzgy, and shangqobyz have long, rich traditions and extensive folk repertoire,
but as solo instruments. The "ensemblization" of Kazakh music (formerly for solo instrument, or voice with instrumental accompaniment) was a
project of the Soviets, which has had very long-reaching consequences. The
2000s and 2010s have seen a proliferation of small Kazakh folk ensembles
that specialize in folk songs and küiler. These ensembles often include the
qobyz, dombra, and sybyzgy as primary melodic instruments, together with
the shangqobyz and reconstructed "historical" instruments, many of them
percussion. These instruments are added for authenticity, color, and to fill
out the small collection of traditional Kazakh instruments. Percussion and
noise-making instruments include the *asatayaq* (a shaman's rod, hung with
bits of metal), the *qongyrau* (bells), *tokyldaq* and *saqpan* (rattles), *syldyrmaq*
(shaken metallic pendants), and *tuyaq tas* (horse hoofs, played by clapping
them together). Small ensembles like Sazgen, Otrar, and Zhetisaz appear in
many performance contexts and are particularly in demand during Nauryz
(Kazakh New Year), as they represent a display of Kazakh musical culture in

an eye-catching, sonically colorful form that is particularly well suited to festival celebrations.

In taxis, cafés, and bars, the soundscape is largely dominated by Russian and Kazakh pop music (mostly singer-centric with synthesized beat and accompaniment, though one can also hear those with backup bands playing electric guitar, bass, and drumset) with a smattering of European and American rock songs and dance hits from the past decade or two. An occasional taxi driver or, more rarely, restaurant owner will play a recording of a Russian jazz band or Kazakh dombra virtuoso. And some bars have live music, such as the Guinness Pub on Dostyk whose house band specializes in 1980s American rock, or the Uzbek-themed restaurant Kishlak, with Kazakh musicians accompanying costumed dancers.

The 1990s and early 2000s also saw the rise of Kazakh rock groups featuring dombra and qobyz, including Roksonaki, ABK, Ulytau, Saz Otau, as well as a constant crop of young virtuosic dombra players. One of the earliest of these groups, ABK, included the singer Kydyraly Bolmanov, husband of the famous folk singer Karakat. ABK was important in planting the seeds for the fusion of Kazakh traditional music and rock music, taking the emotionality of Kazakh folk music and the drive of *tökpe*-style dombra playing (which features very fast virtuosic playing while maintaining the characterstic driving beat) and applying it to rock sensibility. Kydyraly, now a member of the Almaty city government, became a powerful creative and political force behind the Kazakh rock scene. He produced the now-famous group Ulytau, a young hip band performing Kazakh rock (largely instrumental) music in warrior-sexy costuming (also Kydyraly's brainstorm). Ulytau is the name of the legendary place in central Kazakhstan where the Kazakh people achieved unity when the three Kazakh *zhuz* (umbrella clans) joined together as a single state. Ulytau's dombra player Erzhan describes his group: "In general, Ulytau was formed as an experimental collective. . . . From the very beginning, our producer [Kydyraly Bolmanov] wanted to bring to life his dream—to unite Kazakh folk music with classical music. Unfortunately many people often talk about how the 'raisin' [highlight] of Ulytau is the violin. But the idea, the whole point, is all about the *dombra*" (Erzhan of Ulytau, interviewed by Kumysai Sarbasova 2004.[4] Kydyraly Bolmanov talks about his "dream" in an interview: "I formed the group Ulytau in order to awaken the genius within the soul of young people, which comes to us in the blood of our ancestors. There is a musical term 'drive.' The *dombra* has a lot of drive, and it makes the music move like the loud foreign music that our youth is accustomed to hearing. Ulytau works in this way" (Kydyraly Bolmanov, interviewed by Duman Anash 2005; my translation). Indeed, many subsequent bands have tapped into the energy that the dombra brings to this genre, and similar "Kazakh rock" bands have cropped up as well.

LEARNING TO PLAY THE QOBYZ

When I studied qobyz, my first teacher was Sayan Akmolda, a successful Kazakh musician, then in his thirties, who represented an interesting position between the academy and rural life. Though he went through training in the conservatory in Almaty, Sayan is from a rural region in southern Kazakhstan and learned to play the qobyz in early childhood. His musical learning is aurally based—he began to play qobyz küiler and folk songs with his teacher, a noted traditional qobyz player, Symytai Ymbetpaev (who studied with the son of the legendary composer Ykhylas Dükenuly), and only later engaged with the Western pedagogical techniques of scales and arpeggios as an adult student in the conservatory. Linguistically, too, he is an anomaly in Almaty. He speaks Russian with an accent; Kazakh is his native tongue and he speaks it fluently and beautifully. Sayan has important family connections—his brother is a famous Kazakh actor, who appears on television and onstage at the Auezov Theater in Almaty—and he has been picked up by international festivals and concert tours, most notably the Silk Road tour organized by the Smithsonian Institution (managed by the ethnomusicologist Theodore Levin and featuring the cellist Yo-Yo Ma). Culturally and linguistically Kazakh, but with significant international exposure as well as a charismatic onscreen/onstage presence, he was chosen to host a television program on Kazakh music.

My second qobyz teacher, Sersengali (Sersen) Zhumazbaev, was a childhood friend of Sayan's. Now primarily a dombra player, Sersen also learned qobyz as a child from the same teacher as Sayan. Unlike most contemporary qobyz players, who use the flat of the nail to press the strings, resulting in a clean, bright sound closer to the Western classical aesthetic, Sersen plays in the old style, using the fleshy tips of his fingers to push on the strings. His sound is rich and round and slightly muted, allowing more overtones to shimmer around the main note. Sayan, on the other hand (as Sersen explained to me), plays in the new style, with his nail, but he uses the side of his nail, catching part of the cuticle and flesh of the finger, thus approximating the mellow, rich sound of the old style, while taking advantage of the clarity achieved by playing on the nail. Even in his performance style, Sayan mixes traditions, finding a distinct advantage in the middle road.

My experience learning qobyz was composed of equal parts frustration and sheer joy. A difficult instrument, particularly for someone who had never wielded a bow, the qobyz never ceased to enthrall me—once I learned how to produce a palatable sound. The qobyz is bowed with the palm facing up similar to the position you would use to hold chopsticks. The bow itself is extremely light and its horsehair strings are strung very loosely, so that the bowing hand must produce the proper (variable) tension by pulling on horsehair steadily with the ring finger and pinky as the bow is drawn across the instrument strings. The two strings of a qobyz, tuned a fifth or a fourth apart depending on the repertoire, are bundles of horsehair about a quarter-inch thick. The combination of the loosely strung bow and the texture of the horsehair strings makes for slow progress at the beginning. Once I learned to produce a smooth-sounding note, I practiced for hours a day, loving the rich dark tones of my instrument.

The qobyz has quite a resonant lower register, surprisingly so considering the instrument's relatively small size. The body is carved from a single piece of wood and is usually quite thick. There are different shapes for the body, but it is usually some variation of a keyhole shape, with a rounded top, tapering to a narrow base, flat at the bottom. The slightly "nasal" timbre comes from the qobyz's skin head stretched across the narrower half of the body and often with a single pointed edge attached to the inside of the back wall. A qobyz may have very lovely carved, painted, or burned ornamentation on the neck and body. Mine is quite plain, but several of my teachers and colleagues have coveted it for its rich sound. This type of qobyz, called a *qyl-qobyz*, a term that distinguishes it from its modernized cousin of the orchestral variety, is always made by hand. Further, usually the instrument maker (sometimes also a musician) makes each part from scratch, tanning the hide, carving the body and neck, and cutting, washing, and bundling the horsehair strings. Replacing the strings is no easy task, as they are not sold ready-made. When I broke my strings after tuning them too tightly, my first qobyz teacher, Sayan, had to make a long trip to the hippodrome outside of

Almaty, where he searched for hours to find a horse whose tail had not yet been trimmed for the winter.

The first songs Sersen wanted to teach me were simple Kazakh folk songs, mostly in major keys, played in the higher register of the instrument. I really wanted to learn the mournful-sounding küiler of Ykhylas Dukenuly (1843–1916) that I had heard Sayan play and loved for their contemplative feel. This was the first of many times when I had the sense that Sersen was wary of letting our lessons get too far, of teaching me too much, as if he were protective of something he thought I could not understand. As in my fruitless efforts to convince Ulzhan to teach me epic singing, I had the distinct impression that certain genres such as epic singing and some qobyz küi were perhaps tacitly protected traditions.

After much convincing, Sersen agreed to try to teach me küi but only after I had mastered a few folk songs. I first learned "Gul'darigha" and "Gul'deraiym." These songs, though melodically simple were actually not simple to play. They both required learning a second hand position, common for these higher-register, up-tempo songs in a major key. Unlike the küi I would learn later, this type of song often requires a short-bowing technique to produce the lively melodies. In addition, the scale used in these two songs was complicated by the use of a harmonic in rising phrases, but, on the same note, the harmonic was not used in the descent. This was my first clue in qobyz playing that timbre and overtone constitutes a core part of the qobyz repertoire, and that the specific manipulation of timbre is built into certain pieces as firmly as melody.

The next piece I learned, also based on vocal repertoire, was "Aittym Salem Kalamkas," written by probably the most important Kazakh literary figure, the poet and philosopher, Abay Qunanbaiuly (1845–1904). When I told a Kazakh friend about learning it, she was delighted, and said that her mother had sung it to her as a lullaby. This and other songs based on Abay's poetry (with melody also attributed to Abay) tend to have a lovely lyrical swooping melody, in minor mode, with gentle tempos and wide, dramatic leaps, perfect for a soprano voice. These pieces are quite typical of nineteenth-century composed song, many of which have been adapted to the instrumental repertoire. Though I could sing this piece perfectly adequately, I found it difficult to navigate the wide range smoothly on the qobyz, and my endless attempts basically flopped.

Nevertheless, Sersen finally allowed me to graduate to küi, to my great joy. A kind soul, he must have recognized that all those perky melodies were killing me. He introduced me to the wonderful mid-nineteenth-century composer, Ykhylas. Although many küi in the repertoire were adaptations of dombra küi, Ykhylas wrote specifically for qobyz. His pieces make use of sounds and techniques characteristic of this instrument, including rhythmic bowing and timbral manipulations. His compositions are also deceptively simple at first listen, composed of repetitive, subtly evolving melodic cells of only a few notes. The beauty of these küi is in the phrasing. Strict, metronome tempo is not possible when playing Ykhylas, as the movement follows phrasing, and often has an irregular pulse.

Ykhylas's "Erden" seems to have all the ingredients that make the genre of qobyz küi so remarkable. As I described above, it is composed of Ykhylas's signature cellular phrasing, which begins in the lowest register, showing off the gorgeous deep tones of the instrument. The melody moves up to the middle register as the piece progresses, also typical of Ykhylas's compositions, followed by a repetition of the entire first "A" section. This is where it gets interesting. In "Erden," this repetition takes place in the same register, but in a different timbral placement. The bow is placed several inches closer to the bridge, which, in place of the rich, rounded tone, produces a raspy melody with a constant squeaky, scraping addition of overtones. It is as if the sweet melony timbre of the qobyz has been split open and the entire overtone series it holds becomes audible. Valentina Süzükei, who coauthored, with Ted Levin, *Where Rivers and Mountains Sing: Sound, Music, and Nomadism in Tuva and Beyond,* provides a wonderful description of different timbral manipulations in her discussion of timbre-centric music in Tuva (Siberia).[5] "It's easier to express graphically than in words. When you make a sound on the *igil*, it's like spreading open the fan. Inside this one sound is a whole acoustic world created by the spray of overtones that results when you draw a bow across the instrument's horsehair strings."

She continues: "If you pick up snow, pack it into a snowball and throw it, it goes in a single direction and, depending on the force of your throw, it can go quite far. But if you scoop up some loose snow and toss it, no matter how much force you exert, the snow just scatters. Sound is like that. In European music, sound is packed compactly into discrete pitches, with the fundamental frequency and overtones all perceived as one. But Tuvan music is like loose snow, and overtones are like the snow spray" (Levin with Süzükei 2006, 48).

Süzükei's "loose snow" imagery describes a musical practice—a preference for audible overtones and a heightened attention to timbre in listening, performance, and composition—shared throughout Inner Asia, including parts of Siberia, Mongolia, Kyrgyzstan, and Kazakhstan. This Inner Asian complex shares more than musical commonalities, and it is important to understand Kazakh music in the broader context of mobile pastoralist lifeways in the region. Indeed, the shamanic and animist roots of Kazakh solo traditions (of the qobyz in particular), as well as the supernatural aspects of Kazakh epic singing, are closely related to similar practices throughout Inner Asia.[6]

PATRONAGE, COSMOPOLITANISM, AND THE SOVIET LEGACY

Certain aspects of Kazakh music making, like the connection to a nomadic past, have so many intertwining branches; one can trace its links to patronage systems, Soviet cultural policy, and post-Soviet national movements as well as to the ideological maneuverings of cosmopolitanism. Patronage, for example, has been a part of Kazakh musical life from the pre-Soviet context of clan structures, throughout the Soviet era, when family and clan ties were used in conjunction with access to high-ranking party cadres, and into the post-Soviet era, particularly through the difficult economic and political transition of the early 1990s, when many Kazakhs barely avoided starvation and homelessness and only through the aid of family networks. The life of a Kazakh musician is by necessity reliant on this patronage system. Indeed, today's aqynlar often support themselves in ways strikingly similar to those of a century ago. In the popular song-competition (or *aitys*) season, competitive aqynlar throughout Kazakhstan continue to rely on the support of powerful patrons in exchange for their musical "advertising" (i.e., improvised social commentary that benefits their patrons)—essentially the same mutually beneficial relationship between aqynlar and powerful clan heads that could be seen before the advent of the twentieth century.

The patronage of musicians is present on a state level as well as a family or regional level. Sayan Akmolda's television program is part of a recent trend to promote "real" Kazakh music and musicians. With many of the concert venues dominated by pop singers, traditional Kazakh musicians generally have a difficult time finding work, mainly playing at weddings of family members and teaching at local schools—but a lucky few like Akmolda have been singled out, promoted, and funded by the state. In early 2005 several Kazakh performers, including Akmolda, were chosen for state patronage and given choice apartments in the center of Almaty. In a political system that favors patronage for those performers who can serve as a mouthpiece for the state, Akmolda has been very fortunate to be among those chosen.

Sayan is also at the pivot of cosmopolitan musical life in some ways. Adapting the rural solo qobyz playing just slightly to obtain a brighter, clearer timbre, Sayan is well-versed in both the rural tradition he grew up with and in the transnational, cosmopolitan sphere he encountered through the Almaty conservatory and the film industry. In an audition for an international music festival that I helped facilitate, Sayan played beautifully from his extremely virtuosic repertoire, while at the same time emphasizing the older, shamanic aspects of the qobyz performance practice, a combination that earned him a spotlight in the festival. Sayan is a great performer and has an excellent facility for switching musical and ideological "languages," depending on his audience. Musical and social changes during the Soviet era have echoed in the urban cosmopolitanism of Almaty, and can be seen particularly in the centrality of the conservatory, with its capacity to serve as a pivot point for rural musicians to learn cosmopolitan music making and as a gateway to transnational exposure. This process of urbanizing rural musicians and Kazakh solo traditions began during the Soviet era and can still be perceived in the Almaty music scene.

That is not to say that the older traditions have completely disappeared; indeed in rural areas and smaller cities they exist side-by-side with Russian, Kazakh, and Western pop music, accessed through radio, television, and the internet. Kyzylorda, a rural city in south/central Kazakhstan, is home to a school for epic singers, headed by the famous zhyrau, Almas Almatov. When I visited him at his home in 2004, we sat in a large yurt set up in his beautiful yard,[7] which overflowed with apricot, apple, and plum trees—a fertile oasis of greenery in the dusty, desertlike city (if you Google Kyzylorda, you will find an expanse of tan except for a faint green line that traces the Syr Darya river, which runs through the city). The orchards and gardens ran along three sides of his large house, but Almas explained that he usually entertained in the yurt and that he was more comfortable there. Certainly it was well suited to this gathering of ten zhyraular, friends and some former students of Almas, who happened to be in Kyzylorda that evening. Eight men, one woman, and a ten-year-old girl performed portions of epic songs in turn, accompanying themselves on dombra. Some, such as Almas, sang in the low, gruff "epic voice," that I think of as a close cousin of throat singing (or overtone singing); others used a more focused, tense timbre. Between performances, they talked about the piece and about their lives, and how they had become zhyrau. They praised Almas, his school, and his particular legacy of teaching so many of the younger generation of epic singers. The gathering in Almas's yurt, lavishly hung with deep-red carpets and brightly felted Kazakh cloths, served as a reminder that Kazakhstan's rural, nomadic roots are still a tangible reality in some parts of Kazakhstan—even though in Almaty, they appear as a contrived national fiction: idyllic scenes of tranquil, nomadic life colorfully pictured on a billboard in the middle of a four-lane traffic circle. The lives of Almas and Sayan, the teaching of Sersen, and the complex music of the qobyz all bear hallmarks of these important processes, revealing the layers of Kazakhstan's Soviet and nomadic past, which continue to coexist alongside the burgeoning cosmopolitanism of Almaty and the nation-building efforts of Astana, the country's new capital.

CHAPTER 2
AIRING INDEPENDENCE

Performing the Past and the Future on December 16

That kind of historical nostalgia is only available to a certain kind of person....
I can't go back to the '50s because life in the '50s for me is not pretty.

—Zadie Smith

A visitor strolling down the wide, dusty avenues and tree-lined streets of Almaty, Kazakhstan's largest city, would come across various billboards standing at the edge of shady walkways and perched high above the traffic-crowded roads. These roadside advertisements, public service announcements, and seasonal banners display a disparate array of messages: sophistication and luxury in some advertisements, Kazakh nationalism in others, and a sprinkling of certain hot-button topics (environmentalism, family harmony, national development, and progress) on official billboards. Visual and sonic expression in the public sphere reveal aspects of temporality that reflect both popular culture and state ideology. In public squares, felted yurts are set up for holiday celebrations, reminders in the city of Kazakhstan's pastoral nomadic past. Dramatic commemorations of World War II portray emotional tributes to the Soviet Army.[1] Optimistic advertisements display future constructions of luxury apartment buildings, whereas banners for Kazakh holidays show lush green pastures, reflecting nostalgia for a pre-Soviet nomadic past. Statues and billboards occasionally project a wistfulness for Soviet Almaty too, showing a 1970s cineplex of Almaty's "Golden Age of Cinema," and a cozier capital, still lined with bountiful apple trees. Such public displays illuminate emotional aspects of temporality, which are frequently entwined with nationalism and put to the purposes of nation-building in postsocialist Central Asia.

This book is concerned with the concepts of time and its entanglements, particularly those temporal reflections that manifest in Kazakhstan's public spaces and spheres—what one would hear and see while walking down Al-

FIGURE 2.1. A yurt set up for festivities in Almaty, 2005.

maty's streets, gazing into shop windows, listening to the radios in taxis and kitchens, watching television in Kazakhstan's living rooms, and celebrating on its public squares. This ethnographic investigation concerns the intertwining of public and private marking of time, how it combines with emotion and articulates belief and state ideology.

PUBLIC TEMPORALITY

Calendars, whether lived, official, current, or outdated, are used in governing and recording the economic, political, and civic use of time. Like memorials, which stand as concrete and tangible markers of historical events, and yet represent fluid and layered meanings (see Viejo-Rose 2011, 467–71), calendars are similarly multivalent. Rewritten after each regime change, but retaining traces of earlier celebratory practices, calendars function as living palimpsests, revealing the layers of interactions between political and personal beliefs and ideologies. As historical narratives change shape, marked and unmarked days shift and change names, accrue new meanings and temporal valences. Especially after regime change, the old ways of celebrating grate against new calendrical designations, uncovering popular grievances about the state and its new ideologies.

Like memorials and national monuments, calendars are used by the state to "construct mythologies for the emerging power structure" (Viejo-Rose 2011, 469). Seasonal celebrations, new state holidays, banners, slogans, performances, and televised programs all contribute to the maintenance of the new temporal regime. In Kazakhstan, changing celebratory practices revealed newly minted ideas of independence and a renewed sense of what it meant to be an ethnic Kazakh and to be a Kazakhstani citizen. From my vantage point, conducting fieldwork beginning in 2004, I saw firsthand the change of ideological emphasis after the transition from Soviet to independent Kazakhstan. Working in Kazakhstan in the years after the breakup of the Soviet Union was like watching the slowing of a massive steam engine; even now, more than two decades after independence, the hulking mass of Soviet ideology can be seen, rusting, partly obscured by new growth, but still there.

Even in the parts of the calendar that remain the same, there has been a palpable shift in the ways in which the holidays are celebrated, perceived, and framed. Structural permanence and stability in calendars can mask a variability in people's interactions with that structure. In discussing memorials, Dacia Viejo-Rose writes, "Even in the case of cenotaphs built as 'permanent memorials' following the First World War, evolution, movement and change in meaning is inevitable. While the cenotaphs themselves did not move . . . nor their physical form alter much with the years, their relevance, the way they were perceived, what they were understood to represent, their importance and poignancy, and their centrality within their architectural and urban environments did change over time" (Viejo-Rose 2011, 472). Similarly, the date December 16, seemingly fixed in the yearly calendar cycle and on the official state calendar as Kazakhstan's Independence Day, in fact memorializes different events for different groups and signifies entirely discrepant meanings.

EMOTIONAL PUBLICS AND MEDIATED TEMPORALITY

The idea of a public sphere is central to this study, but the meaning of the term "public sphere" is highly contested, varies according to scholarly discipline, and has only become murkier in the past two decades.[2] The public sphere as described by Jürgen Habermas is concerned with freedom of

FIGURE 2.2. Construction-site billboards portraying future apartment complex life.

speech and the lack of coercion in the forming of public discourse. This definition rests on the necessity of an "open society," in which citizens are free to form their own opinions and participate easily in public events and discussion. But even in authoritarian states like Kazakhstan, where Kazakhstani citizens who protest government policies may face reprisals, and the state retains firm control of the media, one can speak of a public sphere, in which state ideology and personal belief coarticulate. Erika Doss, in her *Memorial Mania*, examines interactions with public space, attending particularly to the role of emotion (Doss 2010). Doss and other scholars of emotion, temporality, and public space (Benjamin 2003; Bodnar 1992; Boym 2001; Doss 2010; Olick 2003) suggest that the political uses of emotion come to bear in public framings of temporality. Politicians and advertisers alike rely on the allure of an imagined future and the nostalgic backward glance to sell products and engage its publics.

Recent scholarship in literature, philosophy, and anthropology examine this relationship between desire and temporality. Vincent Crapanzano, who

FIGURE 2.3. Woman walking past construction-site billboards, Almaty, December 7, 2004.

focuses on the emotional pull of the future, writes, "My concern is with the role of what lies beyond the horizon, with the possibilities it offers us, with the licit and illicit desires it triggers, the plays of power it suggests, the dread it can cause—the uncertainty, the sense of contingency, of chance—the exaltation, the thrill of the unknown, it can provoke" (Crapanzano 2004,14).

Sara Ahmed considers our emotional grapplings with the future—particularly in the forms of hope and anxiety. "Hope, we might say, is a thoughtful way of being directed toward the future, or a way of creating the very thought of the future as going some way. . . . If the future is that which does not exist, what is always before us, in the whisper of the 'just ahead,' then hope also involves imagination, a wishfulness that tells us about what we strive for at present. Hope is a wish and expectation that a desired possibility is 'becoming actual'" (Ahmed 2011, 173). Edward Casey (2000), by contrast, considers our fraught relationships with the past, as elucidated in commemorations. Svetlana Boym, in her expansive work on nostalgia, parses the ways that we *feel* the past, and how that relationship with the past is reflected and manipulated in the political sphere (Boym 2001). "Nostalgia," she writes, "works as a double-edged sword: it seems to be an emotional antidote to politics, and thus remains the best political tool" (Boym 2001, 58).

ALMATY, INDEPENDENCE DAY

Almaty is a green, tree-lined city in eastern Kazakhstan, nestled at the foot of the Trans-Ili Alatau, a northern range of the Tian Shan Mountains. Though it began as a sleepy provincial capital, overshadowed by Tashkent as the So-viet hub in Central Asia, arts and cinema flourished in Almaty through the Soviet era, and by the time Kazakhstan gained independence in 1991, it was the economic center of Central Asia, a thriving, ethnically diverse, cosmo-politan city. Walking down the street in Almaty, one may encounter a Kore-an outdoor market, Guns & Roses bar (catering to foreigners), a busker play-ing World War II tunes on a tiny accordion, an elderly *babushka* (Russian, grandmother) selling delicate yellow summer apples on a street corner, and clusters of schoolchildren chattering away in groups on the walk home from school. Among the Soviet gray apartment blocks, occasional old wooden houses and ornately trimmed pale pink, yellow, and blue nineteenth-century buildings crop up unexpectedly. One's field of vision will be accosted by a brightly divergent array of street signs—ideological billboards touting unity among Kazakhstan's people, mixing with advertisements for Dior, Lancôme, and Lipton.

In the early winter, though, the bright colors of the tree-lined city fade somewhat. The air thickens with smoke from coal stoves and a dense fog col-lects in the folds of the mountains' foothills and blurs the bare limbs of the trees along Almaty's streets. It is on such a day that I stood surveying the square, on Independence Day in 2004.

Fieldnotes, December 16, 2004 (Independence Day)

It is December 16 and the day is raw and gray, the sun so dampened it looks more like early morning than nearly noon. The festivities were scheduled to start at noon, but at 11:30 little is happening. A few festival-goers, many of them visitors from out of town, mill about as scattered booth keepers set up along one edge of the square. The Ploshad' Respubliki (Republican Square) is bleak, barely brightened by the holiday banners—scant blue and yellow slivers hung on poles and gathered together in bouquets. A billboard hanging high above the square shows images of Kazakh yurts superimposed over the Almaty mountains and reads "Our goal: Peace and Prosperity." People slowly gather at one end of the square, where the statue of the Golden Man rides the Snow Leopard high overhead on a tall pedestal spike. That corner of the square was the site of an informal Independence Day tradition and people are placing flowers at the foot of the statue to commemorate the bloodshed that occurred on this day in 1986.[3]

The ethnographic center of this chapter focuses on activities and performances held on Independence Day in Almaty, as well as interviews with revelers and mourners. The events on the square that day included concerts by local amateur groups, many based on ethnicity (the Polish association, the Korean association, etc.). Other performances both on the square and in venues around the city featured Kazakh popular and traditional music. I spoke with performers and audience members on the square, and also attended some of the other many events around the city on Independence Day. I also examined concerts and films that were televised on Independence Day, insofar as programs and events in mediated public spaces (such as television and social media) also contribute to public constructions of a nation's past, present, and future.

Independence Day in many countries marks the culmination or resolution of an emotionally charged and often violent event or stage in history. This violence sparks a change in leadership, ripping the present from the past and setting it adrift toward a new horizon. In Kazakhstan, Independence Day officially marks the date when Kazakhstan seceded from the Soviet Union to set up its own state in 1991. The historian Stephen Kotkin writes of Nazarbaev's political positioning in the years leading up to Kazakhstan's independence, "That the Union's demise was 'national in form, opportunist in content' was equally evident in Kazakhstan. In June 1989 Nursultan Nazarbaev became Kazakh party chief, and in April 1990 he was elected chairman of the Kazakhstan Supreme Soviet. Later that year, Nazarbaev was nominated for the post of USSR vice-president, but he demurred. Along with his supporters in the Kazakhstan elite, he manipulated nationalism to consolidate power in the republic, yet, even during his campaign for the new Kazakh presidency in late 1991, Nazarbaev resisted calls for complete independence" (Kotkin 2001, 105–6).

Students, intellectuals, and the disenfranchised rallied for Kazakhstan's independence and called for an end to oppressive measures by the Russian Soviet hegemonic power structure, but political elites (including those at the highest positions in Kazakhstan's government) were concerned that drastic change could dislodge their privilege and political power. Thus the independence gained in 1991 was handed to wary, even unwilling, recipients. The declarations of independence of 1991 unfolded in slow succession (Kyrgyzstan, August 31; Uzbekistan, September 1; Tajikistan, September 9; Turkmenistan, October 27) with Kazakhstan, December 16, the last of all the Soviet republics to declare independence. In the unofficial context, however, this date marks not only Kazakhstan's independence gained on December 16, 1991, but also the turbulent, bloody uprising on that same date in 1986.

After the 1986 ousting of the beloved Kazakh leader of the Soviet Republic of Kazakhstan, Dinmukhamed Konaev, his replacement, Gennady Kolbin (an ethnic Russian) was met with angry resistance by Kazakhs. A group of furious demonstrators gathered on the central Brezhnev Square (now Republican Square) in Almaty to protest what was seen as the last straw in a long history of Russian domination. [4] The journalist Joanna Lillis, in her book chapter about the 1986 uprising, wrote, "Kolbin's appointment appeared to confirm something many Kazakhs had long believed: that their Russian rulers looked down on them as second-class citizens" (Lillis 2019, 162). Lillis describes the demonstration as starting out peacefully. "At first, the demonstration was light-hearted. The high spirited protesters linked arms and sang the song that became the anthem of their protest: 'Menin Kazakhstanym' [My Kazakhstan]" (Lillis 2019, 164). The numbers of protesters grew as student protesters and ethnic Kazakhs voiced their long-standing discontent with Russian domination. Dos Kushim, who had been a prominent leader in the Kazakh community, explained: "This was the last straw, you see. For years this discontent had been accumulating inside us, that we'd become second-rate. The affront had been building up in our souls" (Lillis 2019, 162).

The protest turned violent when police stepped in to break up the demonstration. Reports of beatings, mass jailings, and many deaths of demonstrators at the hands of the military police are generally accepted, though the numbers vary greatly. Police used water cannons in the bitter cold and there are reports that demonstrators froze to death after being drenched with water. Lillis describes this harrowing scene:

As the protest entered its second day, thousands of extra police and paramilitary forces (7618, according to one count) flooded in from all over the Soviet Union—Siberia, the Urals, the Caucasus, other parts of Central Asia—and riot police, special forces, and troops from the Ministry of Internal Affairs equipped with anything from truncheons to sapper shovels began clashing with demonstrators armed with stones, branches, and Molotov cocktails. Helped by 10,000 "volunteers" ushered (or ordered) into civilian militias and using guard dogs rounded up from all over Alma-Ata, they chased down the rioters and dispersed them using water cannons. Some of the drenched protesters were driven out of town and dumped out on the freezing steppe in bitter temperatures; others suffered savage beatings as they were hauled off into custody.

According to a report that was released years later, after consistent efforts to cover up the scale of violence and casualties, the death toll was 168 (including 155 civilians); in addition, 900 people were convicted of crimes, 82 of them were jailed, and 1,400 people "received reprimands that blighted their records as good Soviet citizens" (Lillis 2019, 169). The December 1986 event and the protest movement that emerged from it now bear the name Zheltoksan (Kazakh for December). According to the BBC, about 3,000 people took part in the protest.[5] The poet Mukhtar Shakhanov, who worked against censorship of the reports of the demonstration, asserted, "*Zheltoksan* was the first democratic movement in the whole of the Soviet Union. It was an uprising that sowed the seeds of the destruction of the Soviet Union" (Lillis 2019, 160).

Independence Day as it is remembered in Almaty is therefore split into two commemorations with conflicting agendas and sentiments. Although the actual date of independence in 1991 is central to official celebrations, the more charged and certainly the more contentious remembrance is that of 1986. Until the mid-2000s, the central government scarcely recognized the earlier event in marking Decemer 16. Certainly the focus of the official events I attended was on Kazakhstan's independence in 1991, though in a slight concession, in 2006 (the twentieth anniversary of the 1986 uprising), Nazarbaev marked the protest and publicly honored its victims with the unveiling of a statue dedicated to their memory. In speeches during and after the commemorative events, Nazarbaev and other representatives of the central government emphasized their claim that the bloody protest was not about ethnicity but about the need for freedom and democracy.

In the decades after Kazakhstan's independence, the date December 16 has only gathered layers of meaning, accumulated through years of public protest. In addition to being used by ruling-party politicians to shape public opinion on Independence Day, December 16 is also used by opposition activists and protesters to voice grievances and mourn victims. In 2008 a large group of about four hundred people gathered in Republican Square to protest housing issues and voice criticism of the administration. Ainur Kurmanov, the protest leader who headed a nongovernmental organization addressing the housing crisis in Almaty, stated that they were also there to commemorate the victims of the 1986 uprising (RFE/RL, December 16, 2008). On December 16, 2011, in Zhanaozen, in western Kazakhstan, a large group of protesting oil workers was fired on by police, who killed sixteen and injured more than one hundred people. In subsequent years, since both events (occurring on December 16) involved violent police crackdowns on antigovernment demonstrations, protests in Almaty have included Zhanaozen victims in their commemorations. On December 16, 2015, after the Almaty mayor laid flowers to mark Independence Day, activists were reported laying flowers on the same site to commemorate the victims of the crackdowns in 1986 and in Zhanaozen 2011 (RFE/RL, December 16, 2015). In 2018, following the exiled opposition leader Mukhtyar Ablyazov's call for his supporters to participate in a commemoration in central Almaty on December 16, Almaty officials lined the central squares with militarized vehicles and buses and made preventative arrests of known activists (RFE/RL, December 16, 2018).

During and after the celebrations in the square in 2004, in conversations with revelers at public events, as well as with friends and neighbors, I spoke to people about the meanings of December 16. I found that while many participants treated this day simply as a celebration of independence, others held views that departed significantly from this official designation, particularly regarding the events of December 16–18 in 1986. The details of the 1986 event were described to me in vastly different ways by different people: many of my Kazakh friends described it as a brutal police response to a peaceful student protest; others blamed the protesters for the violence. One of my neighbors, a non-Kazakh, was taken aback when I wished her a happy Independence Day, and replied, "It's not happy for me, too many unhappy memories." She described a group of basically hooligans who started the protest, which quickly erupted into violence. She recalled seeing some of her students, hysterical, with blood on their faces, as they were running from the square through our neighborhood, which was nearby.

Other sources, particularly remembrances of Kazakh intellectuals (who were university students in 1986), insist that it began as a peaceful protest of mostly young people, students. Quanysh Rakhmetov relates his memories of the protest: "We were young students living in the dormitory, but on December 16, 1986, when we were leaving the dormitory friends told us a huge number of students were going to the central square. . . . Two friends and I decided to go immediately. The square was blocked by the police but we managed to get through them and join the demonstration" (Pannier 2006). Kalelkhan Uliy, who was visiting friends at the university on that day, remembered making banners out of sheets, which they hung out of the dormitory windows. According to Uliy, the sheets read, "The Kazakh nation deserves a Kazakh leader," and "Kazakhstan belongs to Kazakhs." He remembers, "We left the technical school and while we were moving toward the central square more and more Kazakhs joined us, like rivers flowing into the sea" (Pannier 2006).

While many intellectual Almatyites I spoke to were critical of Nazarbaev, the oralmandar (returnees) I interviewed, on the other hand, expressed much more positive sentiments. At the oralman concert, attendees from Mongolia and China praised Nazarbaev as a strong and just leader who built Kazakhstan into a stable, economically viable and technologically advanced country. One young Kazakh oralman who has lived in Almaty for two years, said that he was happy living in Kazakhstan, a "democratic" country, as opposed to "communist" China. Interestingly, he especially stressed his love for Astana—when he was asked why, he replied, "[It is] *my* country, my *astana* [*astana* means capital in Kazakh]."

Since the establishment of Astana as the new Kazakhstani capital in 1997, the central government has made a rigorous effort to diminish Almaty's importance in national matters, including Kazakhstani history, and instead establish Astana as the new center. Kazakhstan's new history, particularly as exemplified in Nazarbaev's book *In the Heart of Eurasia*, focuses on Astana (Nazarbaev 2005). One of the benefits of moving the capital is that any old and unwanted associations with the Soviet era can be hastily shed by the current regime. In this context, Zheltoksan is problematic not only because it disputes the official meaning and timing of independence but also because it places Almaty, not Astana, at the center of the independence movements.

The friction surrounding independence can be seen as a tension between collective remembering and forgetting. Nazarbaev has essentially distanced himself from Almaty and the events of 1986 in establishing this new forward-looking capital with virtually no history. Mourners on the square, meanwhile, strive to keep the memory of violence and protest alive.

Many Kazakhs use Independence Day as a memorial service for the protesters who died that day in 1986. Before the festivities began on the square, I saw people gathering in small groups, laying flowers at the feet of the Golden Man statue, the symbol of Kazakhstani Independence. The Golden Man statue depicts a warrior riding atop a winged snow leopard.[6] The statue on Republican Square symbolizes Kazakhstan's independence, reflecting both its prosperity and nomadic past. In her *Memorial Mania* (2010), Erika Doss stresses the function of memorials as sites of powerful emotions. She describes memorials as crucial sites serving affective purposes, important for transmitting not only historical events and actors but also the emotions surrounding these events (Doss 2010, 38). Francoise Choay asserts, "It is not simply a question of informing, of calling to mind a bit of information, but rather of stirring up, through the emotions, a living memory" (Choay, quoted in Doss 2010, 38). Doss contends that memorials are sites of unifying commemoration as well as places of division and conflict. "Memorial mania does not rest on a coherent, collective, or even consensual ideological framework. Many contemporary memorials are marked by conflict, rupture, and loss " (Doss 2010, 47). On Independence Day in Almaty, Republican Square is the site of a highly contested remembrance of the beginnings of independence. Every year, roses accumulate thickly around statues in commemoration of past violence, even as these heavily marked sites provide a meeting place for new protests.

FRIENDSHIP OF THE PEOPLES ON REPUBLICAN SQUARE

One of the ways in which temporality appears in such events is through the endurance of Soviet-era ideologies, which peek through in post-Soviet performance styles and formats. Through examining the ideological residue in these performances, we can observe how the nationalism of today's Kazakhstan is in some ways still tethered to the Soviet past. A particularly stubborn ideological remainder of the Soviet era is the concept of *druzhba narodov* or Friendship of the Peoples. A cornerstone of Soviet nationality policy, druzh-

FIGURE. 2.4. Unity of Nations Day, Almaty, 2005.

ba narodov is a durable and seminal idea that affected a very large stretch of
territory under Soviet influence at the time and continues to inform state policy in contemporary Kazakhstan. Adopted by regimes from Eastern Europe
to mainland China,[7] this ideological concept touts the equality and harmony
of all nationalities, but in practice has supported the primacy of the majority
group while encouraging a surface expression of nationalism for minority
nationalities through "harmless" displays of national costumes, cuisine, and
most importantly for this project, minority music and dance. The superficial support of minority nationalities and simultaneous maintenance of a
majority-dominated power balance was a mainstay of Soviet policy and Soviet holiday events. The Kazakhstani government has mirrored Soviet nationality policy to a surprising degree, and the spirit of druzhba narodov
is still clearly evident in state-sponsored festivals and other performance
genres.

Independence Day celebrations in the central square in Almaty were at
first glance quite similar to Soviet-era performances. They included a long
program of song-and-dance numbers performed by various ethnic groups:

Polish, Turkish, Cossack, Uighur, Korean, Russian, Jewish, Dungan (Muslim Chinese, or Hui), and a grand finale in which all the participants sing together. On the square that day, most of my interviewees spoke about conditions in Kazakhstan in positive ways: prevailing ethnic harmony in the new Kazakhstan, the success of Nazarbaev in building this young country, and optimism for its continued economic development. In this sense, the interviewees' responses were in line with the ideology of the Friendship of the Peoples—indeed, some even used this phrase to describe what they saw as relatively stable ethnic relations in post-Soviet Kazakhstan. The staged festivities at this event were largely amateur performances, in an order typical for this kind of public holiday event—the Kazakh groups performed first, with the Russian act inserted in the middle, and the other ethnic groups followed.

The Kazakh music was dominated by vocal performance, with the marked exception of two acts by young Kazakh performers in which dance and drama were central. The Kazakh songs, both newly composed and reworked folk songs, were sung to a variety of prerecorded synthesized music, including disco tracks, military marches, "Eastern" pop music with an Uzbek or Turkish sensibility and rhythms taken from the Middle Eastern rhythmic modes, and Kazakh orchestral music, with a prominent dombra (Kazakh plucked lute) section. These acts were dominated by middle-aged and older singers with trained, sometimes operatic voices. The songs were from various eras and included a recent pop song and were performed mostly by well-known singers of the Soviet era. Many songs, including "Ata Meken" (Fatherland), "Tugan Zher" (Homeland), and "Menin Kazakhstanym" (My Kazakhstan), were well-known patriotic favorites.

Performances by Kazakh musicians differed along generational lines. Although the older generation sang quite patriotic songs, their cheerful performance style was reminiscent of Soviet-era *estrada* (staged Soviet pop music). The performances of the older generation reflected a Soviet-era quality that is difficult to pin down—reflecting optimism, nostalgia, or a kind of military patriotism reminiscent of Soviet-era performers. The women of this generation performed with an upbeat and industrious brightness and active body language (clapping with the audience and dancing), whereas the military songs were typified by an upright and unmoving performance stance (particularly one performance by two veterans in uniform). Other performances of this same generation reflected sentimentality and nostalgia. One Kazakh singer performed a Russian song popular in the post-war era called "Pesnia ostaetsia s chelovekom" (A Song Remains with You), written by the beloved composer, Arkadii Ostrovskii.

"A Song Remains with You"
Words and Music by Arkadii Ostrovskii

At night stars float in a deep blue river,
In the morning the stars will be extinguished without a trace,
Only the songs stay with a person,
Songs are your true friends forever.

Refrain:
Through the years, through the ages,
On any road, on either side,
You never say goodbye to a song,
A song never leaves you.

We carry with us songs from our cradle,
We travel everywhere with our songs,
How many songs have we sung with our loved ones?
How many we will still sing with you!

Refrain [repeated]:

In the icy cold, a song will warm us.
In the heat of noon it will be like water,
Those who cannot sing and listen to songs
Will never be happy.[8]

This song, unlike others in the celebration, was not patriotic in any definable way and did not celebrate Kazakhstan's independence; rather, it seemed to reflect nostalgia for the Soviet past. Many Kazakhstanis of this generation admitted a special attachment to the old estrada songs of their youth, and they sang these songs at social events like birthdays. The first lines ("At night stars float in the dark blue river / in the morning they are extinguished without a trace, / Only the songs stay with a person, / Songs are your true friends forever") seem to evoke this attachment.

In contrast, the more innovative acts by younger performers had a more creative, dramatic sensibility and focused on a specific political and emotional message. Silver and black costuming and dramatic gestures set a somber, serious mood. In the first act, male dancers used gestures miming horse-back riding and wrestling, very consciously mixing these Kazakh markers with hallmarks of youth culture such as break dancing. The dance was set to synthesized dance music, repetitive and driving, with synthesized strings resembling the sound of a dombra playing over a drone. At the end, a single male performer dressed in white took center stage. Covering his face in a gesture of despair and reaching to the sky with outstretched arms, he "recited" (lip-synched) a poem about the turmoil of Kazakh history. Not only did this performance send a more deliberate message, the mood and methods of conveyance contrasted sharply with those of older generations. Though the *words* of the older generations' songs conveyed patriotic messages about "homeland," the youth acts were more specifically about Kazakh history and independence, a message reflected on multiple levels (visuals, dance, music) in an emotionally charged and dramatic moving tableau.

One Kazakh friend, a single woman in her thirties, who planned to become a Kazakh language teacher, watched the performance with me. She responded positively to the new direction taken by the younger performers, praising their creativity and experimentalism. She was scornful of the old druzhba narodov lineup and said that the people who planned these events needed a new approach, something more in line with the beliefs and tastes of the population. "But," she said, "as long as the older generation is in power, these Soviet-style performances will probably continue."

EURASIANISM AND "THE YEAR OF RUSSIA"

One prominent ideological trajectory in the live performance on the square was Eurasianism. Eurasianism has a long history in the region and has gained prominence and political importance in post-Soviet Russia and Ka-zakhstan. Among the several intellectual strands of Eurasianism, the most salient is that of the Soviet scholar Lev Gumilev (1912–1992),[9] who envisioned a utopian alliance between Turkic and Slavic peoples (an alliance that he viewed as historically and geographically predetermined) and claimed Eurasia as the historic homeland of both peoples. According to Gumilev's theory of ethnogenesis, humans are deeply affected by the territory they inhabit; an ethnic group, or *ethnos*, may be warlike, peaceful, or industrious, depending on their geographical surroundings (see Gumilev 1989b). Terrain, climate, and natural resources dictate what kind of lifeway an ethnos may pursue and succeed at (e.g., fishing, hunting, agriculture, trade, military expansion), which in turn affects the group's sociocultural makeup. He argues that the natural proclivities of Turkic and Slavic people, although inherently different, are mutually complementary and that both can thrive from such a union. Drawing on these concepts, Nazarbaev's Eurasianism places Kazakhstan as an intermediary between East and West. His Eurasianism at once promotes interethnic harmony between Kazakhs (Turks) and Russians (Slavs) and simultaneously implies cooperation between Russia and the Central Asian states.

Both Nazarbaev and Putin are self-declared Eurasianists, engaging with the theories of neo-Eurasianists, the most prominent of whom is Alexander Dugin, a media-savvy Russian philosopher and nationalist who maintains an active website and has written several books about Eurasianism, including a book on Nazarbaev (Dugin 2004). Dugin and other current Eurasianists, among them the Kazakh political theorist Nurlan Amrekulov, envision in Eurasia a second pole of power to balance US political, economic, and military dominance—an ideology with teeth as witnessed by the twenty-first-century acceleration in the formation of transregional partnerships in Eurasia. Dugin sees the rise of a bipolar world order in which a land-based, continental, territorialist power in Eurasia balances the maritime, commercial, capitalist power he calls Atlanticism, which correlates roughly to American-European–driven globalism. Eurasianism meshes well with domestic and foreign policy both in Kazakhstan and in Russia. In Russia, it is used to legitimate a continuation of domination in the region that was formerly the Soviet Union. Under Eurasianism, Russia can promote itself as a powerful *partner* with the Central Asian republics. Where Russian dominance in Central Asia has colonial and Soviet precedence, Eurasianism is strangely forward leaning, utopic, and hopeful, while also drawing from a mythologized Slavic-Turkic partnership in the distant past. Eurasianism thus takes a giant leap over the messy colonial and Soviet history, and forms a bridge from the preindustrial to the postnational. The historian Mark Bassin contends,

"Conventional academic historians tend understandably to be quite critical of Gumilev's word, emphasizing the element of 'unbridled fantasy' in it that undermines any pretensions to serious scholarship" (Bassin 2016, 241). But the fantastical, evocative storytelling that Gumilev's theories spin is perfect for use in nation-building. In Kazakhstan, it is put to use in building the cities (even civilizations?) of the future based on romantic, heroic images of the steppe and forest people.

In a sense, Eurasianism has served as a replacement for the ideology of Soviet socialism, as a way to unify the post-Soviet states in Eurasia and project this partnership into the future. Eurasianism performs that special Soviet sleight of hand: promoting a transnational utopian vision while simultaneously following a nationalist policy maintaining centralized power. Furthermore, Eurasianism is easily blurred with Kazakh nationalism because Eurasianism (particularly as promoted by Gumilev) glorifies Turkic-speaking nomads. Stressing mobility as a distinct advantage on the open steppes of Eurasia (particularly in military and trade), Gumilev wrote that Turkic nomads are the natural leaders in that region and that a partnership with them was essential to the survival of the forest-dwelling Slavs (Russians). Thus, Eurasianism, like Kazakh nationalism, looks to the nomadic past as one of its central myths, while emphasizing a partnership between Slavs and Turkic peoples as the naturalized and historical leaders of Eurasia. Stressing both diversity and centralized power while glorifying a nomadic Eurasian past, Eurasianism becomes a platform that legitimizes Kazakh nationalism as well as an updated Soviet-style nationalities policy.

Nazarbaev's theme for 2004, "The Year of Russia in Kazakhstan," emphasized Kazakhstan and Russia as a key regional partnership, an idea that was echoed repeatedly in Independence Day speeches and in the celebration's single performance by a Russian performer. The opening speech placed this partnership within the context of Eurasianist ideology. The following greeting (in both Russian and Kazakh) opened the Independence Day event:

> Dear Almatyites and guests to the southern capital: Happy Independence Day! Today we mark the main holiday of our country, Independence Day. We feel the sure progress of our young country towards sovereignty and democracy. On the 16th of December 1991, the constitutional law asserting the independence of the republic of Kazakhstan was declared. We are proud that since time immemorial

our country in linking East and West has made a substantial contribution to the development of civilizations. And now, thanks to the farsighted policies of our first president Nursultan Nazarbaev, our state has been recognized by the international community and has set a course for the development and flourishing of Kazakhstanis.[10]

This speech is interesting in that it positions Kazakhstan as an intermediary between East and West, which has implications both domestically and abroad. Implying a balance between "eastern" (Turkic) and "western" (Slavic) peoples, it at once promotes interethnic harmony internally and simultaneously implies cooperation with partners from the former Soviet Union, most notably Russia and the Central Asian states. Further, it is precisely this positioning that is given credit for the "development of civilization" and Kazakhstan's acceptance into the "world community." Essentially, this is a Eurasianist speech. The main theme conveyed is twofold. First, Kazakhstan's role as the fulcrum between eastern and western partners (Russia and Central Asia, or even China) is essential to Kazakhstan's current position of prominence in the region. And second—a key tenet of Nazarbaev's Eurasianism—this speech strongly implies that this crucial intermediary position is a natural, geographically and historically based role for Kazakhstan.

"The Year of Russia in Kazakhstan" theme was particularly obvious in the performance of Maria Dranova, an ethnic Russian, who sang the following:

"Russia and Kazakhstan"

Rivers are joined in the ocean,
The ocean fears no winds.
Kazakhstan and Russia forever.
Russia and we are like brother and sister.

Refrain:
Russia and Kazakhstan,
Two suns, two wings.
Thank you, thank you,
Because I have

One fate, one dream,
Russia and Kazakhstan.

From year to year the Republic is strengthening
Gaining strength in the friendship of the peoples.
The Kazakh steppes are blooming
With islands of Russians roses.

This song is rich with imagery that supports the central ideological bases of the festival (nationalism, Eurasianism, and an updated version of Soviet-era Friendship of the Peoples). In the refrain, the description of Russian-Kazakhstani partnership is combined with nationalist imagery, as the description of Russia and Kazakhstan as "two suns, two wings" refers to the Kazakhstani flag (which depicts an eagle and a sun on a blue background). The phrase "the Kazakh steppe is blooming with Russian roses" conveys images of mutual prosperity, with ecological references used to depict and naturalize the intertwined nature of Kazakh-Russian relations. Finally, in the second verse, the "friendship of the peoples" is credited for Kazakhstan's strength and prosperity.

This performance stood out in the overall festivities in many respects. The act was central in the lineup, sandwiched between two Kazakh performances. It looked more staged and professional than many of the other acts, particularly the groups from the Assembly of Nations, which were clearly amateur.[11] There was also a sudden shift in the color scheme. Many Kazakh singers, the set, and the decorative banners on the square were in blue and yellow (the colors of the Kazakhstani flag), but Dranova was dressed in bright Russian red and gold, colors of the Russian coat of arms and the Soviet flag. Her costume, a Russian *sarafan*, highlighted her Russian heritage. The pairing of Kazakh and Russian performances, the song text emphasizing a partnership between Russia and Kazakhstan, and the color schemes mirroring the Russian and Kazakh flags, combine to echo the Eurasianist rhetoric in this event's "Year of Russia" performances.

After the Russian and Kazakh performances, a long program featured dances by Polish, Turkish, Cossack, Uighur, Korean, Russian, Jewish, and Dungan groups. The majority of acts—including a group of Turkish belly dancers, a Korean choir, and Uighur performers in silver costumes dancing to Uighur pop—fall easily into the Druzhba Narodov pattern, but the Polish group represented a departure from the guiding ideology. The performance consisted of a Polish youth group wearing T-shirts with the Polish crest and singing a song in Polish with lyrics about "following God" set to a reggae beat. A few of the boys wore Polish military uniforms. Though this act could easily be dismissed as a group of teens singing their favorite reggae song (very badly), the display of both Polish nationalism and religious thought made it an anomaly in the Independence Day celebrations. If the unspoken rules of Druzhba Narodov dictate a "harmless" display of national pride, this act arguably contradicts the friendly shoulder-to-shoulder harmony typically depicted in such performances.

It is interesting to compare the rough edges of this performance with the polished, professional performances in the Unity of Nations Day celebration, which was held on Republican Square later the next year, on May 1. In the latter event, the "ethnic" dances were not self-representations, but highly choreographed performances by trained dance troupes (ethnically mixed and Kazakh-dominated). Because they were not representations by various different groups but rather centrally choreographed, the images and ideology were more tightly controlled. Whereas the May 1 event was able to uniformly and unambiguously convey the central concept of druzhba narodov, the Independence Day events were much more loosely organized, and conveyed a number of other themes that strayed from the main concept of ethnic harmony. The homogenizing of each ethnic group in druzhba narodov is easier to achieve when the performance is not a self-representation. In the May 1 event, professional performers, many of them Kazakh, presented a stylized version of Polish or Estonian or Ukrainian identities. By contrast, the Independence Day acts were much more "real," if also more amateur in appearance. When groups represent themselves, other phenomena are expressed *besides* ethnicity; thus the Polish youth group sang about youthful rebellion and God, the Kazakh youth dance brought up themes of struggle, youth, and masculinity, and the older Kazakh group sang nostalgic Soviet love songs.

AIRING INDEPENDENCE

Although this festival was fairly well attended considering the raw weather, many acquaintances I spoke with later admitted they rarely attended these outdoor festivals. In fact, several interlocutors surmised that most attendees were from out of town (a view that did not actually hold up in my interviews; though I spoke with a number of families who traveled from outside the city, and even other parts of Kazakhstan, more that half of the people I interviewed were from Almaty). In any case, for many Almatyites holidays like Independence Day represented a day off from work, a day to relax, hang out, eat, and watch television.

MEDIATING TEMPORALITY

In addition to analyzing live performance, throughout this book I explore the role of television in mediating the intersection of temporality and public feeling. Scholars have examined media's role in shaping the emotional aspects of public temporality.[12] Alison Landberg, for example, stresses the use of media in "public cultural memory." She contends that technologies of modernity, particularly television and cinema, allow people to take on memories that are not their own—*prosthetic memories*—and play an important role in forming political positions. She writes:

> Modernity makes possible and necessary a new form of public cultural memory. This new form of memory, which I call prosthetic memory, emerges at the interface between a person and a historical narrative about the past, at an experiential site such as a movie theater or museum. In this moment of contact, an experience occurs through which the person sutures himself or herself into a larger history. . . . In the process that I am describing, the person does not simply apprehend a historical narrative but takes on a more personal, deeply felt memory of a past event through which he or she did not live. The resulting prosthetic memory has the ability to shape that person's subjectivity and politics. (Landsberg 2004, 2)

Landsberg stresses the use of media, which makes possible the adoption of memories by people who are not their obvious inheritors. Neta Kligler-Vilenchik writes about the media as a "powerful tool in shaping perceptions of the past" (Kligler-Vilenchik, Tsfati, and Meyers 2014, 485) and discusses media's "ability to simultaneously reach mass audiences, and provide interpretations of the past that are hard to avoid" (485). She asserts that mediated representations of the past appear in a narrative form "stressing an emotional aspect, rendering them more resonant than structured learning " (485–86). Media's power to shape our understanding of temporality lies in its mass appeal and large-scale reach, and in its use of emotive narrative portrayals of the past and the future. Public culture, therefore, "is a key arena for retelling the collective past and shaping the public memory" (487) and, I would add, our imaginings of the future. In Kazakhstan, where media are to a great extent controlled by the state, this emotive power to shape temporal perception lies heavily (though not exclusively) in the hands of the government.

Andreas Huyssen, too, stresses the role of media in shaping the way a public perceives, views, and even understands the past. In discussing the mediated past in popular culture, he writes, "Key questions of contemporary culture are precisely located at the threshold between traumatic memory and the commercial media" (Huyssen 2000, 29–30). Although he allows that it may be a stretch to claim that "the specters from the past haunting modern societies . . . actually articulate, by way of displacement, a growing fear of the future at a time when the belief in modernity's progress is deeply shaken," Huyssen asserts that media has a forceful hand in shaping public memory. "Media," he writes, "do not transport public memory innocently. They shape it in their very structure and form" (Huyssen 2000, 29–30).

INDEPENDENCE DAY PROGRAMMING

The television programs that aired on the Kazakhstan channel on Independence Day were quite different in tone and content than most of the acts on the square that day. Whereas the live festivities stressed interethnic cooperation and harmony in the style of Soviet Druzhba Narodov song and dance routines, the television programs instead focused on Kazakh history and culture. The televised programs were entirely in Kazakh and included Kazakh music videos, a concert of Kazakh folk songs, a short film featuring Kazakh musical traditions, and a narrated photomontage tracing economic, political, and historical developments in Kazakhstan.

Two televised features in particular that aired on Independence Day—a film and a music video—showed Kazakh music as a vehicle to transport characters within these stories into other times. But they function as temporal transport in very different ways, and it is interesting to see the contradictory ideas of Kazakh nationhood presented in past and future tenses. The short film *Babalar Uny* (Voice of [Our] Ancestors), which aired on Independence Day, features an array of Kazakh musical traditions, including performances on the qobyz, the Kazakh upright fiddle, and the dombra, the

Kazakh plucked two-stringed lute, and underscores the symbolic role of Kazakh instruments. The plot is straightforward: after a car breaks down in the countryside, its driver is forced to spend the night on the open steppe, where he experiences a kind of cosmic return to a mythical Kazakh past. The main character, played by a famous musician, is transformed from a modern-day Kazakh everyman into a zhyrau (epic singer) and an aqyn (a poet-singer with expertise in improvisation).

The aqyn and zhyrau are important figures in Kazakh history. Aqyndar (pl. of aqyn) functioned as social critics and conveyors of news and zhyraular (pl. of zhyrau) served as a crucial repository for Kazakh mythology and history. The Kazakh language did not exist in written form until the nineteenth century, and early history was transmitted orally through zhyraular. Zhyraular also retained clan genealogical records, as they had to be able to recite the clan lineage back many generations. This was important because Kazakh marriage laws dictated extreme exogamy, forbidding marriage among those sharing a common ancestor up to seven generations back. Although they are still active today, aqyndar and zhyraular function symbolically as a connection to the past, when epic singers served as a main repository for Kazakh mythology and history, and poet-singers provided important social commentary and censure, helping to guide clan decisions and morals.

In the film, as the main character drives through the countryside, shots of his journey are overlaid with various images: ancient petroglyphs of the Altai, herds of wild horses, stylized images of mountains and rivers, and scenes of Kazakh warriors locked in battle with an enemy. Scenes of the past and present are juxtaposed on the landscape. The driver is slowed by a herd of sheep on the road, passes a body of water, and heads into the mountains, where his car breaks down. He walks into the mountains, sits down on a hilltop, and begins to read. As the sun sinks lower on the steppe, he seems to slips into a past era. We hear the sound of a qobyz—then we see that it is being played by our main character, now dressed in traditional Kazakh embroidered coat and stiff, embroidered Kazakh hat.

As is typical, the zhyrau draws out the first note (typically a fifth above the tonic), placed high and tight in his vocal range, and the resulting sound is focused and intense. He then switches to what is sometimes called the "epic" voice, a rough, growling vocal style close to throat-singing, pitched fairly low in the vocal range. It is significant that our hero plays the qobyz, which is fairly atypical for modern zhyraular, who usually accompany themselves on dombra. The qobyz has a long history of connections with shamanism, and still carries a mystic quality. Here, the image of a qobyz player sitting alone in the mountains under a starry sky strengthens the sense that there is something magical happening—that he is magically transporting himself into the past. This excursion that he first began, driving through the mountains, has become a journey into the past. Like the Kazakh shaman who uses the qobyz's deep sonorous tones to transport himself into the spirit world, the main character is in a way detaching from the present. Kazakh music is portrayed as a way of connecting the contemporary hero to a mythologized Kazakh past.

As night falls, the main character, still in traditional dress, sits at a campfire and sings another song, this time with dombra accompaniment. Other men happen upon his campfire and gather to listen. As is typical, the zhyrau doubles his vocal melody on dombra and plays a rhythmic vamp between phrases. As dawn approaches, the men around the campfire slip back into this century. Wearing a T-shirt and black jeans, the main character finishes the epic song, while the others, also in contemporary dress, listen sleepily and warm themselves by the fire as their horses graze nearby. In the morning, it is as if this nighttime encounter with the past never happened; the main character wakes up, alone. He walks back to his car in the early morning, and, after a little tinkering, the car starts up. He continues on his journey out of the mountains, and the film ends abruptly as his car approaches a town.

As in other films and music videos of this type, there seems to be confusion as to what the "real" time is. While the nighttime scene appears as a dream in the bright light of day, it is the heart of the film, while the approaching town signals the film's end. The scenario is fairly typical of Kazakh videos: a journey into the Kazakh countryside, the experiencing of Kazakh lifeways that have disappeared from the city, and then the return trip into the city. This dichotomy of past/rural/traditional vs. modern/urban/postindustrial is often used in "istoricheskii" or "historical" Kazakh music videos, and is fairly common in those of other developing countries as well. The nostalgia in this short film hinges on both fragments from the past (such as the idea that the qobyz is from another time, a mythologized, shamanic past) and the merging of past and present through visual overlay and overlapping narratives (the story of the modern-day journey overlapping with this meeting of Kazakh elders in some past time). As in other films and music videos of this type, it is place that allows the merging of past and present, facilitating restorative nostalgia and nationalist narratives of unbroken lines of history.

Interestingly, one music video, Saz Otau's "Sagym Dala," aired shortly after this movie on Independence Day, seems to mock this modern/traditional, rural/urban dichotomy so common in Kazakh "historical" music videos. This video depicts Saz Otau, a dombra/qobyz duo, flying over a desolate landscape in a wooden orb spaceship. Suggesting a Mad Max–style alternate universe, it blends the preindustrial traditional past with an imaginative space-age future. The woman is seated, playing the qobyz, with the male dombra player standing behind her. The female musician plays with a dry humor, looking directly into the camera, her body upright and almost motionless in an attitude of mock seriousness. Flying in an ancient spaceship, Saz Otau seems to be sidestepping the problematic post-Soviet present. Presenting a tongue-in-cheek mythological worldview, Saz Otau smirks at the canonical view of the Kazakh past as well as its logical evolution to the future. Eschewing both the economic development trajectory and the historicized, mythologized view of Kazakhstan's cultural heritage, this video upends the central tenets of nation-building. It interrupts the flow of progress and modernity, of economic development and cultural flourishing, and instead presents a floating present, disconnected from a historical past or pragmatic future. Unlike other utopian visions of the future, it is futuristic without being nostalgic, and gestures toward a temporality without nation or even place.

The central questions about Independence Day, which I discuss here through an ethnography of 2004 holiday events and programs, continue to swirl around the marking of December 16. Is this day bloody or celebratory? Is it rightly marked by celebration, commemoration, or protest? What does Republican Square in Almaty signify in this era, as a commemorative site that both marks the birth of Kazakhstan's independence and continues to host protests of unfair governance? Contradictions also appear in live performances on Republican Square, which explore ideas that hark back to the Soviet era (like the Friendship of the Peoples) and also reflect newer representations of identity and ethnicity. Rather than resonating homogeneously across the festival, such ideas can show up unevenly, with community-organized song-and-dance acts bringing up off-message topics, such as religion. Televised programs can add another layer of meaning to holidays, picking up and developing state ideology in interesting ways, or, on the contrary, they may contradict the typical construction of Kazakh nationhood. In any case, televised programming, so often a part of the experience of a commemorative or celebratory day, contributes significantly to the construction of meaning around this date. Both mediated and live celebrations elucidate particularly how "sticky" places and dates both connect to the past and point toward the future, continually gathering meaning. Ideologies depend crucially on temporal framing, playing on older layers of cultural heritage, relating to different eras of the past, or promising different futures.

CHAPTER 3

SAME TIME NEXT YEAR

Winter and Rhythmicity on Television

It is a winter evening in early 2005. The snow is swirling outside and the branches of trees in the "dvor" (the interior courtyard of the Soviet apartment block) are swinging wildly in the wind. The temperature has dropped precipitously throughout the day (a local friend instructed me to look to the mountains in the morning to forecast the weather for the day) but our apartment is cozy. I silently thank the Soviet industry that crafted the powerful boiler and built these thick sturdy walls.

Our friends Saule and Dina have stopped by for a visit that evening and we are gathered in the living room, with a bit of local cognac. Later in the night, the two of them will pull out the cards and tell our fortunes—an unnerving experience, and a tradition during midwinter nights—looking, they say, "for love or money." But for now the night is young, the mood is light. Saule, lithe, with a dancer's body and a steely backbone, is perched on a straightbacked chair, her ankles crossed. Dina is lolling on the sofa next to me, telling me jokes. Saule reaches for the guitar. As she plucks the beginning bass line and chords, she smiles. She begins singing a favorite from a beloved Soviet holiday movie, from the 1970s. Dina sings along.[1]

In this chapter I investigate how the repeated cycle of the seasons and the calendar year bears on everyday experience and is reflected on Kazakhstani television. Mary Taylor Simeti writes, "A calendar based on the season, on sowing and harvesting, on death and rebirth, is irrelevant to us now, its recurrent cycle out of step with the linear conception of time and progress that urges us forward" (Simeti 1986, 78). And yet, though daily life in the industrialized world is no longer closely intertwined with the seasonal cycle, we are still attached to ideas and habits related to the seasons. Michael Kammen, a scholar of American cultural history, describes an *increase* of agricultural tropes and images of the seasons after World War II as people became

FIGURE 3.I. Ded Moroz and Snegurochka hold a rooster for the zodiac year, Almaty.

more removed from seasonal agricultural life (Kammen 2004, 210–11). It is as if the greater distance from rural life raises its nostalgic value and fuels the popularity and romanticization of images and tropes of rural life. Seasonal motifs, Kammen argues, became more prominent after the war as their function became monetized: "The four seasons motif emerged with greatly enhanced visibility because it was perceived by all sorts of entrepreneurs as an appealing way to sell and promote things" (Kammen 2004, 211). This process of commercialization of the seasonal themes accelerated and proliferated with the advent of television and other forms of mass media. Widespread cultural ideas about nature and the change of seasons emanate and are popularized by urban, elite centers, rather than rural areas or peasant culture (Shirane 2012). Just as the rural is often connected to the past in the popular urban imagination, similarly, urban, commercialized centers attach a romantic nostalgia to ideas about nature and the seasons.

In the United States, this commercialized and televised seasonality revolves around agricultural traditions and images, whereas in Kazakhstan, commercialized and televised seasonality depends on ideas about preindustrial Russian and Kazakh lifeways. Reflecting this demographic diversity, Kazakhstan's seasonal motifs reveal both its farming and herding ways of life. Until the early part of the twentieth century, Kazakhs were largely nomadic pastoralists living in a region with an extreme continental climate. They necessarily maintained a close connection to weather, livestock, and pasturelands for survival; Tengrism, the animist religion of pre-Islamic Kazakhs and other steppe Turkic people reflected this connection (Amanov and Mukhambetova 2002, 14). Early Slavs worshipped pre-Christian nature spirits of the forest, rivers, and bathhouses (Ryan 1999) and were intimately aware of the seasonal bounty of the fields and forest, which yielded wild greens, berries, and wild mushrooms. In twenty-first-century Kazakhstan, as in other industrialized countries, although seasonal changes no longer connect to lifeways directly, seasonality appears in mediated form, on television, in advertising, and in the seasonal programming of films. Both nomadic and agricultural references to the change of seasons appear in advertisements for food products, cooking aids and spices, restaurants, and even for mobile data plans.

This chapter describes winter in Kazakhstan and its many dazzling ways of celebrating the season, and it also represents a study of the experience of cyclical time. Feminist, queer, and anthropological scholarship has reexamined the linear temporality of modernity, the teleology of modern life, and the forward-facing directionality of progress-centered ideologies (including both communism and capitalism).[2] Such work has posed alternatives to this linearity, shifting the scholarly attention toward nonlinear and nonnormative aspects of time. Cyclicity, perhaps partly because of its relationship to fertility and heteronormativity, rarely appears among studies of alternative temporalities. I suggest that cyclicity and its place in popular culture beg examination. Certainly, expressions and devices of cyclicity and seasonality maintain a prominent presence in advertising and television—but what purpose does cyclical time serve now? As evidenced by the phenomenal popularity of PSL (Starbuck's seasonal return of its pumpkin spice latte), *cyclicity*, the repeated experience of time, can be used as a marketing device to boost sales or viewership and appeal to clientele and television audiences. The seasonal element draws audiences and consumers because of cyclical familiarity—the comfort of knowing what is to come.

According to the sociologist Eviatar Zerubavel, human beings have a strong need for temporal order. Schedules, clocks, seasonal cycles, and calendars all provide a comforting level of predictability, contributing to a sense of well-being. The anthropologist Safet HadžiMuhamedovic writes about the way that the festive, cyclical marking of time, which accords with seasonal labor, creates and strengthens different bonds and relationships in a Bosnian community. He explains that the "annual cycle shaped human activities and various sorts of economies, which in turn structured relationships" (HadžiMuhamedovic 2018, 62). Ordering time also provides a sense of individual planning and agency in imparting a level of control over one's environment. In the same way, a predictable, repeated appearance of seasonal motifs and traditions creates the expectation of a seasonal resting place, a temporal hearth, which brings a sense of belonging and comfort.

This examination of cyclical time attends not only to natural cycles (seasons) but also to political cycles, particularly the making and marking of calendars. Zerubavel describes calendars as temporal maps of marked events in history (Zerubavel 2003, 30). Both maps and calendars reflect and affect ideology in their ability to order space and time and influence everyday life. Maps by their very nature treat space unequally, marking and naming certain places while leaving others anonymous. In the same way, calendars reflect an essential bias in the act of inclusion and exclusion. Because they mark specific historical events and include newly created political holidays while excluding or replacing holidays of older regimes, calendars betray the political inclinations of their makers, and like maps are essential tools of nation-building. On a larger scale, calendars emerge from timelines that chart events central to a particular ideology, such as the birth of Jesus Christ or the emigration of the Prophet Muhammad from Mecca to Medina. In the same way that maps help mapmakers promote their vision of local or national space, calendars promote their makers' ideological or religious leanings. The ways in which people choose to use national maps and calendars provide insight into how they choose to order their environment, what they think of the national agenda, and, ultimately, how they see themselves.

MAPS, CALENDARS, AND REGIME CHANGE

The birth of independent Kazakhstan in 1991 ushered in the post-Soviet era, a sea change that brought new maps and street names, a new calendar and newly established holidays. Thus began the double-layered nature of Almaty's streets and calendar year, a phenomenon familiar to people throughout the former Soviet territory. Anyone unfamiliar with the post-Soviet world visiting Almaty for the first time will remark on the presence of two city maps—the printed map with the new names of Kazakh heroes and historical figures, and the mental map that all Almaty residents hold in their minds, with the old Soviet street names that still dominate in common usage. Taxi drivers may know the new street names (though using them will certainly betray your status as nonlocal), and many residents vaguely know the new names of major streets, but to a great extent the old Soviet map is most often used in conversation. Habits of place-naming die hard. If you grew up going to Elementary School no. 35 on Lenin Street, it is likely that you will not easily call the same street by its new name, "Dostyk" (Kz. *friendship*). Every favorite corner vendor you pass, every carved up bench, every newsstand, belongs on the street named Lenin, not Dostyk. Streets have such personality that it is difficult to change the name without changing something essential about the place. Just as place is embedded in our bodily memory and personal history, so too is the experience of time.

The patterned and habitual experience of time has been shown to provide a source of well-being. Extreme changes in spatial or temporal patterns—in maps, schedules, or calendars—like those that were ushered in after 1991, can thus have a profound destabilizing effect. Bruno Bettelheim wrote of the "endless anonymity of time" in the Nazi concentration camps as a "factor destructive to personality," and conversely, that "the ability to organize time was a strengthening influence" (Bettelheim in Zerubavel 1981,12). Bettelheim and Zerubavel both describe the ordering of time as vital to personality and identity. It then follows that extreme change in ordering space and time deeply affects human beings' social environment, everyday life, and perhaps even, as Bettelheim suggests, sense of self. Zerubavel writes about time in cognitive terms and uses the terms "figure" and "ground" of Gestalt psychology in describing "the way time is perceived and handled by collectivities" (Zerubavel 1981, xii).[3] He explains that we have a continuous perception of rhythmicity—the patterned way that events happen in everyday life (we wake up to the same alarm clock, put on our clothes, start the coffee, see the same people on our way to work). This rhythmicity provides the "ground" in our everyday life. The expected occurrences and usual sequence of events

FIGURE 3.2. The courtyard of the Russian Orthodox Ascension Cathedral, also known as Zenkov Cathedral, in Panfilov Park.

and routine backgrounds contribute to the feeling of rhythmicity. We come to expect this continuity, and therefore anticipate approaching events—holidays, weekends, seasons. If anticipated events fail to come about, their absence results in a perception of instability. New regimes therefore often strive to replace old holidays with new ones on the same date in order to avoid a "felt absence" on that day. Thus the new Kazakhstani regime replaced International Labor Day (May 1), an important socialist holiday, with Unity of Nations Day. The thematic similarity between these two holidays—"international solidarity" in the former holiday and "unity of nations" in the latter—further aids in the success of the substitution.

My interviewees offered many accounts describing this perceived absence of holiday celebrations. I spoke with a middle-aged Russian day-care attendant as we watched bundled toddlers wrestle in the snow. She spoke nostalgically about public celebrations of Maslenitsa, the Russian Orthodox equivalent of Fat Tuesday (or Mardi Gras) that were held in Panfilov Park in the center of Almaty. "They used to make *bliny* [Russian pancakes or blintzes]," she related, smiling at the memory, "and have an outdoor celebration there in the park. Though it was cold they would have it outside every year. They would give out *bliny* to all the children." Panfilov Park is the site of both the war memorial and the ornate Russian Orthodox Ascension Cathedral (also known as Zenkov Cathedral) in the old center of the city. On the weekends the sidewalks leading up to the church are lined with Russian *babushki* (grandmothers) begging for alms. The benches in the churchyard are always filled with teenagers and grandparents, and the large open square on the church's north side offers snacks and games for kids and birdseed to feed the legions of pigeons. Though technically a part of the Orthodox calendar (the last week before Great Lent), Maslenitsa has roots in pre-Christian Slavic traditions of animism and sun worship (the pancakes representing the sun). Celebrated publicly during Soviet times (when atheism was generally the public face of celebrations), Maslenitsa is a holiday that functions in an ethnic rather than religious way, and this woman's nostalgia for it seemed a remembrance of a more "Russian" era in Almaty.

On one level, the post-Independence calendar change created a sharp break with the past, as revealed in nostalgic accounts of Soviet-era holiday celebrations. But on another level—the level of habit—in some cases, a degree of continuity remained years after the transition. The post-Soviet calendar featured a multitude of newly created holidays, but it was still quite common to informally celebrate the officially defunct Soviet holidays, such as February 23, Red Army Day. Early in February 2005, I went with some friends to a Russian nostalgia-laden restaurant, Zhili Byli, whose name signifies the Russian equivalent of "once upon a time." Zhili Byli serves Russian "peasant" food: dumplings, buckwheat groats, and *mors*, thick red juice squeezed from berries. The decor presents a fairy-tale version of the Russian wooden house, and the servers wear *sarafany* (Russian aprons) and embroidered tunics. On that particular evening, cards on the tables announced a "surprise" for men on February 23 to celebrate the old Soviet holiday, Red Army Day. In the Soviet era, Red Army Day became a day when men were toasted and hosted—the masculine equivalent of March 8 (International Women's Day). When my husband asked about it, the waiter replied with a grin that there was going to be a stripper. But when we returned on Red Army Day, no "surprise" appeared. We asked again about the promised festivities and were told that they were canceled for today, but that we should come back again on the new equivalent holiday, May 7, Kazakhstani Army Day, and there would be a similar celebration. Red Army Day was one of those officially defunct holidays that had no place in the new calendar, but still was marked in casual, familial, and semipublic ways. What is interesting is the *partial* nature of these celebratory gestures and the uncertainty as to how (and even when) to make them. The restaurant Zhily Byli attempted to present an updated, commercialized, sexier version of Red Army Day, aimed at playing with Soviet traditions and motifs while retooling them for another purpose—marketing. Whether because of censure or uncertainty about the acceptable limits of this playful twist, the restaurant managers decided to simply move the celebrations to the parallel holiday (Kazakhstani Army Day) in the new calendar.

On the same February day we visited some friends at their workplace— two fast-talking, vivacious and brightly clad professional women, both nearing fifty. We sat for a while in their office, chatting and playing with our three-year-old daughter. After their younger officemate left for lunch, they locked the door to the office. One of them magically produced *zakuski* (snacks to accompany drinking); the other took out a bottle of vodka from her desk drawer. And so we spent the afternoon. When anyone called, our intrepid companions yelled into the phone instructing the callers to try again when they were not so busy. Although Red Army Day no longer appeared on the calendar, it clearly still exists in habits of celebration, hidden in desk drawers, and in "surprises" in restaurant advertisements. When I asked friends about the holiday, I received predictably divergent responses. Some said only people of the older generation paid attention to such holidays; others said that it was quite common for men of all ages to celebrate Red Army Day in bars. Not quite family holidays, and not completely public, these mini celebrations of Soviet-era holidays do not fit into a neat box. Lacking an official place on the calendar, they are still remembered, marked, it seems, mostly by informal toasting and spontaneous celebrations. There is something off-kilter, off-center about these temporal habits that no longer have an official place. Playful, winking celebrations, stashed mischievously, not quite forbidden, but also not publicly marked, they are remnants of the Soviet past peeking through cracks in the present.

Old New Year, another curious temporal anomaly, is the only remaining secular holiday from the era when the old Orthodox Church calendar (based on the Julian calendar) was the norm. Used exclusively in Russia before the modern Gregorian calendar was adopted in 1918, the old Orthodox calendar is still used for all religious celebrations. It is thirteen days behind the Gregorian calendar, thus Orthodox Christmas occurs on January 7 and New Year's Eve according to the old calendar, or "Old New Year," is celebrated on January 13–14. Now that the calendar is only used in the Orthodox Church, Old New Year is the lone remnant of a time when that calendar guided secular as well as sacred life. Much like the leftover Soviet holidays, it is not written on any current calendars, but still holds a place in the annual cycle of Kazakhstani celebrations. One snowy Almaty winter in mid-January, I wrote in my journal, "Old New Year seems to have survived the century solely through the habits of eating and drinking." The change of calendars and the official omission of old holidays can leave a gap in the cycle resulting in a perceived absence, a nostalgia, and perhaps a sense of loss, but there is a concurrent tendency to continue celebrating the omitted holidays from previous regimes. Like the mental presence of the old Soviet maps, the emotional presence of the old Soviet calendar is still prevalent, whether marked by celebration or reminiscence.

NOSTALGIA, CONSUMERISM, AND POLITICS IN HOLIDAY TELEVISION

Holidays, Food, and Time

In studying cyclical time, it is impossible to miss the ways food and feasting participate in marking the significance of calendrical cycles. Zerubavel writes eloquently about the habits of eating, drinking, and cleaning that accompany—and anticipate—holidays and the Sabbath and contribute to the sense of weekly and seasonal rhythmicity. As he describes Jewish households in a particular community, they clean "toward the Sabbath" and, as members of the community note, "by the smell of the street water . . . you can tell what day of the week it is" (Zerubavel 1981, 18). One temporal aspect contributing to this heightened awareness of *marked* days—especially holidays—is anticipation. Zerubavel's term *rhythmicity* concerns the experience of temporal regularity, but also encapsulates this sense of expectation—a regular, repeated waiting (and preparing) for anticipated future events. In his description of Jewish households he explains that cleaning prior to the Sabbath contributes to such anticipation. Similarly, habits of cooking, eating, and even grocery shopping contribute to our awareness of calendrical cycles. In my household, Thursday is currently soup-making day, and the presence of the giant steaming pot of soup on the stove marks the imminent approach of the weekend and the anticipation of rest. Certain foods, for example, the fresh cranberries that appear in American stores in November, signify the approach of late fall and carry an association with Thanksgiving. Similarly, pumpkins for Halloween and Thanksgiving and oranges for Christmas are connected to natural growing seasons, and help to ground these holidays in the cycling of the seasons. Zerubavel also writes about the importance of seasonal grounding with regard to historical origins of celebrations. He writes, "Whereas eating the 'same' unleavened bread on Passover helps present-day Jews identify with the ancient Israelites who allegedly came out of Egypt three thousand years ago, the fact that it takes place at the same time of year as the Exodus is specifically designed to make the link between them seem more 'natural'" (Zerubavel 2003, 47).

In an effort to uncover the emotional links between feasting and our experience of cyclical temporality, I turn to the flourishing of food studies scholarship in anthropology, sociology, and psychology (e.g., Belasco 2006; Claflin and Scholliers 2012; Do 2013; Farquhar 2002; Kershen 2014; LeBlanc 1999; Parasecoli 2008). In such studies, scholars ask why food and the act of eating are emotional, indexical, political, nostalgic, and communal. In other words, our connection to food seems to be both personal *and* political; eating means childhood and home, community and nation. Ronald LeBlanc (like Marcel Proust before him) muses that the pleasures and communal experiences surrounding certain foods hark back to our childhood. "Those 'happy days' of childhood past that people seek nostalgically to recapture in their imagination are, in turn, often associated with fond memories of food and festive meals; reminiscences of those culinary delights that brought them such warm feelings of pleasure, security, and even love as a child" (LeBlanc 1999, 245).

The psychologist Catherine Rouby, in her study of taste and smell, has found that taste and smell are more emotional modes of perception, but may also be less reliable as an aid to memory than vision and hearing (Rouby 2005, 117–18). The historian Caroline Byman notes the religious connotations and associations of eating and fasting, and the fellowship of sharing a meal: "Eating in late medieval Europe was not simply an activity that marked off fine calibrations of social status and a source of pleasure so intense and sensual that the renunciation of it was at the core of religious world-denial. Eating was also an occasion for union with one's fellows and one's God, a commensality given particular intensity by the prototypical meal, the eucharist, which seemed to hover in the background of any banquet" (Byman 1987, 5).

Many scholars write about eating (and *commensality*, or eating together) as an important marker of identity and community builder. Do Tess writes, "To eat is therefore not just to feed oneself, but to enter a system of signs and symbols that shapes one's collective identity" (Tess 2013, 6). Food also carries associations with home. Anne Kershen writes of diaspora communities: "Diet is one means of preserving identity and links with home. . . . For it is within the private sphere that the eating and ceremony of ethnic diet enables the retention of links with, and memories of, kith, kin and homelands left behind. Indeed, the food of home is one of the last links with "over there" to be relinquished" (Kershen 2014, 203). Like Proust's madeleine, food can be about recapturing a lost time—not only constituting a reminiscence of childhood, but a way of marking (or noting the passing of) different stages of modernity. Richard Coe muses, "It is not so much that the child itself, now an adult, has forever outgrown the splendors of the past, but rather that civilization and 'progress' have annihilated, perhaps totally and irretrievably, an ancient way of life and replaced it with something crude, rootless, and modern" (Coe in LeBlanc 1999, 245).

In Kazakhstan, food is a way to bridge the distance between Soviet ways of celebrating and present celebrations. Mediated feasting—watching holiday meals on television—is often part of contemporary celebrations. Television enriches the experience of food and the holiday feast with images, music, and conversations from past celebrations of the holiday. The food studies scholar Fabio Parasecoli asserts, "Pop culture constitutes a major repository of visual elements, ideas, practices, and discourses that influence our relationship with the body, with food consumption" (Parasecoli 2008, 3). Holiday television thus builds on and expands the emotional experiences of feasting and familiarity.

Winter Television

The Soviet film, *The Irony of Fate*, which originally aired on January 1, 1976, is a favorite of Kazakhstani revelers, and watching it on television is a necessary part of twenty-first-century New Year celebrations. Nostalgic television viewing in Kazakhstan around holidays evokes competing nostalgias and layered temporalities, as viewers feel the draw of the Soviet past and wax reminiscent about the time before Kazakhstani independence.

An experience from my fieldwork during New Year, 2004–2005:

Snow falls on 1970s Moscow. First tracing the uniform contours of Soviet apartment blocks, the camera slowly zooms in on an ornate, brightly gilded orthodox cathedral wedged between massive gray buildings. A beloved golden-voiced singer, Sergei Nikitin, the troubadour of 1970s Russia, croons a guitar ballad set to verses of Boris Pasternak's poem about snow, isolation, and waiting. Viewed through the frame of a boxy gray Panasonic television from a crowded perch on a faded floral divan, this scene from a Soviet holiday film is at the focus of another tableau—a New Year's celebration in Almaty, Kazakhstan, 2004. As our small, intimate gathering watches the film on television, we eat, argue about the film's star-crossed lovers, and sing along with the soundtrack. Pulled up to the couch, the dinner table is loaded with New Year dishes—Russian potato salad, smoked fish, oranges, champagne, vodka; it mirrors, nearly exactly, the cozy New Year feast in the film.

Holiday television in Almaty underscores the seasonal, culinary, and consumptive aspects of holidays, and supports social memory of the Soviet period. Much like the viewing of *It's a Wonderful Life* around Christmas in the United States, the annual viewing of Soviet holiday films has become a part of holiday tradition for many Kazakhstanis.

Simon Huxtable and Sabina Mihelj have written about the mediation of "festive time," especially in the Soviet sphere: "Different kinds of holidays and commemorations were marked with different kinds of programming" (Huxtable et al. 2017, 49). They describe the same kind of "festive viewing" that I have experienced in Kazakhstan, and explore the ways festive television has shaped holiday experience in the Soviet bloc. Indeed, following Daniel Dayan and Elihu Katz (1992), they find that festive media perform a "symbolic alchemy," which "reaffirms society's sacred center" (Huxtable et al. 2017, 51). In this same sense, winter television as it is consumed in Almaty reaffirms ideas about New Year and midwinter—thoughts that contain layers of disparate eras—from the mixed up, heady nostalgia of a Soviet New Year romance (and drinking too much at the sauna/bathhouse), to the older embedded layers about midwinter, magic, and cosmology.

In addition, by screening stories about feasting, television and old films support impressions of seasonal habits of eating and drinking while establishing holiday habits of viewership. In the film *Old New Year*, which recounts the story of two family dinner parties on this holiday, one of the first scenes shows two women preparing the holiday dinner. In a scene familiar to many Kazakhstanis at this time of year, the two friends discuss which salads to make—"olivie" (Russian potato salad) *and* "vinegret" (beet salad), or only one? One blogger describes the integration of film viewing and feasting in his New Years' celebration, stating that *The Irony of Fate* "is one of those films that I can watch over and over again . . . and I just can't imagine my New Year day/eve without it, and a bottle of "Soviet" champagne, and Russian salad, and the proverbial jellied fish that Ippolit referred to as 'muck'" (trionon07 2006). This nostalgic blogger not only describes his own New Year's feast (complete with Russian potato salad, of course) but also incorporates descriptions of a dish by a character (Ippolit) in the film, thus folding the televised feast into his own experience.

The viewing of the film *The Irony of Fate* is embedded in winter celebrations across the former Soviet territory, and along with its songs, the film has grown into a phenomenon of Tolkien proportions. Many people I spoke with described it as an essential part of the holidays. One blogger writes on IMDB:[4]

> This film has celebrated its 30th anniversary on this 2006 New Year['s] Eve, and there was a special programme about the creation of the film, actors etc. Apparently, the whole country (then USSR) watched it when it was first shown in 1976, and they wanted to see if the rating would be the same 30 years later. I have to say, I have been watching this film religiously since [my] early teens every New Year and when I moved to live in the UK, the video recording of "Ironiya" [*Irony of Fate*] was one of the essential items I brought with me. It's one of those films that I can watch over and over again, [an] instant mood lifter, and I just can't imagine my New Year['s] Day/Eve without it. . . . On my way back from Moscow to London in January, I tried to purchase a DVD copy in the airport but was told by the assistant that they are permanently sold out!!!" (trionon07 2006)

From the same website, a blogger from Ukraine writes: "I love this movie. I watch it every 31st December with my family" (spaceblossom). A blogger from Latvia adds, "Watching this movie has become a tradition each new year in Latvia.... Another thing that amazes me is the way the system of Soviet Union is sho[wn]. All the situations are unpredictable and one can really enjoy the characters and the way...they [solve] their problems" (soviet chick).

The tradition of watching particular Soviet films such as *The Irony of Fate* during the holidays, much like shared holidays marking important events in Soviet history (e.g.,Victory Day, May 9), has helped to maintain ties to the Soviet past and to maintain a Soviet cultural connection with fellow post-Soviet states. Films such as *The Irony of Fate* and *Old New Year*, so evocative of Soviet life, seem to feed nostalgia for the Soviet past, but also provide continuity, a bridge over the great jagged edges of the political transition. Seasonal viewing of Soviet films contributes to a rhythmicity of the holidays, underscoring core ideas about midwinter and solidifying cultural connections. In hearing songs from the late Soviet period, reexperiencing life in Soviet apartments and Soviet modes of work and leisure, present-day viewers reconnect with Soviet life in a very tangible way. Habits of feasting, consumption, and viewership become linked, together making up much of what is considered core to the season. The fact that this viewing is often collective and synchronized with real-life celebrations further connects past and present ways of celebrating midwinter.

Midwinter and *Sviatki*

Soviet films viewed during the holiday season not only reflect Soviet-era modes of celebration but also include much older ideas about midwinter. Midwinter, along with midsummer, was considered a magical time in pre-Soviet Russia. A number of its rituals and associations persisted through the mid-twentieth century, with remnants such as midwinter *gadanie* (fortune-telling) still appearing to this day in post-Soviet states. Like important life-cycle transitions (birth, death, and marriage), these two pivotal transitions in the solar cycle—winter solstice and summer solstice—became a focus for rituals and holidays as well as magic and divination. In his comprehensive tome on Russian magical folklore, *The Bathhouse at Midnight*, W. F. Ryan writes, "In Russia, as in many other parts of Europe the time around Christmas and Midsummer were particularly suitable for magic and divination. The practices varied a little locally but the period from Christmas Eve to the Twelfth Night was a time of festivity, which included all kinds of *gadani-*

ia or divination, sometimes to find out what the new year would bring with regard to the weather or harvest, often to discover a future husband. Of the days in this period the commonest for divination were New Year's Eve and the eve of Epiphany" (Ryan 1999, 46).

This period of midwinter holidays from Christmas Eve to Epiphany was known as *sviatki* in Russia. It is, in literature and television alike, a time when the boundary between our world and the spirit world is thin—a dangerous and liminal time, full of chaos and magic. *The Night before Christmas*, a 1950s Soviet animated film based on a short story of the same name by Nikolai Gogol, is set in the Russian period of sviatki. In this film the devil appears on the night before Christmas and runs wild through the Ukrainian countryside—slipping down chimneys, hiding in ovens, playing tricks on lascivious lovers. Liminal times are times when chaos rules, when the ordinary rules of the universe are temporarily suspended. In *The Night before Christmas*, this inconsistency is evident in a very physical sense—objects fly through the air, or become extraordinarily heavy—as if gravity were no longer a constant but rather mercurial, flexible.

Liminal time involves a reordering not only of time and place but also of the self. A rift in the "normal" fabric of life, a liminal period is a time for reexamining priorities and reinventing the self, albeit temporarily. Indeed, in pre-Soviet Russia the period of sviatki was (as elsewhere in Europe) a time of mumming and ludic activities that involved "playing" at another self. Ryan writes, "Yuletide was also the time of various kinds of mumming, crossdressing, dressing as animals, wearing masks, wearing clothes inside out or upside down, and dramatized rites such as 'playing at corpses'" (Ryan 1999, 46). Unlike everyday life when a "continuous self" is most often required for everyday purposes (Zerubavel 1981, 2003), sviatki allows a jagged, chaotic, discontinuous, contradictory, creative, and uncharacteristic presentation of the self. Just as the ordinary constants of everyday life can no longer be relied on, so too the self becomes mutable and inconsistent during the dark nights of midwinter.

Two Wintertime Soviet-era Films

The chaos of sviatki, when observed through a Soviet lens, reveals a subtler version of midwinter instability: a philosophical, slapstick confusion of time, place, and the self. It addresses a particularly Soviet sense of place and displacement, focusing on the uniformity of Soviet space. It examines personal aspects of Soviet life at a time when communal, public life was emphasized. Through this Soviet lens, the liminality of midwinter appears as displacement, confused identities, and a kind of trying on of different lives.

Two Soviet-era movies hold a prominent place in postsocialist Kazakhstani holiday programming: *The Irony of Fate or Enjoy Your Bath* and *Old New Year*, set in Leningrad and Moscow during the Brezhnev era. Both are concerned with a disordered sense of place, and both use this disruptive period of sviatki to examine the superficial interchangeability of Soviet apartments (and Soviet lives?), and the uniformity of Soviet space. The Soviet apartment is, in a way, the focus of *The Irony of Fate*. In this Soviet classic, the hero, Zhenya, gets drunk in the bathhouse with his old schoolmates. Then, while seeing his friend off at the airport, Zhenya, too drunk to notice, is mistakenly put on a plane to Leningrad in place of his friend (also too drunk to notice). On arriving in Leningrad, Zhenya is unaware that he has flown to a different city. He hails a taxi "home," giving the address of his apartment in Moscow. But Soviet cities being so alike, the taxi actually takes him to the very same address in Leningrad, which looks exactly like his own building. His key works in the lock and he makes himself at home, falling asleep on the couch in the Leningrad apartment belonging to the beautiful Nadia, who is alternately irate and charmed when she returns home. The plot spins out from this basic misunderstanding, as the two alternately tangle and find compatibilities with each other. The joy of the film is in the ridiculousness of this night, in following the twists and turns of happenstance that can lead one to slip, haphazardly and happily, into another life. Sviatki has wrought its chaotic power and injected a dose of unpredictability into these predictable Soviet lives.

Old New Year also takes the Soviet apartment as the central plot device. This holiday film is a study of two families living in the same apartment block in Moscow around 1980. The first family is well-established and intellectual, the second is up-and-coming, newly well-off, having just moved into their apartment on this Old New Year's Eve. The film alternates between the two celebrations of Old New Year in these two apartments, separated by one floor. A philosophical film involving more dialogue than fast-moving plot, it is a study of class in an ostensibly classless society. Colorfully disparate dialogue shows the sharply contrasting lifestyles of these two families. Both families are at a turning point in their lives, and in a way, each strives to emulate the other: the intellectual hosts speak about living like the *narod* or "the people," and the working-class family strives to accumulate the possessions that are the mark of the upper class. It is a film about our relationship with the material world—the possessions with which we surround ourselves and the physical structures that house us. It also seeks to understand what is below the surface of materiality.

Throughout both films runs the idea of the Soviet sense of place, the uniformity of the buildings and the overwhelming nature of public life, as contrasted with the intensely personal and protected space of home. *The Irony of Fate* is prefaced by an animated short film about the proliferation of the Soviet apartment block. An unwitting architect originally designs a beautiful edifice, complete with balconies and curlicue ornaments, which the building committees one by one delete, leaving a plain cement apartment block. Replicas of this building march in legions over Soviet territory, from the Central Asian deserts to the Far North, surprising camels and polar bears alike, until Soviet apartment blocks finally cover the entire globe. Following this short cartoon, the beginning of the actual film interestingly focuses in on an ornately magnificent Russian Orthodox church, covered with snow. The camera then pans out and reveals it to be surrounded and dwarfed by rows and rows of prototypical Soviet apartment blocks. The focus on the church in the context of Soviet architecture can be understood as representing the duality of inner life versus the utilitarian nature of Soviet public life and space. Throughout these films we see a similar contrast, the sterility of the external facade of these apartments, contrasted with their "alive" interior.

Appearing at key points in both films, the *banya* (bathhouse) represents a bridge between public and private life and a catalyst for the chaotic unfurling of the New Year's Eve plot. Though strictly speaking a public space, the bathhouse seems to be a realm of the semiprivate, a place for philosophical discussions and close-knit celebrations. In *The Irony of Fate*, the banya appears to be a spatial catalyst for the unfolding of the film's events, a bridge into the unknown (just as it traditionally functions as a kind of gateway into the world of magic and spirits), for it is in the bathhouse that Zhenya's engagement is toasted, and there that the small group of friends gets him so drunk that he ends up in a different city. In contrast, in *Old New Year*, the banya appears at the end of the film and is similarly a place for rather drunken philosophizing, a place where the characters all rehash the events of the night before and attempt (unsuccessfully) to make sense of them. As Ryan and other scholars assert, the bathhouse is strongly associated with magic in Russian culture. Connected to purification rituals and childbirth, guarded by a *bannik*, the bathhouse spirit, the bathhouse is essentially a pagan place, underscored by the necessity of removing one's cross before entering (Ryan 1999, 50). Just as midwinter is a supernaturally chaotic time, the bathhouse is traditionally a site of heightened supernatural activity, and seems to function in these films as a liminal, catalytic space.

The uniformity of the Soviet apartment and the reordering of this Soviet space provide the basis for the plots of both movies, in which the theme of moving and the rearranging of the apartments' interiors—the making and unmaking of place—figure prominently. Both Zhenya and Nadia in *The Irony of Fate* have recently moved to their respective identical apartments and, as in *Old New Year*, their furniture and possessions are in disarray. In the latter film, the new family is moving its furniture in, while the head of the second household, disillusioned by the conspicuous consumption of the season and the proliferation of his family's own possessions, decides to throw out all his furniture. As his well-heeled guests arrive, they help to move out every last object in his living room until they are sitting on the floor in the dark (which one of his guests proclaims to be very chic and "modern") and discussing the true meaning of life. The characters in the two movies are in transition and the chaos and disorder in both apartments sets the stage for the reordering of their lives and life priorities.

The theme of mistaken places is key to both films, in a way creating the impetus for these changes. In *The Irony of Fate* displacement happens on a large scale, as the hero mistakes his apartment for another identical apartment in another city. Because of this misstep, Zhenya meets Nadia, rejects his old life (and his previous fiancée), and goes through a transformation from an awkward, hesitant fiancé to an intrepid, persistent lover. In *Old New Year*, the old man who is a guest of the new family continually (and drunkenly) mistakes this intellectual family's apartment for that of his friends and repeatedly joins their celebration in an impromptu fashion. He gradually becomes a conduit between the two families as he participates in the two ongoing discussions and relates the sometimes-misunderstood dialogue to both parties. In each case, displacement provides an unexpected look into the lives of others and prompts inner reexamination.

Original soundtracks were written specifically for each film, and their songs are integral to the enduring meaning and popularity of these films. Of the *avtorskaia pesn'* (balladeer's song) genre popular in the Soviet Union from the 1970s on, these songs, particularly those from *The Irony of Fate*, have enjoyed enduring and widespread popularity throughout the former Soviet Union. Written for solo voice with accompaniment on the Russian seven-string guitar, with memorable lyrics and simple chord structures, they are often still played at informal gatherings, particularly around the New Year (the scene I describe at the start of this chapter is a good illustration). Some of the song texts are written by singer-songwriters; others are taken from the works of great Russian poets such as Boris Pasternak (1890–1960). In two songs from these films, "Snow Is Falling" and "No One Will Be at Home," the poetry of Pasternak, whose own life bridges preindustrial Russia and Soviet Russia, manages to convey the remnants of old Russian midwinter into the Soviet era.

"Snow Is Falling," with music by Sergei Nikitin, opens the film *Old New Year*. Set in midwinter and replete with architectural imagery, Pasternak's poetry draws attention to the film's focus on place and the season and complements the cinematic imagery of snow-covered Soviet cities.

"Снег идет"—Борис Пастернак[5]	"Snow Is Falling"—Boris Pasternak (translation by the author)
Снег идет, снег идет.	Snow is falling, snow is falling.
К белым звездочкам в буране	To the white stars in the storm
Тянутся цветы герани	Stretch the geranium blooms
За оконный переплет.	Across the window-sash.
Снег идет, и все в смятеньи,	Snow is falling, and all is in commotion
Все пускается в полет:	All is turning to flight:
Черной лестницы ступени,	The stairs of the black staircase,
Перекрестка поворот.	The turn of the crossroads.
Снег идет, снег идет,	Snow is falling, snow is falling,
Словно падают не хлопья,	Appearing not as snowflakes,
А в заплатанном салопе	But as the dome of the sky
Сходит наземь небосвод.	Falling to earth in a patched-together coat.

Словно с видом чудака,	Looking like the crazy person,
С верхней лестничной площадки,	Who lives upstairs,
Крадучись, играя в прятки,	Creeping, playing hide and seek
Сходит небо с чердака,	The sky descends from the attic,
Потому что жизнь не ждет.	Because life doesn't wait
Не оглянешься, и—святки.	Don't look back, and—*sviatki* is here.
Только промежуток краткий,	Only a short span of time,
Смотришь—там и новый год.	You look, and the New Year is there.
Снег идет густой-густой,	Snow is falling thickly,
В ногу с ним, стопами теми,	Is perhaps time passing,
В том же темпе, с ленью той	In step with it, following along
Или с той же быстротой,	At the same tempo, with the same laziness
Может быть, проходит время?	Or with such speed?
Может быть, за годом год	Maybe, one year after another
Следуют, как снег идет	Follows, like the snow flies
Или как слова в поэме?	Or like words in a poem?
Может быть, проходит время...	Maybe so too will time pass.
Может быть, за годом год...	Maybe, one year after another.
Снег идет, снег идет,	Snow is falling, snow is falling,
Снег идет, и все в смятеньи:	Snow is falling, and all is in commotion
Убеленный пешеход,	The whitened pedestrian,
Удивленные растенья,	The surprised plants,
Перекрестка поворот.	The turn of the crossroads.
Снег идет, снег идет.	Snow is falling, snow is falling
Снег идет, снег идет.	Snow is falling, snow is falling.

Describing the contemplative and chaotic aspects of sviatki (midwinter), Pasternak describes the falling snow and its obscuring qualities, depicting sviatki as a time when things are out of place. "Snow is falling, and all is in commotion [confusion, or disarray]." Pasternak focuses on perception, as the narrator's inner thoughts meet the external world. He describes how the snow confuses objects and places, and generally wreaks chaos, as objects and places become unmoored from their usual context. "All is turning to flight: /

the stairs of the black staircase, / the turn of the crossroads." The next stanza continues, "Snow is falling, snow is falling, / Appearing not as snowflakes, / but as the dome of the sky / Falling to earth in a patched-together coat." So while earthbound objects are seemingly "turning to flight," the sky is "falling to earth," in a reversal of their usual state. Displacement—a shift in the natural order—again appears as a theme of midwinter.

The poem, "No One Will Be at Home," also by Boris Pasternak, appears in the song of the same name, in *The Irony of Fate*. The song is composed by Mikael Tariverdiev and performed by Sergei Nikitin.

"Никого не будет в доме"[6] **—Борис Пастернак**	**"No One Will Be at Home"—Boris Pasternak (translation by the author)**
Никого не будет в доме. Кроме сумерек. Один зимний день в сквозном проеме Незадернутых гардин. Незадернутых гардин.	No one will be at home. Except dusk. One winter day in the drafty opening[7] Of undrawn curtains. Of undrawn curtains.
Только белых мокрых комьев быстрый промельк моховой, только крыши, снег, и кроме Крыш и снега никого. Крыш и снега никого.	Only the quick mossy flash of white wet clumps Only roofs, snow, and besides the Roofs and snow no one . . . Roofs and snow no one.
И опять зачертит иней, и опять Завертит мной прошлогоднее унынье И дела зимы иной. И дела зимы иной.	And again the frost scribbles, and again I am spun by last year's sadness And the things of a different winter.
Но внезапно по портьере пробежит сомненья дрожь. Тишину шагами меря. Тишину шагами меря. Тишину шагами меря, ты, как будущность войдешь.	But suddenly along the portiere a tremor of doubt ripples. Measuring the silence with footsteps. Measuring the silence with footsteps. Measuring the silence with (your) footsteps, you, like the future, will enter.
Ты появишься из двери в чем-то белом, без причуд, В чем-то, впрямь из тех материй, Из которых хлопья шьют. Из которых хлопья шьют.	You will appear from the door in something white, without whimsy, In something just like the kind of material From which flakes are sewn. From which flakes are sewn.

The use of architectural language in both songs stresses the attention to place and also contributes to the feeling of liminality. Pasternak uses precise, old-fashioned architectural vocabulary: portiere, window-sash, and embrasure (window opening). Set against the film's visual backdrop of Soviet architecture, the slightly archaic descriptions evoke the interior of an old Russian home—the effect is temporally jarring, cleaving a split between aural and visual messages. The song text also conveys a state of suspension or flux. The structures he describes—windows, doorways, stairs—are all inherently transitional spaces, from the outside in, from one room to another, from up to down. His poetry depicts not only the structures of place themselves, but what is happening within, and particularly *through* these architectural spaces. The geraniums stretch "across the window-sash . . . to the white stars in the storm," and (in the poem "No One Will Be at Home") "along the portiere [door curtain] a tremor of doubt ripples," anticipating an arrival.

Just as thresholds and doorways represent in-betweenness in space, midwinter appears as a liminal time in these films and song texts. In "Snow Is Falling," New Year's Eve is depicted as a kind of temporal doorway, a transition that makes us aware of the passing of the years, the passing of time. Pasternak's words comment on the elasticity of time. He writes that time may pass "with a lazy tempo, or with such speed," and continues, "Maybe one year will follow another, like the snow flies, or like words in a poem. Maybe so too time will pass, one year after another." Time flows not in straight lines, but chaotically, in spurts, like the falling of snow. In "No One Will Be at Home," winter both obscures the outside world and throws the inner world into confusion, in which the experiencing of disparate times overlap: "And again the frost scribbles, and again / I am spun by last year's sadness / And the things of a different winter." Pasternak's poetry, like the Soviet films it accompanies, reveals time and place not as definite, concrete, but as mutable, subject to perception.

In *The Irony of Fate*, the liminality of sviatki and the New Year lifts the mask, suspends one's ordinarily consistent persona, and allows uncharacteristic and confused presentations of the self to emerge. Ippolit, a normally upright and sober professional man, starts to come apart at the seams when he realizes that Nadia is falling for Zhenya. Ippolit returns again and again to Nadia's apartment, the last time completely drunk: "Ippolit! This is the first time I've seen you like this," says Nadia; "This is the first time I've been like this," says Ippolit. When Zhenya suggests a trip to the banya, Ippolit proceeds to take a shower, fully clothed, with his fur hat on, in Nadia's bathroom. It is the incongruity—the wrong combination of person, activity, place, and "costume"—that makes the scene so funny. All the aspects of the scenario—being drunk, being Ippolit, being fully clothed, taking a shower, going to the "banya"—taken separately are part of "normal" life; it is this particular combination that makes the scene ridiculous.

Thus the liminality, the "uncommonness" of midwinter creates a chaotic upheaval in the everyday. The chaos that displaces people and things also creates channels between these separate spheres/lives (between Zhenya and Nadia, and between the two families), opening up new possibilities and ways of looking at life. But, in the true sense of liminal periods (Turner 1969, 1974), there is also a return to normalcy once the liminal period is over. Thus, as dawn breaks in the New Year, Nadia pronounces, "New Years is over, and everything remains in its own place," and insists that Zhenya must return home to Moscow. Similarly, after the magical craziness of Christmas Eve in *The Night before Christmas*, the devil is banished and village life returns to normal. The liminality, the "uncommonness" of midwinter creates a chaotic upheaval in the everyday. But this chaos does not change anything permanently; rather it provides depth, revealing what is under the surface of everyday life.

These films thus include threads from an older conceptualization of winter, sviatki, while simultaneously presenting a very Soviet picture of the season. The Soviet apartments (and by extension, lives of Soviet individuals) are depicted as uniform and interchangeable, and the swapping of lives, roles, and apartments underscores the superficial uniformity of Soviet life and space. At the same time, the examination of midwinter as a chaotic period of transition provides a glimpse into the inner lives of individuals. These films thus show both sides of the coin: the communal, uniform, utilitarian nature of public life and the inner, personal, and protected space of home and thought.

Environmentalism, Winter Forest Scenes, and Holiday Mumming

Kazakhstani television and advertising reveal the intertwining of cosmological framings—images and traditions from the Kazakh nomadic wintertime and folk characters from the Russian forests, the quiet time of *kystau* (winter camp) and magical, chaotic period of sviatki. Children's theater and holiday pageants and games meld Russian and Soviet mumming traditions with creatures from the eastern zodiac. Mumming traditions, prevalent during sviatki in pre-Soviet Russia, show up in public children's celebrations of New Year in Kazakhstan. Soviet skits and games involving Ded Moroz (Father Frost) brought Russian mumming traditions through the twentieth century and these traditions have continued into the post-Soviet era. I attended several such holiday skits at day-care centers and children's puppet theaters, all with similar casts of characters. Because most of the post-Soviet Kazakhstani New Year traditions come from Russian folklore (the old Central Asian new year is in March, on the vernal equinox), the use of the natural world images and creatures pictured in holiday plays and advertisements are typical of northern, forested regions of Russia, incongruous with the typical nationalist images Kazakhstan's landscape (i.e., forests rather than steppe).

In Kazakhstan, seasonal children's skits, a leftover from Russian mumming traditions, usually included forest animals—bunnies, squirrels, foxes, bears—common in Russian children's stories. The stories of Ded Moroz and his granddaughter, Snegurochka, also often took place in the forest. The cast of characters in the holiday skits and games also often included other fairytale fixtures such as the evil witch Baba Yaga and the swamp witch Kikimora. A skit I watched in a holiday celebration at the Almaty State Puppet Theater was a typical example of the many I attended. In this New Year's skit, the children, dressed in animal and angel costumes, sang New Year's songs, and then were encouraged to call out "Snegurochka!" and "Ded Moroz!" to try to draw them into the festivities. First Baba Yaga appeared disguised as Snegurochka, and was then discovered and entreated to release the real Snegurochka. Kikimora also came out, ragtag and chaotic, before Snegurochka finally made an appearance.

Many television advertisements included forest scenes around the winter holidays, with cute animals, Snegurochka, or Father Frost. In the winter of 2004–2005, public service announcements aired by the political party Asar (All Together), headed by Dariga Nazarbaeva, daughter of the president, Nursultan Nazarbaev, were set in the wintry forest. Featuring short holiday stories, these political advertisements combine Asar's general emphasis on "family" (Asar's logo was a red roof, indicating its family-centric politics) with a very timely political platform—environmentalism. Two of

Asar's advertisements focus on the tradition of decorating New Year trees—
the Soviet-era version of Christmas trees (in an effort to capture their various
meanings, I will call them Yule trees). The first of these vignettes opens with
a scene of a lively winter gathering in the middle of a snowy forest. Young
people decorate the live trees with ornaments and tinsel while a table is set
with oranges and champagne. It is New Year's Eve and the countdown is approaching when a rough-looking man sneaks up to one of the trees and men-
acingly brandishes an axe. Two of the young people rush to save the tree
from his axe, scolding the man, and later (no hard feelings) inviting him to
join the celebration. One of the rescuers was dressed as the Russian Snegurochka, Father Frost's granddaughter. As midnight strikes, Father Frost himself appears, and leads a merry chase through the forest to the tune of "Jingle
Bells."

The music accompanying this public service/political advertisement is a
newly composed pop ballad that puts a twist on the Russian children's tune,
"In the Forest a Yule Tree Was Born." Written to publicize the ban on cutting
down fir trees for the New Year, the song's lyrics are:

"Little Green Yule Tree"
Our holiday approaches,
There is a holiday bustle in the city,
And all rush to buy a beautiful tree for their house.

And thousands of trees
For thousands of people
Bring happiness, but only for a few days.

Refrain:
Little green Yule tree . . .
Do not cut down trees anywhere in the world.
Little green Yule tree, don't bring her pain.
Little green Yule tree, preserve her for the children.

You wouldn't see a dressed up beauty, and tear out her eyes.
The clock is striking twelve and we must make our wishes in time.
The wishes of each person are fulfilled by the holiday hour.
We all love life and so let her live too, among us.

The short video message combines holiday images ("dressed up beauty," the "holiday bustle in the city,") with an environmental message. The link between environmentalism and the holidays takes place on an emotional level, in the urgent appeal to save the evergreens. Indeed, environmentalism was an expedient political platform for Asar—one aimed at young voters in particular.

A second televised public service announcement, also sponsored by Asar, is about a young mother and her son. It is an animated short with a similar theme, this time stressing family as well as youth appeal. The animation has an early 1960s retro feel, with clean lines, simple color schemes, and a pretty hourglass mama, reminiscent of U.S. Christmas specials such as *A Charlie Brown Christmas*. The young mother is out in the woods with her son decorating a small snow-covered tree with red ornaments, as friendly forest animals (rabbit, squirrel, fox, and hare) gather to watch. Suddenly a man jumps out from behind the tree with a saw in his hand, but the next moment, in a clever comic twist, he takes out a violin bow and starts playing the children's song "In the Forest a Little Yule Tree Was Born" on the saw.

"In the Forest a Little Yule Tree was Born"

In the forest a little yule tree was born,
In the forest she was born,
In winter and summer
She was strong and green,
In winter and summer
She was strong and green.

The breeze sang her a song
Sleep, little yule tree, sleep!
The frost covered her with snow:
"Be careful, don't freeze!"
The frost covered her with snow:
"Be careful, don't freeze!"

The timid little gray rabbit
Hopped around under the tree.
And from time to time the wolf, the angry wolf, loped by.

And from time to time the wolf,
the angry wolf, loped by.

Oh! The snow-covered forest
On the fields something scraped
A horse with shoed hooves
Came hurrying, running.
A horse with shoed hooves
Came hurrying, running.

The horse pulled a sleigh
And on the sleigh was a driver.
He cut down our yule tree
Right down to the roots.
He cut down our yule tree
Right down to the roots.

And here she is all dressed up
Come to visit us for the holidays.
And many, many happinesses
Has she brought the children.
And many, many happinesses
Has she brought the children.

Both advertisements manipulate the children's holiday traditions, using the well-known children's song (and its pop incarnation) as a springboard to address environmental issues and at the same time target a young, family-oriented audience.

Environmentalism resonates well in children's holiday themes partly because of the central role that the forest and its wildlife plays in folklore about Ded Moroz. Unlike Santa Claus, an industrial-era character who heads a toy factory (an interesting idea in itself), Ded Moroz is essentially a spirit of the forest. In contrast to benevolent depictions of Santa, the Kazakhstani plays, skits, and puppet shows about Ded Moroz portray him as a fierce and sometimes frightening protector of the woods. The State Puppet Theater in Almaty, the venue of the holiday mumming described previously, annually

FIGURE 3.3. *Morozko* placard, Kazakhstani State Puppet Theater, Almaty, 2005.

shows the play *Morozko*, which tells the story of Snegurochka. The little girl named Morozko (who eventually becomes Snegurochka) is kind to the animals in the wintry forest. She gives her gloves to the rabbit, and her hat to warm the fox, while her naughty stepsister steals the sleeping bear's horde of berries and ignores the pleas for help from other forest animals. In the end, Morozko is rewarded with furs and jewels, and becomes Ded Moroz's helper and adopted granddaughter, while her selfish stepsister is left to freeze in the snowy woods.

The play *Morozko* is set in the snow-covered forest, and like many Soviet children's plays about the New Year holiday, prominently features forest animals as main characters. Both the play *Morozko* and the song "In the Forest a Little Yule Tree Was Born" take a protective, almost motherly stance toward the natural world, and the forest in particular. In the song, the Yule tree is in need of protection, the snow provides a blanket for it through the harsh winter, the wind sings a lullaby to it, and the forest animals befriend it. The environmental advertisements cleverly adopt this protective approach toward the natural world prevalent in Russian folklore. In incorporating the children's song about protecting the Yule tree, these advertisements tap into a larger body of holiday folklore to support environmental/political messages.

Winter as a theme is rich with imagery, history, and folklore. It is striking to see how its many facets have been highlighted in Kazakhstani television, which provides a Soviet perspective on the holidays while also connecting to older Russian ideas about sviatki. In bringing the seasons inside, television and films underscore basic ideas from folklore and sviatki traditions as well as modern ideas about Christmas and the New Year, and weave these into other holiday activities—like drinking, feasting, and singing.

THE KAZAKH ZODIAC AND NOMADIC SEASONALITY

In contrast to the sviatki-based concepts of midwinter originating in Russia, another framing also has an effect at this time of year—the eastern zodiac, used from East Asia to Central Asia. In addition to forest animals and fairy-tale creatures, the sign of the animal year from the Eastern zodiac has been incorporated into Kazakhstani winter holiday celebrations as well. In the eastern zodiac, 2005 was the Year of the Rooster, and the image of the Rooster appeared in holiday celebrations and on holiday banners all winter, from January 1 to the lunar New Year to Maslenitsa. Kazakhstani friends have asserted that the eastern zodiac characters leaked into the Soviet mumming traditions during the Soviet era. In the skit I watched at the Almaty State Puppet Theater, after Ded Moroz finally arrived, two final characters arrived on the scene—these were characters not from the Russian mumming traditions, forest animals, and Russian fairy tales, but from the twelve animals of the eastern zodiac. As the year 2004 was the Year of the Monkey, the character of the Monkey appeared and was subsequently chased away by the Rooster (2005). In this way, the characters from the eastern zodiac were incorporated into the older New Year's tradition, whose function was essentially to part with the old year and welcome the new.

Kazakh conceptions of the calendar and the seasons share the main ideas of the eastern zodiac, but they also diverge. In Kazakh the twelve-year zodiac is called *mushel*. Asiya Mukhambetova, a Kazakh ethnomusicologist, has written extensively about the Kazakh zodiac and how it is built into Kazakh lifeways. According to Mukhambetova and other Kazakh and Soviet scholars, the sixty-year calendar, which is made up of five twelve-year cycles (and which is known in the West as the Chinese zodiac) originates not in East

Asia but in Central Asia. Mukhambetova and others assert that it is a Tengrian calendar,[8] originating in the region of the Altai (the mountains that lie
between Kazakhstan, Siberia, and Mongolia), and is an integral part of the
nomadic tradition and lifeways there.

Like Zerubavel, Mukhambetova discusses calendars and the ordering of
time as an important basis of community. She writes, "Conceptions of Time
are one of the basic foundations of any civilization. They bring together its
[civilization's] many faces, putting them together into a structural whole
through the unifying forces of their temporal code. Systemic understandings
of Time, as a rule, are concentrated in calendars, which . . . coordinate all
aspects of life. The calendar carries the basic information about time-space
and appears as a structural genetic code of culture" (Amanov and Mukhambetova 2002, 11).

So for Mukhambetova, the structuring of time in the form of calendars
(and zodiacs) is a core base of "culture." In describing the "genetic code of
culture" Mukhambetova refers to a "Tengrian ethnos." Her writing clearly
invokes the Eurasianist Lev Gumilev both by using his term "ethnos" and
in her discussion about how climate and terrain affect and *effect* culture and
society. Muhambetova continues, "The nomads made this complex calendar
in order to survive conditions of the extreme continental climate of Central
Asia. It was one of the necessary bases regulating the . . . economical, political, spiritual and cultural life, and also the rhythm of the personal life of the
individual—in a word, all aspects of life in nomadic society. The animal calendar fulfilled these functions because it was based upon a profound study
of the Cosmos and its effect on earthly life" (Amanov and Mukhambetova
2002, 14).

For Mukhambetova, the calendar or *mushel* essentially emanates from
nomadic life. Conditioned by extreme continental climate, dependence
on weather conditions and other natural forces, nomads needed to predict
weather far into the future. A particularly catastrophic climatic event was
zhut, a hard spring frost that left the tender green grass inaccessible to herds
and made movement to other pastures impossible. A zhut could mean starvation for an entire group of mobile pastoralists and their herds. Because
inclement weather could spell success or disaster for very large groups of
people traveling together, weather prediction was a highly prized and spe-
cialized skill, and one of the main duties of the clan's astronomer, or *esepshi*.

So the mushel, for Mukhambetova, encapsulates all of this—Kazakh conceptions of nature, seasonality, and nomadic lifeways, which also form the basis of Kazakh nationalism.

Mobile pastoralism has become less common in Kazakhstan, but Kazakhs in Mongolia and parts of northwest China are still at least partly nomadic. Kazakh nomadic seasons are divided into four parts: *küzeu*, the fall migration period, *kistau*, the winter campground, *kökteu*, spring migration, and *zhailau*, the summer campgrounds. Though scholars of the region describe many different kinds of mobile pastoralism, this pattern seems to be the most common among Kazakhs.[9] Many herd owners in Mongolia live in permanent dwellings in the winter and move to zhailau with some or all of their family members into the high pastureland in the summertime. In Kazakhstan, though mobile pastoralism is now fairly rare, it still holds cultural meaning. Many aspects of mobile pastoralism—cooking and eating outdoors, entertaining and sleeping in yurts, and the importance of the herd animals in everyday life—are not so far removed from modern life, even for city dwellers. Many Kazakhs in the countryside own land and herds and it is fairly common to sleep, entertain, and host relatives in yurts erected nearby the family home in the warm summer and autumn months. Urban Kazakhs often have firsthand experience with life in the countryside from visiting relatives in the *aul* (village).[10] Quintessential aspects of nomadic life like the zhailau and zhut are well-known to city- and country-dwellers alike, and often appear in Kazakh television, films, and music videos.

Kazakh conceptions of seasonality often appear in nationalist contexts. This is more visible in spring when the "Kazakh" (Central Asian) holiday of Nauryz dominates public and institutional celebrations. At this time, themes of pastoralism such as the first milk of spring, the springtime clearing of streams and natural springs, and greeting the first dawn of the vernal equinox, appear frequently in celebrations and on television. Winter depictions of Kazakh seasonality are less common, but the music video by Tamara Asar, "Bul en burynghy ennen ozgerek" (This song is different from past songs) with words by aqyn Shekerim Kudaiberdiuly (1858–1931),[11] vividly depicts a nomadic experience of winter. This video is set in a wintry forest covered by deep snow. The yurt looks warm and protected from the cold, as light from the hearth fire fills the yurt, and the walls and floors are covered with rich red carpets. Two aging grandparents are at home with a mother and her young son. The video alternates between the snowy forest and the yurt's interior, as the young mother (Tamara Asar), sings the song "Bul en." Outside, she is draped in thick furs, surrounded by the spectacular scenery of the wintry forest. Inside she variously reads from a thick leather-bound book, holds her sleeping son, and braids her long hair. There is a feeling of dormancy, of waiting, as she anxiously scans the forest, looking for signs of her husband who is out hunting.

Wintertime survival for Kazakhs traditionally depended on meat, and hunting success was crucial to augment the household stores of dried meat. Inner Asian mobile pastoralists switched from dependence on meat products to milk products around March, marking the end of the long winter and the beginning of spring. Whereas spring and autumn were periods of change and motion for Kazakh mobile pastoralists, zhailau and kistau (summer and winter camping periods) were relatively static times for them. Summer was a time of plenty, when herders relaxed and celebrated in large communal groups while the animals fattened up in the rich pasturelands; in contrast winter was portrayed here as a time of relative isolation and uncertainty, dependent on chance and the whims of nature. Like the Russian imagery of midwinter, Tamara Asar's video reflects a kind of temporal suspension—waiting for the resumption of "normal" activity.

In focusing on calendars, zodiacs, and the celebrating of the winter season, this chapter has examined how Kazakhstanis experience and order temporality, particularly through celebration. I have focused on televised time in Kazakhstan, where seasonal television portrays the same ritual/holiday cycles onscreen as those happening in real time, mirroring and adding to the cyclical temporal experience. In addition to creating anticipation of the same seasonal programs every year, television time augments and tints seasonality by refracting the seasonal changes in political, historical, and culturally specific ways. Televised time, in following the rhythm of the seasons and the calendar year, continually reveals and shapes cultural framings of time, and of the present.

Similarly, children's skits and banners portray an amalgamated and multifaceted representation of winter holidays. Holding the legacy of Soviet culture and habits as well as strains of postindependence nationalism, holiday imagery and celebration in Kazakhstan are historically layered and multivalent. Like the eastern zodiac, which alternately signifies nomadic mythology (and the Tengrian "ethnos, à la Lev Gumilev) and an inclusive adoption of East Asian traditions, such imagery supports a range of ideologies, from Kazakh nationalism to the "Friendship of the Peoples." Kazakh scholarship that insists the zodiac should be called by its Central Asian name, *mushel*, thus acknowledging its Altaian roots, makes it clear that temporal ordering also reflects spatial ordering. Using the mushel consciously as a Kazakh calendar not only supports the idea of a Kazakh conception of "big time" but also, in a way, reorders the globe, placing the Altai (and the region of Inner Asia) at the center. Like maps and place naming, calendars—and the celebratory marking of time—are both political and personal, emplaced and embodied reflections of personal and national beliefs.

CHAPTER 4

AN ARCHAEOLOGY OF NAURYZ

The Ancient Past in Public Culture

Where is it, this present? It has melted in our grasp, fled ere we could touch it, gone in the instant of becoming.

—William James

We need to look into the past in order to understand the present and foresee the future.

—N. A. Nazarbaev

The unearthing of traditions—and their reintroduction into a present that has already forgotten them—is a process integral to nationalist cultural reconstruction. This chapter uncovers uses of the ancient past in Kazakhstan's construction of nationhood, particularly during the Kazakh spring holiday of Nauryz, by drawing on archaeological approaches to time. The idea of time as successive moments following in an orderly straight line has been held up for scrutiny in many scholarly disciplines including anthropology, archaeology, literary criticism, and queer studies.[1] Given the nature of archaeology, engaged in uncovering the past, perhaps it is unsurprising that this discipline has yielded appealing and theoretically productive approaches to temporality. The anthropologist Shannon Dawdy, in her explorations of alternative approaches to temporality (Dawdy 2010, 2016), proposes the use of archaeological concepts in examining temporality in anthropology and popular culture. Theorizing time as layered and disordered, as "folded, chiasmic, and entangled" (Witmore 2006, 269), other archaeological scholarship (Olivier 2011, 2013; Olsen 2012; Witmore 2006) develops the temporal concept of *percolation*, a chaotic bubbling up of the past into the present. The image of archaeology, with its exploration of overturned layers, of churned up pasts folded into the present, is useful in many ways to the study of nationalist discourse.

DIGGING UP THE PAST

Nauryz, the Central Asian New Year, has become perhaps the most widely celebrated holiday in Kazakhstan. Of pre-Islamic Zoroastrian origin, Nauryz is celebrated throughout Central Asia, as well as in Iran, Azerbaijan, and parts of Turkey and the Caucasus. Zoroastrians were sun worshippers and Nauryz, occurring on the vernal equinox, is a celebration of the sun's return after the long winter and the arrival of spring. Capitalizing on Nauryz's indigenous origins, public Nauryz celebrations and televised programs feature a heightened presence of Kazakh nationalism, traditions, and language use, all of which support Kazakh-centric nation-building policies. Mining this rich vein of ancient steppe history for the source of Kazakh national culture, public Nauryz celebrations incorporate images and cosmological symbols from petroglyphs found in present-day Kazakhstan. Carved into a rocky canyon not far from Almaty by steppe inhabitants nearly four thousand years ago, these images have found their way into all kinds of Nauryz pageantry in post-Soviet Kazakhstan, from celebratory banners to concert logos and decorations. By planting the roots of Nauryz deep in the Bronze Age, the implication is that Kazakhs are descendants of the ancient Turkic steppe people and inheritors of their long legacy. Such temporal anchoring in the distant past allows the claim of Nauryz as an indigenous sacred holiday (not one from an imported calendar, religion, or cosmology), and in general lends legitimacy to nation-building efforts.

The Kazakhstani government's recent efforts to establish lineage with an ancient past bleed into cultural events and celebrations, a process particularly evident during Nauryz. Sak-era motifs, Chingizid references, and twelfth-century Islamic texts appear under an umbrella of claimed "Kazakh" cultural heritage. Underpinning the recent quest to uncover the "ancient" roots of Kazakh culture is a large-scale policy of ethnic redress undertaken by the Kazakhstani government shortly after independence. A Kazakh-privileged policy aimed at counteracting centuries of Russian hegemony in the region, ethnic redress has taken several forms. First, since independence, a concerted Kazakhization of the state has infused every level of government with greater numbers of ethnic Kazakhs. Second, demographic redress aims at repatriating ethnic Kazakhs from other countries in order to achieve a titular majority. And third, Kazakh culture has been promoted through the funding and engineering of cultural and historical projects.

The effort to connect modern Kazakhstan with an ancient past has been promoted through various institutions, including academia, elementary education, and state-controlled media. Edward Schatz writes that in the 1990s, "newspapers routinely devoted ample space to explaining ethnic traditions and covering Kazakh cultural events. In academia, any topic that covered pre-Soviet [Kazakh] history . . . received blanket endorsement. According to several informants of the Institute of History and Ethnography, the Institute's director, a powerful ally of Nazarbaev, issued an order (*instruktazh*) to researchers to find the roots of Kazakh statehood in the Sak period (first millennium B.C.E.)" (Schatz 2004, 82). The fruits of these labors are plentiful: Sak-era motifs appear everywhere from the local televised weather report (which shows the local temperatures on the right side of the screen as Sak jewelry decorates the left side) to Kazakh music concerts, and have come to signify Kazakh nationhood. To aid in the search for the deep roots of the new Kazakhstan, archaeological digs, ethnographic and linguistic studies, and historical reconstructions have been well-funded by the state, with the goal of bridging Kazakh history (which, by most accounts only begins in the fifteenth century) with that of Central Asia's oldest civilizations. Two children's encyclopedias of Kazakhstan, commissioned by the Kazakhstani Ministry of Education and Science and published in 2003 and 2004, highlight the following: archaeological finds from the Sak era, the eleventh-century carved stone statues in central Kazakhstan, the tomb of the twelfth-century Sufi Yassaui, which was recently restored in southern Kazakhstan, as well as later Kazakh heroes like Zhanibek (Zhanaidarov 2003; Zhumakhanov et al. 2004). In 2009 the Ministry of Education and Science sent scholars and linguistic experts to India to peruse the Mughal texts concerning the rule of the great Mughal emperor, Babur, apparently with the intent of identifying their linguistic roots (ostensibly as more Turkic than Persian, and thus closer to the Kazakh language).[2]

The Tamgaly petroglyphs in the Semirechie region of Kazakhstan, 170 kilometers from Almaty, are a particularly rich source of Kazakhstani historical reconstruction. With carvings dating from the second millenium

BCE, these images, including depictions of warriors, hunting scenes, and sun idols, appear often in advertisements, on television, at concerts, and in movies. Many television programs and concerts feature images from Tamgaly and a kind of runic script is often used when advertisers want to index ancient Kazakh roots. The petroglyphs appear often on the Kazakhstan channel, most noticeably in its logo—a petroglyph image of a rider on horseback carrying a flag. One advertisement for the channel shows petroglyphs morphing into thumbnail videos depicting scenes of contemporary Kazakhstan, including images of scientists, universities, factories, and oil wells. The emphasis is on development and advancement, a teleological progression from ancient history to modern times.

According to the UNESCO World Heritage site, "The Archaeological Landscape of Tamgaly features a remarkable concentration of some 5,000 petroglyphs, associated settlements and burial grounds, which together provide testimony to the husbandry, social organization and rituals of pastoral peoples from the Bronze Age right through to the early 20th century." This striking site, a clustered outcropping of black stones containing thousands of carved images, was likely a ritual space, as areas thought to be sacrificial altars are found in the sheltered space of the canyon. A wide array of sacred petroglyph images, including solar deities portrayed with gloriously shining sun heads, provide a symbolic logic for connecting the dots between an ancient sun-worshipping people, pre-Islamic Zoroastrians, and the present-day Nauryz holiday. These symbols—used in Nauryz concerts, banners, billboards, and televised advertisements—have become the visual totem of Nauryz, a shorthand for the sacred cosmos of the ancient Turks, a legacy inherited by their descendants, the Kazakhs. Many Nauryz events include the Tamgaly solar images, using the indigenous Zoroastrian roots of Nauryz and the theme of sun worship to bridge the ancient and modern celebrations of the holiday. The set for the Kazakh music concert *An men Anshi* (Songs and Singers), which took place at the Republican Palace in Almaty on Nauryz, featured large floor-to-ceiling sun god images painted on hanging translucent screens. The concert was largely composed of pop singers and a light show that lit up the screens with flickering colors, changing with the mood of the songs. In one act the petroglyphs seemed to dance in a psychedelic frenzy of green, pink, and yellow bubbling colors, images from a past civilization percolating up to the surface. In the process we see these fragments from the past dislodged from their original context and embedded in the present, gaining new meaning with this transference.

The solar images and other petrogyphs appear significantly in the Sultan Khodzhikov's historical musical feature film, *Kyz Zhibek* (Kazakhfilm 1971), which was aired on Nauryz in 2005. The story of the film *Kyz Zhibek* is taken from an epic poem (*zhyr*) set in the sixteenth century when feuding tribes on the Kazakh steppe engaged in bloody battles. Dubbed "the Kazakh Romeo and Juliet," this folk legend is a classic story of an ill-fated love between a young warrior named Tolegen and a beautiful girl, Zhibek, from feuding families. One scene featuring the Tamgaly petroglyphs comes just before the big battle scene, in a calm, still place just before the film's climax. At the start of this scene, the hero, Tolegen, played by Kuman Tastabekov, says good-bye to his sweetheart (Meruert Utekesheva, in the title role of Zhibek), and rides off with his friend to the rock outcropping where the petroglyphs appear, elaborately carved, above the steppe. The two dismount and look up at the cliffs with their fantastically illustrative carvings—sun deities with their radiantly shining heads, rams, riders on horseback, and a deer with majestically curling antlers stretching up like the branches of trees. Tolegen approaches a large, flat rock carved with ancient runes (created for the film), blows the sandy dirt off the surface and begins to work out the meaning, reading, "My people. Your strength is in unity." Turning to his friend, Tolegen comments, "Our ancestors left their testimony." The image of the sun god flickers briefly in the next frame, high above on the cliff face. "If we want to unite (through marriage) with the Shekty,"[3] Tolegen continues, "we should carve our mark next to theirs." Tolegen begins to chisel a sigil (tribal mark) in the cliff face. Like their ancestors, whose marks persist after death, Tolegen and his companion carve their mark into their present, so that their lives too will endure into future times. In so doing, they seek not only to mark temporal layers—a kind of temporal graffiti—but also to maintain ancestral links connecting these temporal layers, thereby creating a relational, familial, civilizational connective tissue between the past and the present.

The film *Kyz Zhibek* has also left an indelible mark on the landscape—a wall of "petroglyphs" near Tamgaly made specifically for the movie remains there today. Set among the petroglyphs, telling a story of these ancient people, *Kyz Zhibek* not only intervenes artistically in that history (as any work of historical art or literature does), it also inserts the present imaginary of the past into the very landscape. In this way, by disrupting the accumulation of temporal layers, shuffling the present and the past, and jumbling the timeline, *Kyz Zhibek* provides an example of how film, television, and other media can set *percolation* in motion.

NAURYZ ON TELEVISION

Though Nauryz was originally a Zoroastrian celebration of the new year and the return of the sun after the short days and long nights of winter (*nowruz* means "new day" in Persian), in Kazakhstan it has acquired additional meanings over time. Hints of Nauryz's Zoroastrian origins in Kazakhstani celebrations include a nod to sun worship (Kazakhs traditionally climb a high hill to greet the sun on Nauryz), the use of solar imagery, and a sense of the ancient origins of Nauryz. But in general Nauryz is connected to nomadic springtime traditions and, occasionally, associated with Islam, a connection supported by the state in media events such as the opening of the Islamic Cultural Center and mosque on Nauryz in 2005. This is possibly because Zoroastrianism, though originating in Central Asia, was a prominent religion in Persia and remains culturally relevant in Iran. Zoroastrianism is therefore more closely associated with the Persian world and the settled oasis culture of Central Asia, rather than that of the northern nomadic Central Asian Turks, like Kazakhs. Kazakh Nauryz traditions are most often connected to the seasonal lifeways of Eurasian mobile pastoralists, including the first birthing of lambs and other livestock, the first milk of the spring, the clearing of natural springs after winter.

A documentary program, *Traditions of Kazakhstan*, aired on Nauryz in 2004, highlights these nomadic connections. The channel Mediaset, which features cultural programs produced in a documentary, academic, and slightly colonialist-explorer style reminiscent of *National Geographic*, aired twin programs on Kazakh traditions, one in Russian and one in Kazakh, though the topics covered were somewhat different. The Kazakh program included a section on childbirth and fertility, followed by a section on Nauryz traditions. The film on Nauryz was presented in an ethnographic style, filmed in a mountainous pastureland and featuring Kazakh nomadic family life, with participants in traditional Kazakh dress. The first section was followed by this passage:

The Kazakh people kept the traditions of nomadic life until the 1930s. Their way of life, spiritual richness, poems and songs were all connected with the specifics of nomadic life. And the appearance [color] of the grass and the heavenly sphere (the sky) the Kazaks called by one word: *kök* [pronounced "cook"].

Had winter passed? Are the herds all right? The earth has freed itself from its wintry cover, and most importantly, the sheep have finally fattened up. If the livestock [are] healthy and well, then everything else, everyday life and existence, goes well. When everything turns green, the herds' newborn animals bring happiness and good fortune. Usually, after the first birthing [of livestock], people go out to the pasture. In the ancient understanding of the nomads, a person's age is determined by the number of times he has met the spring.

Since ancient times, Nauryz was considered the beginning of the year, and the main dish of this holiday is Nauryz *közhe*. It is prepared with seven ingredients: wheat, millet, milk, meat, salt, water and *kurdiuk* [mutton fat from the rump]. This signifies: unity, prosperity, success, good fortune, and health. Making *közhe* with the colostrum [the first watery milk] of cows who have just given birth, and inviting guests to share it, is considered an ancient tradition.[4]

The ethnographic film focuses on aspects of nomadic life: Tengrism (Central and Inner Asian animism or nature worship), dependence on livestock, seasonal renewal, and the spring birthing of the flock. The reference to the first milk (colostrum) of newly lactating cows is particularly interesting. Milk and milk products are especially important in Nauryz celebrations, and the first milk of spring after the livestock birthing is considered to have almost magical qualities. One practice at Nauryz is to sprinkle milk on newly planted trees while reciting a *bata* or blessing. The mention of the Kazakh word *kök* is also significant. Literally translated as blue or green, it is a Tengrian concept that describes living things and resists simple translation. The sky is kök, eyes may be kök, spring greenery is kök, but another word is used to describe inanimate objects (*zhasyl*: green). Kök comes directly from Tengrism, implying something sacred. The word for spring, *köktem*, contains this root.

News programs also highlighted traditions associated with seasonal nomadism, birth, and renewal. The Kazakhstan channel aired a news story about a gathering in Astana on Nauryz morning in which participants conducted a practice known as the "awakening of the spring":

> Astanites began the morning of Nauryz with the folk wisdom "Bulaq közin ash" or "Open your eyes, spring [natural water source]." Since 8 a.m. the people gathered at the spring believe the superstition that [this will ensure that] the year will be prosperous and happy. In Astana, the planting of saplings on Nauryz has acquired particular popularity. Twenty saplings planted on the grounds of the central mosque were named after babies born on this day. Elders gave their blessings. Thus, the twenty Astana seedlings, having received nourishment from mother earth, in proof of their existence, rapidly begin to stretch to the blue sky.

> In the words of the mayor [of Astana], Ömirzaq Shukeev, "Nauryz is based on good traditions, which should be continued. It's a holiday of renewal, of youth! The greatest news for nomads is considered the appearance on the earth of a new baby. Therefore we wanted this tradition to take form in the city and in the country."[5]

The continuation of Kazakh tradition, as seen in ethnographic films and media events like the planting of trees in Astana, was supported by "ethnographic expeditions" undertaken as part of the larger cultural-historical project of ethnic redress promoted by the state. Schatz writes about these "ethnocultural expeditions" undertaken in 1998, which were generously funded by the state. "Instructed to spotlight ethnic cultural traditions, teams of scholars were dispatched to each of the fourteen *oblast*'s to examine which sayings and proverbs, traditions, customs and toponyms had persisted into the post-Soviet period" (Schatz 2004, 83). Such expeditions, which sought to document and preserve Kazakh traditions that seemed to reflect those of a pre-Soviet era, came on the heels of a larger political imperative, when 1998 was declared the "Year of People's Unity and National History." As Abish Kekilbaev, the Kazakhstani secretary of state at that time, described, the stated aim of 1998 was to "systematize all historical events and phenomena, revive historical memory and provide spiritual cleansing. This is necessary in order to deeply recognize and to better understand the many-centuries aspiration of the people to state independence, unity, freedom of spirit, and human dignity" (Kekilbaev in Schatz 2004, 84). Kekilbaev's words imply that through the "revival of historical memory" and promotion of historical and cultural projects, the Kazakh people could "forget" the Russian/Soviet legacy, erase its residue from their cultural past and begin to reclaim their cultural heritage as their own. Documentary films like those discussed above clearly reflect this directive. Interestingly, they are not necessarily accepted as a current part of Nauryz celebrations. A young woman (a Kazakh-speaker from Astana) who watched the ethnographic film on Nauryz with me commented, "Wow, I learned so much about Nauryz!" She then cautioned, "You know, Maggie, no one actually celebrates Nauryz this way." This leads me to wonder whether such films are really bridging the gap between ancient and modern. The goal after all seems to be to try to present Kazakhstani traditions as an unbroken line, not a revival of long forgotten pre-Soviet traditions.

THEORIZING TRADITION

The sociologist Diana Kudaibergenova has written about the ways artists, politicians, and other political actors shape, take apart, and reconstruct concepts of tradition. Kudaibergenova discusses one artist, Askhat Akhmediyarov, whose work was harshly criticized for using large overturned Kazakh pots or cauldrons (*kazan*) to create a giant installation depicting a string of beads scattered over the ground. His critics chastised the artists arguing that an overturned kazan means bad luck, loss of fortune, or famine. Kudaibergenova argues that artists and independent actors often work to *retraditionalize* traditions, particularly in an unstable regime or in the aftermath of sharp transitions. In postsocialist cultures, Kudaibergenova contends, the reinvention of tradition is "seen as a stabilizing effort. In other ways, under conditions of constant crisis, transformations, and ruptures, inventing and re-inventing help many social actors and collectives to create a sense of continuity with the lost past, and traditions that might have appeared to be lost under . . . the Soviet state. (Kudaibergenova 2017, 307).

In my own work on tradition, I am interested in how media and entertainment participate in this construction and reconstruction of tradition. Kudaibergenova writes about using material in unfamiliar ways (the kazan) to comment on tradition. Some of my interlocutors considered the television shows I viewed with friends on Nauryz as outdated and overly pedagogical representations of Nauryz traditions. In contrast, in popular comedy and music programs, I frequently came across the use of satire to poke at the staid traditions. In one such comedic exchange, two program announcers discuss the tradition of making Nauryz *közhe*, a kind of liquid porridge of grains and meat. One announcer comments that everyone knows Nauryz *közhe* has seven ingredients, and one by one names the various grains and fat. This assertion is contradicted by the second announcer who protests, "Modern *közhe* now has eight ingredients. The eighth is ketchup!" While many Nauryz programs give the impression of an "ethnographic present"—an unquestioned and unchanging permanence of cultural traditions—others, like this comedy routine, take a more flexible approach to the holiday, challenging the static presentation of Nauryz traditions.

Anthony Smith discusses this rub between concepts of "authenticity" of national traditions and the gradual change in these traditions that inevitably comes with time. "According to the new nationalist vision, the idea of 'authenticity' was regarded not just as signaling what is 'mine,' 'my own' and nobody else's, or 'ours' alone, but as that which is 'original,' innate' and 'pristine' to us, stripped of all later accretions, and therefore 'true,' genuine' and 'real.' Hence the increasingly widespread rejection of all that was 'false,' 'corrupt' and unsubstantial as 'inauthentic,' *in particular the artifice and corruption of modern civilization*" (A. Smith 2013, 90; partially cited in Kudaibergenova 2016; emphasis added). Like the humorous addition of ketchup to the list of seven sacred Nauryz ingredients, the comedic questioning of the "original" is a way of challenging this binary between modernity and tradition, between modern "artifice and corruption" and that which is "natural," "original," and "pristine."

TELEVISED NAURYZ FILMS, CREATING NAURYZ IN THE PRESENT

Although the ethnographic-style films discussed seem to present a "pure" museumized version of Nauryz traditions, more recent films place Nauryz traditions in the context of "modern" life. Rather than taking an ethnographic approach, they are presented as stories of present-day Kazakhstan, with didactic vignettes injected into the storyline, educating viewers about Nauryz traditions, while at the same time indicating that these traditions are still alive and vibrant in Kazakhstan. A made-for-TV movie produced in 2005 and shown on Nauryz on the Kazakhstan channel is set in the aul (countryside, or Kazakh village). It opens with a young boy just waking on Nauryz morning to the sound of Nauryz "carols" or *saulmalyq*. He opens the door to find sever-

FIGURE 4.1. Sculptures depicting *mushel* (Kazakh zodiac) in Almaty.

al young boys, his friends from the village, singing saulmalyq, as his mother distributes candy to them. He opts not to participate in the caroling, and the film that follows revolves around his gradual social involvement in Nauryz alongside his growing crush on a fellow classmate.

In a later scene, the boys, cavorting outside, present impromptu skits about Nauryz. As in *Kyz Zhibek*, this scene is set among ancient stone sculptures, the durable remainders of the ancient past. The scene opens on a gentle sloping hillside golden with last year's tall grass, and the main action takes place around a group of famous stone sculptures called the Karkaraly stones (*Qarqaralydaghy balbal tastar*), which appear mostly in Almaty oblast (province) and date from at least the ninth century. The stones are believed to be memorials of fallen Turkic and Kipchak heroes. According to the archaeologist Lyubov Emolenko, a specialist in the stone memorial statues of Central Kazakhstan, "the ancient Turkic statues . . . depict warriors . . . fallen in a battle" (Kuzmenko 2015). The stone figures discovered in the territory of Kazakhstan "trace back to the period beginning from the late Bronze Age (the second and first millennium b.c.) to the developed periods of the Middle

Ages (at least, before the Mongolian invasion in the beginning of the 13th century)" (Kuzmenko 2015). Setting the scene among the ancient Karkaly stones helps direct our attention to Nauryz's deep historic roots. In casually setting disjunct temporalities in one frame, the film leaves the viewer to do the work of associating the present with the ancient past.

Another link to the ancient Turks in this scene is the reference to their cosmological representation—mushel, the Kazakh zodiac. In the boys' first skit, called *tülik zhyry* or "epic of the animals," the boys each play the role of an animal of the mushel. The Kazakh zodiac, though of unclear age and origin, is held in both scholarship (Amanov and Mukhambetova 2002) and popular culture to be an ancient, indigenous representation of the cosmos.

In this playful incantation of the cosmos, the boys' parts are as follows:

Mouse: Listen, people, I will be the head of the year. Who are you next to me? . . .

Cow: This year's eyes are [as small as] a little finger! Don't pay attention to robbery; there is no trickery; don't keep secrets. As I command it, I am the Cow. I will be the head of the year.

Tiger/Snow Leopard: I am strong! I fight with anybody who attacks me, and defend the others. And who are you [in comparison with me]?!

Rabbit: I am the Hare. I am not a coward, but harmless. A lot of snow falls during my year. I feed the people's livestock. There is good sowing (harvest of hay) in my year. I will be the head of the year.

Snail: My deeds are respected among insects. I am a snail, suitable for the beginning of the year. I drag my long tail. Beware! I am a snake.[6]

Snake: I am the great pockmarked Snake. I am treacherous. Don't stand in my path. Give me the beginning of the year.

Horse: The Horse is the wings of men, and is always with humans. I am transportation, and my milk—*kymyss* [fermented mare's milk]—has healing properties. No one can compare with me.

Sheep: I am the humble Sheep. Many people praise my years. In my year there is much good fortune. And in the year of the Monkey, there is *zhut.*[7] The beginning of the year will be prosperous if it is mine.

Monkey: Yes, I am a monkey. Don't tell anyone about my harmful/negative character. In my whole humorous being, I am the most careful and prudent of all. Who is better than me? I will be the head of the year.

Rooster: I am the winged Rooster. I feel all dangers. In the morning I wake you with my crowing, in the evening I call you home. Wherever we go, we always return to our people. We are responsible for the beginning of the year.

Dog: I can withstand the cold. At night I guard the livestock from wolves who run at a trot. And I do it without compensation. The year of the Dog is a good year. I will be the head of the year.

Pig: And don't forget about me. Don't leave me out of the year. When I come I squeal, and you run away, afraid. I am also needed. I will be the head of the year.[8]

This scene depicts a Kazakh legend in which each of the animals is vying for primacy in the calendar. Each tells Tengri (the Kazakh nature god) why he is the strongest and most important to Kazakh life. Finally it is decided that the calendar will be divided into twelve-year cycles, with each animal in charge of one year. To decide which will head the first year, it is agreed that the animals all go to the top of a hill, and the first one to see the sun will be the first animal in the zodiac. The mouse climbs onto the camel's back and from this high vantage point manages to see the sun first, winning the contest.[9] Here Nauryz is presented as New Year, not just in a seasonal sense but also in a calendrical sense. Although Nauryz is often portrayed as a seasonal beginning—the beginning of spring, the start of new life, with the new growing season and the birthing season among the livestock—it is less often connected to the zodiac. This allows a stronger link to an older representation of the cosmos, and a connection to Tengrism.

A second skit, portraying a struggle between summer and winter, is linked to the celebration of Nauryz as a vernal new year, marking the return of the sun at the spring equinox, celebrating new growth, new life. Two boys, one dressed as Summer (with a halo of greenery encircling his head) and the other as Winter (dressed in layers of clothes), present a mock battle between the two seasons to determine whether spring will start. After circling each other threateningly and improvising short speeches about their relative strengths, Summer overcomes Winter, bringing about the end of winter's reign and the beginning of spring. This dramatic portrayal of spring's beginning reflects the dualistic nature of Tengrism. Tengrian traditions and Inner Asian folklore (including that of Kazakhstan, Kyrgyzstan, Mongolia, and Siberia) often feature pairs of opposites: black and white, good and evil; similarly, Nauryz is celebrated as the balance between night and day, the vernal equinox as the seasonal pivot between the summer and winter solstice. While this scene clearly reflects the indigenous belief system, it is also replicates aspects of other current Kazakhstani New Year's Eve children's plays, in which the animal of the coming year challenges the animal of the old year (in 2004–2005, it was the Rooster and the Monkey). This chasing away of the old year was a staple of Soviet children's performances. It is significant that it appears here in a Nauryz skit as well, connecting Nauryz through performance to other New Year celebrations.

A particularly didactic moment in the film occurs when the children climb a hill on Nauryz morning to pick snowdrops, the small white first flowers of spring, and they happen upon a withered old man sitting high up in a treetop. It is the Kazakh storybook character Qangbasha, whose name means "tumbleweed." He asks a number of riddles to which the children must supply the answers, all of which have to do with Nauryz (e.g., about the ingredients in Nauryz közhe, the significance of Nauryz). Again, this scene appears as a lesson, almost a public service announcement, in which this character from Kazakh mythology faces the present time and instructs the public in traditional Nauryz celebration. The film, in conveying Nauryz traditions through skits, games, and storybook characters, participates in the effort to revive, strengthen, and maintain older Nauryz traditions, as they are pulled from the edge of extinction and firmly (re)planted in the present.

A number of these traditions are still maintained in rural areas (notably the tradition of climbing a hill at dawn on Nauryz morning to welcome the first sunrise of spring), but others are not common in Kazakhstan. Like *Babalar Uny*, the made-for-TV movie aired on Independence Day described in chapter 2, this short film weaves instructional lessons about Kazakh culture into a contemporary storyline. In presenting these didactic scenes in the context of a story of a boy on the verge of adolescence and his life in the aul, and interweaving these vignettes into the story of his crush on a schoolgirl, they seem to be striving to make older Nauryz traditions more accessible. Unlike the documentary style of the films produced in the late 1990s, these made-for-TV movies aim to connect Kazakh traditions to the present, rather than relegating them to the nomadic past. At the end of the film, the boy's older brother, played by a Kazakh pop star, sings a song about love and romance. Such injections of modern Kazakhstani life help to distance this film from the frozen, timeless style of the ethnographic documentary. Instead we are offered a mishmash of past and present celebratory practices, an amalgamated version of the holiday that makes for a strangely temporally flexible sense of Kazakh life and Nauryz traditions.

SATIRE, COMEDY, AND ANACHRONISM IN A NAURYZ CONCERT

An men Anshi (Songs and Singers), a concert held during Nauryz at the Republican Palace, is an annual event featuring an impressive lineup of Kazakh pop singers. In 2005, two announcers provided commentary and comic banter between the performances of national stars such as Karakat, Indira Rasylkhan, and Makpal Zhanpeisova.

One act in this concert was presented as a traditional *aitys*, an improvisitory competition between two aqyndar (poet-singers), played by comedians, who spar verbally while accompanying themselves on dombra. The two masters of ceremonies (MCs) each called out one aqyn in the following skit:

MC1: Serzhan, I have a personal *aqyn*, whom I praise, look after and prepare for competitions like this. I'm a teacher.

MC2: You can't be an *aqyn* yourself but prepare another man?

MC1: You don't know the whole of my ruse. I will tell you about it, acquaint you with my creative work. And now we'll see my apprentice.

MC2: Which *aqyn* is he? [Who is he?]

MC1: Oy, just wait, I will let you know in good time. He is a little like that [pointing his finger to his head, indicating "crazy"].

MC2: Like that?

MC1: Sometimes he can't stand still and acts nervous. And if his competing rival is unworthy, he will destroy all of us here.

MC2: Who? Us?

MC1: You and his rival.

MC2: You are mistaken if you think that he will get the better of me. And I have an *aqyn* too! Let's have a competition!

MC1: OK!

MC2: Call your *aqyn*!

MC1: Where is my *aqyn*? Hopefully he didn't get nervous and go away somewhere.

MC2: Call him!

MC1: He doesn't come out to just any invitation [i.e., you must address him respectfully]. Respected gentlemen! Dear spectators! My personal *aqyn*, sportsman, karateist, footballer, boxer—Dora!

[The *aqyn*, Dora, comes out dressed in gym clothes and begins doing exercises, bending into a squat and lifting his dombra over his head as if in weight training.]

How are you? Are you ready? Ok, bend . . . enough. . . . You are not in training, why do you dance like you're in a disco? [Addressing the second announcer:] Call him!

MC2: Conqueror of many competitions, Ulan-Ude!

MC1: That's your *aqyn*?

MC2: Yes, that's him. Take your seat, whoever came first.

[Ulan-Ude is dressed in traditional Kazakh dress, complete with a Kazakh felt hat topped with an enormous feather. As there is only one chair, Dora sits, leaving Ulan-Ude standing.]

MC1: [to Dora] Hey, play more quietly, you woke up a sleeping hunter. Play quietly!

Dora: In honor of Nauryz, with honest and kind intentions I welcome you my friends! *Ayay, ayay, ayay* . . .

MC1: [to Uland-Ude] Sit please.

[Ulan-Ude looks around and sits cross-legged on the floor next to Dora's chair]

Ulan-Ude: So now I will sing "ayay"! I bow and welcome my people! Then I bow and welcome my earth! And then I bow and welcome my rival! I come from abroad.

Dora: The eagle-owl feather sits too high on your head. Careful, an airplane can bring it down!

Ulan-Ude: I'm an *oralman*, who came here, who misses his own people and homeland. I bow to my homeland. I will bow for the sake of my people and take knowledge. I bow to the people of Kazakhstan and if need be I will kiss the stones of your people. Kiss stones . . . kiss stones . . . Where are the stones? Do you have them?

Dora: No, there are none here.

Ulan-Ude: If there are no stones, I will kiss the head of the *aqyn!* [Kisses his rival's bald head.]

Dora: People of course can't refuse a greeting like this. Friends, now Yuldash [Ulan-Ude]! I didn't bow like him, because we have nervous heads!

Ulan-Ude: I learned to welcome people, and it's proof of my creative work, my bowing to you. If it's not enough, I will bow in French!

Dora: He tries to turn somebody's head, let's see! But I greeted you and I have finished my speech.

Ulan-Ude: Hey wait! I want to greet you, but you run away! Anyway I will catch you and greet you.

The contrast between the oralman aqyn from Mongolia and the local aqyn is striking. The local aqyn is dressed in a tracksuit, and the oralman is in traditional dress, including a hat with an enormous feather, which his opponent ridicules. The oralman ridiculously bows to everyone on the stage, then to each corner of the audience, and even tries to greet each member of the audience separately before the hosts stop him. He represents tradition and a kind of down-to-earth naiveté, whereas the Almaty aqyn is condescending and modern, joking that an airplane might crash into the tall feather in the oralman's hat. The oralman sits cross-legged on the floor, while the Almaty aqyn sits on the chair. The oralman's mention of stones is interesting too, implying an affinity with natural surroundings. The oralman, however, uses this to ridicule his urban counterpart, saying in the absence of stones, he will have to kiss the bald head of his opponent.

This mutual ribbing highlights the oralman–local divide, which is premised on the general (though somewhat flawed) understanding of oralman Kazakhs as rural, more traditional, and closer to nature, whereas the local Kazakhs are thought of as condescending, out of touch with their roots and their land, and too caught up in cosmopolitan culture. This comic routine rests on economic, social, and linguistic differences between oralman Kazakhs and local Kazakhs, and represents the fraught relationship between the two groups. Local Kazakhs complain that oralman Kazakhs receive special considerations from the state (the Kazakh government rewards oralman Kazakhs monetarily for their "return" to Kazakhstan), and oralman Kazakhs for their part are often dismayed at their chilly reception in Kazakhstan and at the lack of adequate job prospects once they arrive in their supposed homeland. Further, even highly educated, multilingual oralman Kazakhs face the stereotyping of oralman Kazakhs as rural and uneducated, partially because of their lack of Russian-language skills, so important in Kazakhstani cities, particularly Almaty and Astana.

FIGURE 4.2. A Kazakh yurt alongside more permanent dwellings, Bayan Olgii, Mongolia.

Highlighting the undeniable culture clash and mutual resentment between oralman Kazakhs and local Kazakhs, this comedy routine also raises another important aspect of Kazakh diaspora politics—a temporal discrepancy in portraying Kazakh "homelands" in Kazakhstan and Mongolia. In contrast to the nativist search for the Kazakh past inside Kazakhstan's borders (as with the appeal of the Tamgaly petroglyphs), in the above comedic portrayal, the nomadic past is elsewhere, over the border, while the present (modernity, civilization) lies in Kazakhstan. Mongolian Kazakhs are often seen as repositories of traditions that no longer exist in Kazakhstan—and nomadic lifeways are indeed much more prevalent among Kazakhs in Mongolia. Because of this, Mongolian Kazakh lifeways are sometimes ridiculed, but just as often, are portrayed in romanticized, nostalgic hues in Kazakhstani media.

Kazakh cultural areas outside of Kazakhstan, such as Bayan Olgii in western Mongolia (an area that is 90 percent Kazakh), are relatively remote and largely rural. Because nomadic lifeways are more prevalent in these areas, they are perceived as maintaining more "authentic" Kazakh traditions and language use. Additionally, unlike their coethnics in Kazakhstan, Mongolian

FIGURE 4.3. A Kazakh yurt in Bayan Olgii, Mongolia.

Kazakhs have not incorporated Russian culture and language. For this reason, recent ethnographic expeditions, such as that of Kazakh music scholars
from the Kazakhstan Academy of Sciences in 2005, have traveled to regions
like Bayan Olgii in search of more "pure" versions of Kazakh culture outside
of Kazakhstan's borders. Like an archaeological dig, such expeditions seek to
uncover past layers of Kazakh culture, to collect cultural "artifacts" such as
Mongolian Kazakh folk songs to bring back and examine, thereby reclaiming a piece of Kazakh national heritage. This relationship with Kazakh areas
outside of Kazakhstan establishes a time–space framework in which the traditional–modern dichotomy takes on spatial dimensions. In this framework,
Kazakhstan represents the image of "modern" Kazakhs, globalism, technology, and the future of modern Kazakh life, while the outlying Kazakh regions in other states stand as repositories of Kazakh culture, traditions, and
folklore. In short, outer Kazakh regions represent the past; Kazakhstan the
future. Thus the movement of oralmandar (Kazakh returnees) into Kazakhstan represent a flow of past traditions into modern life, the gathering of the
Kazakh past to support and strengthen a forward-facing Kazakhstan.

Heeding the archaeologist Christopher Witmore's insistence that we consider not only the recent past but also the ancient past as proximate to the

present, I have paid particular attention to archaeological concepts of time in this examination of Nauryz. I have discussed the use of ancient imagery in contemporary Nauryz celebrations, the retelling (and re-viewing) of Kazakh mythic past in stories like *Kyz Zhibek*, and the curious, crooked, satirical, and whimsical use of time in didactic and comedic Nauryz television shows. Accepting the ancient past as proximate to (or even coexistent with) the present—that ancient layers of culture lay just under our apartment blocks and thoroughfares—we are left to decipher what significance this proximity holds for us, living in the present. The Nauryz television programs and concerts discussed here participate in a purposeful mining of the past, with mediation participating in this disruption of temporal layers. By investigating how such programs dredge up and illuminate past practices, and examining which aspects are magnified and embellished, we can more fully understand the present.

CHAPTER 5

TRAVELING HISTORIES

Ethnicity, Mobility, and Religion in Spring Celebrations

The steel ran South and North, presumably, springing from some inconceivable source and shooting toward a miraculous terminus. Someone had been thoughtful enough to arrange a small bench on the platform. Cora felt dizzy and sat down. Caesar could scarcely speak. "How far does the tunnel extend?" Lumley shrugged, "Far enough for you."

. . .

They waited.

—Colson Whitehead

Border crossings in Kazakhstan are freighted with meaning and heavily implicated in Kazakhstan's temporal and ethnic makeup. A train traveling between northwest China and Kazakhstan affords small trade routes and more established transborder businesses, and connects Kazakh and Uighur families split at the border—a legacy of centuries of crossings, back and forth, traversing this well-traveled border during times of famine, political and ethnic strife, regime change, or in search of opportunity. They bring with them the spoken and sung histories of migrations and past homelands. Borders move, evaporate, or solidify with the whims of empire, drawing the temporal and moral geographies of entire communities. Kazakhstan's population owes its diversity in part to forced migrations of the mid-twentieth century—traveling histories that have shaped individual lives and inscribed the roots and branches of family trees. In Kazakhstan, religious spring holidays—Purim, Passover, and Easter—cluster in a way that allows an examination of these moving histories of the diverse population groups living there. Celebrations at an Almaty synagogue, two Korean churches, and an Uighur commemoration event trace the complicated histories that brought these groups to Kazakhstan.

Calls to reexamine and retheorize border studies have yielded rich areas of scholarship at the intersection of mobility, border crossing, and temporality (Andersson 2014; Ballinger 2012; Behar and Suarez 2008; Donnan, Hurd, and Leutloff-Grandits 2017; Hayden 2010; Smart and Smart 2008; Tosic 2017). This reexamination has taken up topics such as inequalities in the slowing of mobility at crossings (Andersson 2014; Smart and Smart 2008,), the use of time as a tool to exert power over migrants at crossing (Andersson 2014), enclosure and mobility (Andersson 2014), displacement and "replacement" (Ballinger 2012), staying and "stayers" (Gaibazzi 2015). New terms and concepts introduced in these studies, such as "prefrontier," "punctuation," and "rhythms of displacement" (Ballinger 2012), point to the temporal reframing of border studies.[1] Such scholarship highlights the intersection of subjective temporality with political temporality at borders, and underscores the significance of border temporalities to political change. Although there is a large body of work on mobility and migration in ethnomusicology (for example, Manuel 2012; Robinson 2013; Sanadjian 1995; Shannon 2007, 2015; Watkins 2009; Wong 2012; Zheng 2010), little overlap exists between studies of mobility and temporality.

In probing the sonic histories of mobility in Kazakhstan, this chapter examines three phases of political change and migration: Stalin-era migrations, post-Soviet emigrations, and the redrawing of borders after the collapse of the Soviet system. I discuss the effects of these mobilities on family histories and their creation of temporally inflected mobile conceptions of "home" (Donnan, Hurd, and Leutloff-Grandits 2017; Tosic 2017). Through waves of internal migrations, evacuations, and border crossings, home becomes not a place but a *traveling*, in which each chapter, each episode is linked to its own location. This episodic temporality, moving from place to place through decades or centuries becomes an important force in shaping communities and families (see, for example, Werner and Barcus 2015). The people I spoke with in Kazakhstan who were involved in forced or voluntary migrations described how their family histories map, in stages, onto the past, present, and future. Some related and performed stories of forced migrations;,others told of the economic and family networks in other countries tying them to past homelands. In some cases, these same connections now enable their children to emigrate back to their country of origin. Songs performed at community gatherings and in private homes told of siblings left behind, of funerals unattended abroad, of life continuing on without them in their abandoned homelands.

HISTORICIZING MIGRATIONS

In examining the intertwined trajectories of mobility and demography in Kazakhstan, it is crucial to look at both Soviet emigration and internal migration across the Soviet Union. Scholars who study the former have described four waves of Soviet emigration: 1917 (directly after the Russian Revolution), 1941–1947 (World War II and its aftermath), 1948–1986 (particularly important for Soviet Jewish emigration), and since 1987 (up to and following the fall of the Soviet Union) (Dietz, Lebok, and Polian 2002; Vishnevsky and Zayonchkovskaya 1994). In the first two case studies discussed here—Korean and Jewish communities in Kazakhstan—the center of the story pivots around World War II. An examination of forced migrations from western and eastern regions of the Soviet Union into Kazakhstan provides a look at how these communities trace their histories and pathways into this vast country. The other major shift discussed here took place in the post-Soviet era, which brought, along with mass emigrations among certain ethnic groups (German and Jewish, for example), an influx of foreign investments and missionizing to fill perceived "vacuums" in post-Soviet states. Both the World War II and Post-Soviet waves of mobility and migration catalyzed crucial changes in Kazakhstan, as if some great tectonic plates shifted, altering Kazakhstan's demographic landscape.

KORYO SARAM

Stalin's forced migrations of Poles, Germans, Kurds, Iranians, and Koreans in the late 1930s and 1940s brought large numbers of deported peoples from the Soviet borderlands to Central Asia. The ethnic Korean population, located in the Soviet Far East, was one of the most heavily affected by the forced migrations; the entire population was forcibly relocated from the far eastern edge to the center of Soviet territory, with the majority being resettled in Kazakhstan. Known today as Koryo Saram, Kazakhstani Koreans maintain a strong sense of local community. With the largest numbers residing in Almaty, ethnic Koreans in Kazakhstan have also strengthened ties with Korean and Korean American communities. This is partly achieved through family and business connections, but a major link to Korea and the Korean diaspora has been facilitated through Korean evangelical church communities. By way of introduction to the Koryo Saram, I begin by relating the family histo-

Figure 5.1. Sveta Kim, Almaty, 2014.

ry of Sveta Kim, whose story closely intertwines with the winding path of the Kazakhstani Koreans.

Sveta Kim is an elegant middle-aged woman who works as a housekeeper and, on Sundays, is a regular congregant at Almaty Central Evangelical Baptist Church (ACC).[2] Her family history now spans five countries in Asia as a consequence of migrations and shifting borders. From her parents' deportation to Kazakhstan in 1937, to her own tumultuous childhood and early adulthood in Soviet Central Asia, to her son's recent "return" to South Korea to work and attend seminary, the arc of Sveta's family journey attests to the transnational familial, religious, and business networks Central Asian Koreans draw on.

The first Korean families came to the Russian Far East in the 1860s, and were welcomed by tsarist officials, who sought to settle the sparsely populated area. Following a particularly poor harvest in Korea in 1869, the numbers of Koreans immigrating to Russia drastically increased. The first Koreans settled along the Amur and Ussuri Rivers near the coastal region of Far Eastern Russia. Sveta's great-grandparents, born in Korea in the late nineteenth century, were among those who emigrated from Korea to Russia, fleeing famine and seeking better opportunities across the border. Through the late nineteenth and into the twentieth century, many Koreans crossed overland across the Tumangan River or via the sea route from Pusan to Vladivostok. In 1917 Koreans in the Soviet Far East numbered 85,000 (G. Kim 2004). At the time of Soviet annexation of the Far East Republic on November 22, 1922, ethnic Koreans resided in three districts of the Far East region, including the the Posyet national Korean district with 55 Korean village councils (Polian 2004, 98). In 1926 their numbers had swelled to 169,000, according to the 1926 Soviet census, and by the 1930s, there were well-established communities in Vladivostok, Amur, and Khabarovsk, including hundreds of Korean agricultural and fishing kolkhozes, Korean theaters, and other educational and cultural institutions (G. Kim 2004). Both of Sveta's parents were born into this well-established Korean community in the Soviet Far East.

The forced migrations of ethnic Koreans were undertaken in several deportations, beginning in the fall of 1937, but in the end, the entire Korean population of the Soviet Far East had been resettled in distant Central Asia. The wheels of change were put in motion in the spring and summer of 1937. According to the Russian geographer and historian Pavel Polian, "Following the resolution of the All-Union Central Executive Committee and Council of People's Commissars of 17 July 1937, special defense zones, or border zones, were to be introduced along the USSR frontiers" (Polian 2004, 98). Certain ethnic groups living in these border zones, including Poles, Germans, and Koreans, were considered threats to Soviet security; indeed, on April 23, 1937, the Soviet newspaper *Pravda* reported Koreans to be key agents of Japanese espionage in the Far East (Polian 2004, 99). As a result of this perceived threat, in 1937 Stalin closed Soviet borders and instituted a "frontier zone cleansing" that would drastically alter Soviet demographics, particularly in the Soviet Far East and Central Asia.

Through the fall and winter of 1937, Stalin forcibly moved some 200,000 ethnic Koreans from the Soviet Union's eastern edge into Central Asia (Diener 2009; Polian 2004). The majority of Korean deportees were settled in Kazakhstan and Uzbekistan. Sveta's parents, teenage newlyweds in 1937, were swept up in this massive deportation, which took approximately one month and directly claimed at least five hundred lives (G. Kim 2004), although with epidemics and poor conditions during and after the deportations, the number of deaths was more likely in the thousands. Upon arrival, resettled families were greeted by official incompetence, often a dire lack of food and basic necessities, and extremely harsh living conditions. One group of four thousand ethnic Koreans, arriving on December 31, 1937, in Kostanay, northern Kazakhstan, where the extreme continental climate brings frigid winter temperatures, "spent about one week in their carriages before there was any sign of activity from local authorities" (Polian 2004, 100). Korean deportees were settled largely in urban areas, though about ten thousand were relocated to northern Kazakhstan in areas recently settled by Polish and German deportees.

Sveta was born in Tashkent, Uzbekistan, in 1950. During her childhood and early adulthood she lived in three Central Asian capitals, Tashkent, Bishkek, and Almaty. Her father was sent to work in a *trudarmiia* (labor army) mining coal in Karaganda. Rather than being conscripted into the army, the so-called punished peoples such as Koreans and Germans were sent to serve in labor units, especially coal mines. Polian writes, "On 10 January 1943, a State Defense Committee resolution was issued stipulating that some 8 thousand Koreans be demobilized from the army and subsequently recruited to labor battalions and transport convoys" (Polian 2004, 101). Her father, having been sent away to work in the mines, abandoned the family when Sveta was young. Sveta's mother supported her family by making Korean sweets to sell and maintaining a "riumochnaia" a kind of backdoor watering hole for drinking shots of vodka and *samagon*, a homemade liquor.

Sveta remembers how her mother missed the home of her girlhood in the Russian Far East. Here is an excerpt from our conversation in a 2015 interview:[3]

MA: So your grandmother and grandfather died in the Far East. Do you know what city your mother was born in?

SK: Suchan.[4] I remember I asked her where she was born and she said Suchan. Suchan was a large port city. Vladivostok, Suchan, they are right on the sea. And after they moved here she always dreamed, "I want once before I die, just once, to go back there again, to Suchan," where she lived in her youth. And she said it was so beautiful there. There were mountains, well not very high mountains, and there grew ginseng—do you know ginseng, the roots are very medicinal, good for your health. Yes, ginseng, it actually grows in the mountains. And she said, "There were so many beautiful flowers, it was SO beautiful." She talked about it with us all the time.

MA: She remembered?

SK: Yes, she remembered it. You see, in 1937 (she was born in 1919) she was grown up already. She was already a young woman. She would always remember it, she would always tell us about it. And she told me they lived by the sea and there was a lot of fish, seafood, and that "kim" [using the Korean word for seaweed] (you know what that is—kim, have you tried it?) and they went out to the seashore and they gathered that, the seaweed—gathered it, dried it, and ate it. . . . She talked about that, that there by the sea, they could just catch everything and eat. And that's how they lived.

Unable to return to the Far East as she had once wished, her mother made a life for herself and her children in Central Asia, growing rice, distilling spirits, and making Korean food to sell. Eventually she reunited with her husband in Kyrgyzstan, where he built a small house. Sveta's half brother lives there still. "The house is still standing," Sveta marveled (S. Kim 2015).

THE KOREAN COMMUNITY IN ALMATY

Through the Soviet era, Almaty became an important center of Soviet Korean life, with a Korean theater, radio station, and newspaper (Diener 2009, 476). While the rural Korean population also flourished in the decades after deportation, with Korean collective farms well-established in rural Central Asia, in the late Soviet era and after independence (from about 1980 to 2000), the importance of Almaty to Korean culture became pronounced, as a rural–urban shift pushed the urban Korean population to 87 percent (according to the 1999 census; Diener 2009, 476). Identifying as Koryo Saram ("people of Koryo"), Central Asian Koreans are largely Russian speaking. Since language instruction in Korean was for the most part not available after deportation, Korean-language retention in later generations was very low. Like many Koryo Saram, Sveta is a native Russian-speaker, but has now been learning Korean on her own and can speak some Korean, which she says she has learned mostly from watching Korean movies and soap operas. Language classes for children and adults have been popular in Almaty for more than a decade and there are dozens of Korean associations and amateur performance groups.

Like many ethnic Koreans in Almaty, Sveta has gradually become more connected to South Korea, not only through her heritage and language but also through her children, her church, and her work. She worked for many years for a businessman from South Korea who ran a wedding banquet venue in Almaty. When I spoke with her in 2014, one of her sons had gone to live and work for three years in South Korea, where he served in a church. Sveta explains, "Yes, he serves there in the church. You know how many churches there are in Korea? There are as many churches as there are stores! At night you can see—so many crosses. And do you know who he ministers to? He serves Russian-speakers! Now there are many who have gone there to work—from Uzbekistan. . . . . They made an agreement, one month without a visa. They can come here; we can go there."

THE KOREAN EVANGELICAL MISSION IN ALMATY

The Korean mission to Central Asia that began in the late 1980s was a response to what Korean and Korean American missions saw as an enormous opportunity. Like the Chabad-Lubavitch branch of Judaism, the Korean evangelical churches saw the former Soviet states as a kind of tabula rasa, where decades of enforced atheism left a spiritual lacuna that presented foreign religious institutions with an obligation—and immense opportunity. The flood of missionary activity into the former Soviet states, particularly on the part of evangelical and fundamentalist religious organizations, was a direct response to this perceived need for spiritual guidance and opportunity to missionize.

A website run by Korean evangelical missions details the Korean missions to Central Asia over the past two decades. "After the dissolution of the Soviet Union, the Korean church and mission organizations began their ministries in the North. Missionaries from Korean churches in Korea and America began ministering to *Koreyskiy*, diaspora Koreans. Most of the missionaries in the beginning targeted Russian-born Koreans and native Russians with the help of Russian translators among the diaspora Koreans. . . . The first ten years of mission work resulted in a high level of evangelization among Russians and diaspora Koreans, establishing many impactful ministries and numerous registered churches" (D. Kim 2014). The author, Daniel Kim, a Korean missionary, goes on to describe how the involvement of missionaries in community building activities, such as the funding and organizing of schools, day cares, language classes, and arts programs, helped the missions to skirt the

FIGURE 5.2. Korean food stand selling kimchi and tofu outside the Almaty Central Evangelical Baptist Church.

watchful eye of the state, particularly through pairing with nongovernmental organizations. He describes the role of missionary teachers and professors who not only offer Korean and English classes but also teach "sound ethics and . . . a Christian worldview" (D. Kim 2014). Thus, the religious teaching of the Korean missions in Central Asia was entwined, it seems by design, with community-building efforts and Korean cultural activities.

The Korean mission to Central Asia that began in the late 1980s relied on transnational networks involving a flow of funding, leadership, and religion through triangulated diasporic routes (Korea, Kazakhstan, the United States). Both the Agape Church and the Almaty Central Evangelical Baptist Church, where I attended several services, were recipients of funding and religious leadership from abroad that flowed into Kazakhstan at the end of the Soviet era and continued after independence.

ALMATY CENTRAL EVANGELICAL BAPTIST CHURCH

Almaty Central Evangelical Baptist Church, where Sveta and her family attend service every week, was founded in February 1991. In September of that year, the church received governmental registration, a significant hurdle for new religious organizations in Kazakhstan. (I also worked with Seventh-Day Adventists, for example, who had not been granted legal rights to organize as a church.) The original church was quite small, but after rapid growth through the 1990s, a much larger building was constructed on the same site in 2001. The church's original name, Hosanna, was changed to Almaty Central Baptist Church in 1997 and in 2012 the name was changed to the Almaty Central Evangelical Baptist Church.

On a brilliant, warm Sunday morning, parents with young children, groups of teenagers, and a number of extended, multigenerational families, gathered in the courtyard outside the ACC. Unlike other churches I had attended in Almaty, which tended to be quite diverse, this congregation was largely Korean, with just a few exceptions. From the street, the bustling activity and large brick exterior of the ACC is mostly hidden from view by a solid steel gate, though passersby might note the handful of vendors outside the church selling tofu, kimchi, and Korean sweets. Sveta, who attends the ACC every week with her adult children and their families, chatted with her many friends in the sunny courtyard. On this particular Sunday, several baptisms were scheduled for the 9:00 a.m. service. Sveta and her friends, a lively group of self-named "koreiski babushki" (Korean grandmothers), had plans to take one of the newly baptized members out to lunch after church.

The baptisms took place in a round brick baptismal pool—so large that the pastor, Alexander Han, and the newly baptized could both stand in it. In white robes, the pastor called each person separately to the pool. The congregants presenting themselves for baptism entered through a break in the blue curtains at the back of the stage like gameshow contestants. The first woman came down and stepped gingerly into the pool. The woman, who was in her fifties, had struggled with alcoholism and had trouble supporting herself and her family. The pastor joked with her genially and blessed her as he placed one hand over her head. Then he dipped her as if they were ball-room dancing, submerging her for a second or two before bringing her back to the surface. He then asked if she was OK and gently placed his hand on her head for a moment. After the church service, I went to lunch with Sve-ta's group in celebration of this new member of the church. There the newly baptized woman recounted a time of terrible trouble during which she was in debt and unable to support her two daughters. She wept as she related her story, and said she hoped that her life had now turned around. The baptism of the newly converted is a regular part of the ACC, and of Korean evangeli-cal churches in general. As is so often the case, these new inductions into the church are the result of the coinciding of the church's proselytizing mission with the precarious social position of the new members. The church's large, active congregation (the church holds five full, very well-attended services on Sunday) attests to the church's extremely successful efforts to make church members feel included, protected, and part of a living body of faith.

The close physicality and interactivity involved in worship seemed to constitute a conscious maintenance of the congregants' strong involvement in the church. Performance during the service was multifaceted and elab-orate. Teams of dancers in modest matching costumes performed gestures and simple dance moves to illustrate and illuminate the sung text. A small choir of robed singers and a soloist accompanied by electric guitar and key-board performed throughout the service. One of the most interesting aspects of the worship was how gesture was performed in different ways through-out the service, accompanying prayer, singing, and even congregational an-nouncements. Several different gestures were used regularly by the partici-pants. One was the receiving gesture—hands out palms up—for receiving blessings. The second was a blessing gesture—hands up about head height palms facing forward—used for actively directing healing prayers and bless-ings on another congregant or group. Finally, the praise gesture—hands above head palms relaxed, facing forward and swaying—used by some con-gregants when singing or listening to music during the service.

At the beginning of the service, the pastor called up the children from the wings of the worship space, set up like a stage in the front of the church. As the children entered, the congregation applauded them enthusiastically, the

Figure 5.3. Agape Church.

children waving to their parents like rock stars. The pastor asked the congregants to give the children their blessing and the entire community raised their hands palms facing the stage as if radiating goodwill toward the children. The children, in turn, received the blessing with palms up, hands slightly extended. The pastor gave a vigorous, fast-moving, emphatic blessing, urging us all to protect and bless all the children. One small boy cried quietly. It was an intense moment of support and almost violent caring—and it was a regular part of *every* service. In addition to these gestures, considerable physical contact was required during the service. At one point the pastor asked the congregation to stand close to and directly facing a neighbor. He then instructed congregants to pray together, out loud, with prayers directed toward their partners, while holding hands. Clearly, one cannot passively experience this style of worship; if you are in the church, you are obliged to be an active participant. Though this begs further research, I suggest that this kind of hyperparticipatory worship affects the congregation's self-understanding as a community.

AGAPE CHURCH

The Agape Church, where I attended services on Easter Day in 2005, was well attended by a mixed congregation of Kazakhs, Russians, Koreans, and

some of mixed ethnic heritage. Fairly typical of many "new" religions in Kazakhstan, Agape was very inclusive, with many mixed marriages within the
church community. The young woman who brought me to the church had
grown up in an orphanage and was as she put it a "metis" (of mixed ethnic
heritage). She had known Kim, the pastor, for many years, and he was instrumental in her religious education. She was introduced to Christianity
through missionaries at the orphanage where she grew up, and said that religion saved her from the fate of the streets met by many of her fellow *detdo-
movskie* (orphanage kids), including many who ended up in prostitution. At
Kim's prompting, she attended seminary in her early twenties and, ten years
later, she maintained deep religious convictions and a strong, almost familial
attachment to him.

The pastor, Joseph Kim, was born in Korea and emigrated in his early
twenties to the United States, where he "found" religion, went through religious education, and became a pastor in Los Angeles. He came to Kazakhstan in the 1980s and founded the Korean Agape Church in Almaty. Though
he lived for many years in Almaty, his main languages remained Korean and
English, as he had never become proficient in Russian. Kim had children and
grandchildren in the United States and traveled back and forth frequently
to visit family. The church was built in part with funding from the Korean
American Christian organizations, and Kim was careful to maintain both
Korean and Korean American connections in the service.

The service was conducted in Korean with simultaneous translation into
Russian. Of the songs accompanying worship, many were American worship
songs, translated into Russian with lyrics projected onto a large screen in the
front of the church. One song, titled "He Lives" (*On zhivoi*), featured a male
soloist standing centerstage with an electric guitar, flanked by two female
dancers and backed by a small choir in robes as well as five backupsingers
with handheld microphones, singing in unison. The main singer played electric guitar, joined by a drumset and electric keyboard. I was struck by the
dynamic nature of the performances, many of which included dance. Many
parishioners clapped and moved with the music as they sang, and some singers shouted out expressions of praise like "Hallelujah!" and "He is risen!" between musical phrases and during the instrumental tags at the end of songs.
My friend admitted that they strove to emulate a black gospel style of worship and prided themselves on active, expressive participation.

When I reluctantly allowed my (half-Jewish) three-year-old daughter to attend Sunday school on Easter, she emerged after the service with a large present wrapped in Christmas paper. The box contained all sorts of kiddie mementos from the United States: colorful hair fasteners, fancy colored pencils, a flashlight engraved with the words "Jesus is the light," peppermint drops, and of course, a Barbie doll. The church, with its connections to Korean American Christian organizations and its use of the Korean language, American commercial goods, and American musical culture and style of worship, reflected its pastor's transnational migrations. In a way its cultural and linguistic makeup traced his path from Korea to the United States and then to Kazakhstan, and its existence depended on the personal, religious, and financial networks of which he became a part.

PURIM AND PASSOVER IN ALMATY

It is thought that Jews first came to Central Asia in the fifteenth century as traders on the Silk Road. While Central Asian or Bukharan Jewish culture flourished for centuries in the beautiful city of Bukhara, now in Uzbekistan, the first record of Ashkenazi Jews in Kazakhstan was in the nineteenth century (EAJC). Throughout the twentieth century, the small Jewish community in Kazakhstan was in flux, culturally and numerically. Mass evacuations of European Jews into Kazakhstan during World War II and emigration from former Soviet states after the collapse of the Soviet Union in 1991 created upheavals in the Almaty Jewish community and had lasting effects on Jewish worship practices in Kazakhstan.

At the start of World War II, to preserve Soviet industries while war raged in the west of the country, a mass evacuation was ordered of Soviet citizens from western regions of the Soviet Union (particularly from Leningrad and Moscow) to Kazakhstan. In 1941 and 1942, a total of 532,500 people were evacuated to Kazakhstan from western regions (Zhanguttin 2016); precise numbers are difficult to obtain, but by some estimates as many as 100,000 of the evacuees sent to Kazakhstan during these years were Jews. Although most of these evacuees returned to western cities after the war, still the Kazakhstani Jewish community saw their small community grow and strengthen as a result of this influx.[5]

During the Soviet era, there were officially sanctioned synagogues in Almaty, Shimkent, and Kyzylorda. In Almaty, one of the key figures in the de-

FIGURE 5.4. Postage stamp featuring the Almaty Chabad-Lubavitch Synagogue.

velopment of the Jewish religious life, Levi Yitzchak Schneerson (1878–1944), in fact came to Kazakhstan as an exiled rabbi under Stalin. Schneerson was the chief rabbi of Yekaterinoslav, Ukraine, where he lived for most of his life. In 1939, after his arrest and imprisonment for protesting the crackdown on Jewish observances and learning, he was exiled to Kazakhstan. He lived first in a remote village near the border with China then moved to Almaty, where he met frequently (for both socializing and religious observance) with other Jews in the community, many of whom were wartime refugees from the western republics of the Soviet Union. He died in Almaty in 1944 and the Chabad-Lubavitch Synagogue in Almaty was built in his honor near his gravesite (Chabad of Kazakhstan).

The influence of Chabad-Lubavitch in Almaty is undoubtedly due not only to Levi Yitzchak Schneerson but also to his son, the seventh and last Chabad-Lubavitch rebbe, Rabbi Menachem Mendel Schneerson (1902–1994), an extremely important figure who was responsible for expanding the small religious group in Brooklyn to an international network. Menachem Mendel Schneerson grew up in Ukraine where his father was a rabbi, married the daughter of the sixth Lubavitcher rebbe, and after traveling and studying abroad, he moved with his wife to Paris, where they lived until the outbreak of World War II. In 1941 he fled Paris to escape the Nazis and settled in the United States with his family, where he lived until his death in 1994. Headquartered in Crown Heights, Brooklyn, the Lubavitch movement grew under his direction to become an international network spanning seventy countries (EAJC; Ferziger 2012). The historian and biographer of *The Rebbe: The Life and Afterlife of Menachem Mendel Schneerson*, Samuel Heilman, who studies what he sees as increasing fundamentalist tendencies in Judaism, describes him in this way: "The Lubavitcher Hasidim . . . think that their Rebbe is the Moshiach, or messiah, and that they can bring him back and usher in a messianic end of history by converting all Jews into Lubavitcher Hasidim" (Heilman 2005, 259; see also Heilman and Friedman 2010). The documentary journalist Carolyn Drake writes, "A small, vocal faction of Lubavitchers believe that Schneerson is the Messiah and revere him as such. But most simply honor the memory of the man who helped energize a religion devastated by Hitler and Stalin" (Drake 2006). Almaty, as the last home and final resting place of the rebbe's father, is then unsurprisingly a focus of attention, and the Jewish community there the recipient of funds and religious leadership from the Lubavitch headquarters. Thus, these forced migrations and evacuations of World War II that brought Polish, Korean, German, Jewish, Kurdish, and Iranian people to Kazakhstan also brought Lubavitcher leadership—ironically, a religious leadership now at odds with Kazakhstan's diverse population.

PASSOVER AT THE ALMATY CHABAD-LUBAVITCH SYNAGOGUE

On the first night of Passover, I traveled with my husband and young daughter to the Almaty Chabad-Lubavitch synagogue for seder. The synagogue, located far from the city's center, was barely visible from the street. Set back in an abandoned-looking lot, the synagogue, gated and guarded, resembled a castle, its large windows showing off an enormous chandelier hanging in the two-story worship space. The local population was very mixed, but the Lubavitch rabbis (brothers, Elchonon Cohen, chief rabbi of Almaty and Yeshaya Cohen, chief rabbi of Kazakhtan) conducted a rigidly structured seder. The brothers, born in Israel and educated in the United States, were from a large Lubavitcher family in Jerusalem, where their father was still an active rabbi. We arrived early, and before the seder started I sat outside on one of the lacquered wooden benches, talking with a woman, Nadia, as our children played in the ramshackle playground.

Nadia spoke about the Lubavitcher rabbis and their patchy reception in the Almaty Jewish community. She herself did not quite seem to know what she felt about them, alternately complaining and speaking warmly about them. "They didn't used to let in our (non-Jewish) relatives and those who had been baptized," Nadia said, but then she assured me that the synagogue subsequently became more welcoming and anyone, even Russians and Kazakhs, could come to the seder. "But they are strict, very strict, the Lubavitchers," a reference, I gathered later, to their rather didactic style of worship, which discouraged active participation and enforced a strict gender divide. The construction of the new synagogue, Nadia explained, was supported through Israeli funding (though I noticed the meeting hall was funded by a Brooklyn couple and much of the furniture was also purchased through private U.S. donations). "We could never build such a place ourselves." The synagogue was erected in 2003; previously, services were held in a makeshift synagogue on Tashkentskaia Street.

The seder was conducted in three languages, with prayers in Hebrew, explanations and instructions in Russian, and some Yiddish spoken between the two brothers. An American woman who sat with us mentioned that she recognized many of the songs from her stay in Israel—Hebrew children's songs and folk songs. The participants sat at long tables where there was a constant flow of food, served by Kazakhs. The main action of the ceremonies took place in the center of the large hall, where the rabbi-brothers conducted the service. Because most of the participants did not know the songs or prayers, the rabbis were the sole actors, as the hundred or so participants merely looked on and tried to follow their instructions, given in heavily accented Russian. The lack of active participation speaks to the distanced nature of its leadership and the incongruence between religious ideology and the realities of the Jewish population in Almaty.

PURIM IN ALMATY

Purim in Almaty was a festive affair, held not at the synagogue but in a small public concert hall, the Kazakhconcert Hall in Almaty. When I arrived with my family, my husband explained that we did not have an invitation but learned about the event through the Almaty Jewish organization Mitzvah. The man at the door waved us in, saying smilingly, "We can recognize our own [nashi]." Purim, ludic and exuberant, often involves active participation by children and young people and frequently includes musical and dramatic sketches complete with masks and costumes. The theatrical nature of Purim

celebrations makes it a fitting vehicle for the presentation of multiple snap-
shots of Jewish life. The celebration we attended included many skits, both
historical and playful, that reflected various aspects of Jewish culture. Stressing different periods in Jewish history, it also tugged strongly in several directions toward multiple "home" regions.

The Purim celebration was clearly a community-organized event. Adults
and children took part in the performances and while the main action took
place on the stage of the large hall, there was also much activity within the
hall, as attendees milled about greeting each other before and after the event.
The event began with a family trio (father and son on violin with a daughter
flutist) playing a Soviet Jewish song, "The Jewish Shtetl" (*Evreskoe Mestechko*,
by A. Lunev and M. Tanich). The announcer then introduced the Purim pageant with these words:

> The Jewish shtetl. It gave the world such wonderful composers, poets, writ-
> ers—it is enough just to say one name: Sholem Aleichem! We decided that we
> will also present the Jewish shtetl, in which people gathered in ancient times to
> celebrate such wonderful holidays on just such a square [indicating the central
> area of the stage]. So, let's celebrate Purim!!

> Now enter our heroes, residents of the shtetl Kostrilovka. But first I want to
> introduce the heroes of a legendary time . . . [introduces Mordechai, Esther, and
> all the characters of the Purim story].

The setting of the pageant was revealing. It framed the Purim story of ancient Persia within the context of a parallel narrative of Purim celebration
in the shtetl, the Jewish village, invoking simultaneously ancient Jewish
history in the Persian Empire and Jewish village life in pre-Soviet and early Soviet Eastern Europe. The mention of Sholem Aleichem referenced the
nineteenth- and early twentieth-century Jewish writer, one of the first modern male literary authors to write in Yiddish about shtetl life, and whose pro-
digious work marked the beginning of the shtetl as an acceptable literary
source and subject.[6] The frame of the shtetl for this sketch provided the backdrop of a rich Jewish cultural life.

The program also included several songs in Russian, mainly romantic songs of the Soviet era. One of the characters in the Purim story sang a
Soviet-era love song—a bard song, accompanied by guitar—and later in the

FIGURE 5.5. Dancers at a Purim celebration, Almaty.

program the cast performed a popular Soviet Jewish song, "We Melt, We Melt" (*My Taem, My Taem*). Later in the program, performers sing the Soviet-era song, "Just Like That" (*Tol'ko Tak*), whose refrain is as follows:

Не кружись над головою, черный ворон,
А кружись, шар голубой, над головой!
Don't let a black raven circle over your head,
But instead let the blue sphere circle above you!

This song was written in 1984 by a well-loved Soviet/Russian bard duo, Aleksei Ivaschenko and Georgii Vasilyev. Known simply as "Ivasi," in the 1970s–1980s the duo wrote many popular songs, which were recorded on the Soviet classic Melodiia label. These songs, romantic and nostalgic, seemed to take a comfortingly optimistic view of life's trials, and their inclusion in the program constituted a potent, positive evocation of Soviet life.

After the rabbi's speech, in which he enjoined the revelers, "Today we unite with our sacred city Jerusalem, . . . with our fellow Jews in Jerusalem," a group of belly dancers in partial veils and flowing sheer costumes took the stage. Recorded music began with an oud (a Middle Eastern plucked lute) solo followed by a female vocalist singing in Hebrew. The choice of music and dance was striking. The music was *muzika mizrahit*, a genre of the Jewish diaspora featuring songs in Hebrew with instrumentation, ornamented performance style, and tight, nasal vocals typical of Middle Eastern Arab music. Criticized for mixing Arab and Jewish musical elements when it first emerged in the late 1950s, *muzika mizrahit* is now performed widely by Jewish musicians throughout the Middle East and in parts of North Africa, the Caucusus, and the Balkans. Although earlier references to the shtetl seemed to privilege eastern European roots of Jewish culture, and later Soviet life, this part of the performance clearly pointed to Israel and the Middle East. The belly dancers swirled around the edges of the stage to the sound of the oud and the sultry vocals, with the Israeli flag displayed directly behind them.

Through the high energy and festive mood of the Purim celebration, there were references to three pasts—naturally, there is the story of Purim set in ancient Persia, along with a simultaneous reach back to the eighteenth- to nineteenth-century shtetl, a reliable, rich source of Ashkenazi Jewish culture and language. But there is also a nostalgic pull back to Soviet urban life, back to the time before the Jewish community was split by multiple emigrations. In addition to all these pasts, all these backward glances, there is also a forward-facing view. If the Jews in Kazakhstan are the "stayers"—those left behind when others have emigrated—for them, there exists a forward inclination toward Israel, which has always represented a *possible* future for Soviet Jews. The performances we enjoyed in the Purim celebration thus resonated with the idea of home as associated with multiplicity and motion, rather than fixity.

BETWEEN KAZAKHSTAN AND CHINA, TWO STORIES ON A WELL-TRAVELED ROUTE

Although the connections and migrations portrayed in the Jewish and Korean communities in Almaty involve long distances and triangulated networks of funding, family history, and religious missions, the crossings of the Kazakhstan–Chinese border are of a different scale and texture. The Kazakhs and Uighurs I spoke with described families split by a single border that over the centuries was so well-traversed it seemed to have worn a groove connecting the two countries. Families and indeed whole communities, having crossed over so many times in both directions, are really making their histories in both places.

AN UIGHUR SINGER IN ALMATY

I sat at the dinner table in the home of an Uighur singer one evening in Almaty in early spring. I had heard her perform a week earlier at an Uighur event, and, stunned by her powerful performance, I asked if she would agree to meeting again and perhaps recording some songs, which brought me to her dinner table, listening to her beautiful voice. Meryam emigrated to Kazakhstan as a girl in the 1950s from Xinjiang. The two songs she performed, both in Uighur, represented two very different aspects of Uighur immigrant life in Almaty. The first, a beautiful, keening tune, was about separation from family in Xinjiang. The second was a raucous song about a penniless Uighur youth trying to impress his date in an Almaty café.

The event at which I had met Meryam was a celebration at the Assembly of Nations to commemorate a young Uighur war heroine who died during World War II. The venue, affectionately known as Dom Druzhby (House of Friendship), is a remnant of the Soviet "Friendship of the Peoples" concept in which some "harmless" aspects of minority culture (e.g., song and dance) should be celebrated and preserved. In this building each official "minority nationality" has a representative office that organizes cultural events. Meryam, a middle-aged woman with a shy demeanor and a huge voice, does not consider herself a professional singer, but is well-known in the Uighur community for her strong and beautiful performances. She has five sons, all born in Kazakhstan, but she also still has family members across the border in Xinjiang, northwest China. The song she sang at the World War II event, "The Seven Siblings,"[7] is about a family in which six of the siblings departed Xinjiang to settle in Kazakhstan with their mother. It is written from the perspective of the one sibling who stayed behind, and describes his grief about having been absent from his mother's funeral. The event was very Xinjiang-dominated, and this song was just one of the many narratives about Xinjiang as the original homeland for Almaty Uighurs. The event stressed the Uighur war experience as separate from that of the Soviet Union, and in a way identified Uighurs as outsiders with a "real" homeland across the border.

The Seven Siblings

1

FIGURE 5.6. "The Seven Siblings".

Meryam performed "Seven Siblings" in a full and throaty a capella. Her moderate tempo was both languid and forceful, with the held notes at cadences building dramatic temporal suspension. Her powerful voice, rich and deep in the lower register and just slightly nasal in the projected upper range of her chest voice, conveyed intensity of emotion, and she ornamented the melody throughout not in clean grace notes but an emotionally wrought bending and sliding between pitches (for example, in the E–A–F♯–A figure, in mm. 1 and 3). Her performance was the highlight of the evening, met by a burst of applause from the otherwise rather indifferent audience in the large hall. In contrast to this heart-wrenching performance of "The Seven Siblings," Meryam later revealed a completely different side of her versatile performance style.

When I visited her at home, Meryam performed another song, which captured the cosmopolitan life of Almaty, her second home. This song, which Meryam described as "shutochnaia" (humorous), was from the 1950s, she guessed. It tells the story of a young man who takes a girl out to an expensive Almaty café. He has 30 rubles, considered a lot of money at that time, and he orders "Russian salad, Kazakh meatballs, Dungan noodles, White Sea cigarettes, and a bottle of vodka." He ends up not having enough money and the waitress tells him he has to leave his suit behind instead. His girl stands up to leave, saying "Do svidaniia! Hosh!" (Good-bye! [Russian]; See ya! [Uighur]). Meryam sings it with the gusto and merriment of a drinking song, punching each menu item and the thrown-off "See ya!" with bawdy good humor. Unlike the poignant lyrics in the "The Seven Siblings," which reflect a longing for the Uighur homeland in Xinjiang, this humorous song describes a cosmopolitan view of Kazakhstan, where diverse groups share cities, cuisines, lifeways. Meryam's life clearly includes both these elements: she left Xinjiang as a young girl in the 1950s and lives in Almaty, where one can hardly escape the sort of cosmopolitan scene described in her second song. At the same time, she still has ties in Xinjiang and recently returned for the memorial service of a close relative. Caught between nostalgia for Xinjiang and adaptation to life in Almaty, her vastly differing performances illustrate the rhetoric of cosmopolitanism as well as the fracturing nature of transnational family ties.

TRAIN TO KAZAKHSTAN

The overnight train from Almaty arrives in the early morning in Urumqi (the capital of Xinjiang) and carries with it cross-border trade and related business. A small hotel in the Uighur section of Urumqi is the site of many such transactions. The arrival of the train from Almaty causes a flurry of activity in the hotel, as local translators, guides, and personal shoppers arrive in the lobby to greet the Kazakhstani travelers in hopes of securing short-term jobs. One young woman I noticed, Meruert, stepped up confidently to several businessmen, proferring her card without success (I stayed in this hotel for a few months and noticed the comings and goings, the changing cast of characters). Meruert finally found success with a small group of middle-aged women from Kazakhstan, here on a furniture shopping expedition to take advantage of the Kazakh connections in this region of northwest China while avoiding Almaty's skyrocketing prices. After I spoke with her, she offered her services as a tour guide and took me up the bumpy winding road off a terrifyingly steep highway to her boyfriend's family's house in the mountains outside the city. There she turned me over to her boyfriend and made the long trip back to the city, waving and looking distractedly at her phone. For these two—young and hungry looking, tethered to a scrappy business by their cell phones and living in several places at once—at the present their survival, their only constant, was waiting for that train.

I tagged along on one of these shopping trips with two Kazakh women, an Almatyite looking for furniture for family members and a young Xinjiang Kazakh who was assisting her with her purchases, providing Chinese-language bargaining and local shopping smarts. The Almatyite, Aigul, was a lovely, polished newlywed, with a handsome and successful husband moving up the ladder in a joint-venture construction company. We had met the year before in Almaty and I had thought I would find her happy and doing well after her storybook marriage. Instead I found her miserable because her main job—to set up and maintain a household in Xinjiang—was made nearly impossible by her lack of Chinese-language skills. She was reluctant to put the effort into learning Chinese since she was convinced they would not stay many years in China. She managed to do daily shopping by seeking out Kazakh vendors at the bazaar. Aigul, like Meruert, was trapped in a constant present, stuck in this place where her life could not move forward, and she could not (yet) return.

I also met Kazakhs who had made the opposite trek, Kazakhs from Xinjiang who had come to Almaty looking for opportunities and eager to adopt Kazakhstan as their new homeland. Despite the state's efforts to integrate these "returnees" (oralmandar) into Kazakhstani life, the complicated relations between diaspora and homeland Kazakhs, their difficulties with language and employment in Kazakhstan, and continued attachment (physically and psychologically) to the diaspora regions of their birth refute the concept of unbroken Kazakh nationhood.

This chapter has examined the histories of these migrations in sonic form, in the music and family lore of communities whose histories are defined by movement. Neither cyclical like agricultural time, nor linear in the way that national time would draw history, such episodic time is uneven, with sudden starts and stops and wide-swinging geographic shifts. Evacuations and forced migrations can be seen as interruptions in time, breaking the continuity of community, nation, and family. Sveta Kim, who had a fractured kind of life and family history that spilled across the Eurasian continent, found a sense of community in the Korean church in Almaty. Indeed, religion frequently seems to figure into these histories of mobility, particularly around the post-Soviet transition. In Korean churches and Jewish synagogues in Almaty, missionizing ushered in new forms of outside influence (both economic and religious) to the Soviet republics and then newly independent nations. The transition brought outward flows too—emigration and the strengthening of transnational business ties, in both the Korean and Jewish communities.

Many of the mobilities I have discussed are by-products of political change—with large-scale, devastating consequences. Others have been pressured or motivated to leave for economic and political reasons; these separations can enact a more private devastation, leaving behind a bereft remnant of families and communities. In the Uighur case I discuss, the singer's separation from Xinjiang is expressed in her performances; she sings about the separations that set siblings on opposite sides of the border and on different life paths. Such a geographic split, whether permanent emigration or a more complicated movement back and forth, results in family histories that are defined by separation.

In considering the economic aspects of these mobilities, I have looked at businesses that are built around cross-border travel. The young Kazakhs in business in Xinjiang capitalize on these kinds of cross-border splits (and ties) in the Kazakh population—offering translation services and local trade smarts to Kazakhs from Kazakhstan coming to shop in Xinjiang. I examine the cluster of activity that revolves around the train schedule—the comings and goings from the near abroad, which shape their current lives, daily schedules, and livelihoods. Such ethnographies speak to the temporality of the border as well as to the precarity of those whose lives depend on it.

CHAPTER 6

PLAYING AT WAR

Musical Commemorations of World War II on May 9

Commemorating . . . is an especially efficacious remedy against time's dispersive power

—Edward Casey

It is May 9, 2010, and we follow the crowds of young people, families and veterans, all here to celebrate the holiday in the bright sunlight. War songs pipe through the speakers in Panfilov Park. Guided as much by sound of war songs as by the flow of the crowd, fathers and young mothers with toddlers in tow, elderly grandfathers in uniforms decorated with medals, small girls with big puffy bows in their hair, all walk toward the eternal flame and the war memorial, where row after row of visitors leave flowers and take pictures by the enormous bas-relief of soldiers in battle. Alongside the black-and-white photomontage of war images, mournful popular ballads and patriotic marches provide a continuous soundtrack to accompany the ongoing commemoration of Victory Day.

In the month of May, it is impossible to escape the references to World War II in Kazakhstan, as a barrage of imagery, stories, and songs about the war appear daily in the media beginning at least a month before the May 9 celebration, commemorating victory in World War II—or the Great Patriotic War, as it is known in the post-Soviet states. Still an important holiday in Kazakhstan, May 9 references an era when Kazakhstan was part of the Soviet Union, and it provokes conflicting emotions about the Soviet past—patriotic pride for a country that no longer exists and ambivalence or hostility toward a repressive Soviet regime. This chapter examines the temporal and emotional work of commemorations, and their enduring political and personal meanings in Kazakhstan.

FIGURE 6.1. Families pose in front of Victory Day banners and war photos in Panfilov Park during Victory Day (World War II) celebrations, May 9, 2010. The banners read, in Kazakh and Russian: "A Million Bows [A Deep Bow (Russian)] to the Heroes of the Great Victory!"

COMMEMORATION, TEMPORALITY, AND RITUAL

Edward Casey, along with many other scholars of memory and commemoration,[1] has written extensively on the phenomenology of remembering. His monograph, *Remembering* (2000 [1987]), includes a study of commemoration that focuses particularly on temporality and ritual. In this study, Casey introduces the term *perdurance*, a "neglected temporal mode," which, Casey argues, "has received scant attention in Western thought" (Casey 2000, 228). Less absolute and comprehensible than *eternity*, more alive and immediate than generic *time*, perdurance is an active, reaching, human temporal mode. It is this temporality that is involved in commemoration. Casey contrasts the meaning of perdurance to a sibling term: *duration*. Despite the family resemblance, *duration* has a more straightforward, direct demeanor, essentially conveying the distance between two temporal points. Perdurance, on the other hand, containing something of the sense of *lastingness*, possesses a more emotional, human constitution.

This active lastingness, as described by Casey, borrows from Heidegger: "What is present concerns us, the present, that is: what, lasting, comes toward us, us human beings" (Heidegger in Casey 2000, 228). Casey writes similarly about lastingness—describing *perdurance* as that which lasts (memories, for example), and comes toward us from the past into the present, and engages us (and we it), and *endures through* this encounter.

Perdurance, according to Casey, is a most important and characteristic temporal form in the regular (annual, centennial, etc.) commemorating of past events. If we consider Paul Ricoeur's discussion of *chronosophy*, which concerns assigning meaning to time, then commemorating is chronosophic in that its purpose is to assign lasting, relevant meaning to past events. Commemoration is a way of actively pulling past events into the present, with a sense of tangibility and immediacy. According to Casey, commemoration as a "ritual transmitting tradition," need not, indeed, *must not* be performed precisely the same way every time through the ages. Instead, to preserve the essential nature of a tradition, the "spirit of the rites,"[2] it is necessary to alter the ritual commemoration to serve the present, so that "the ritual is compatible with modification and innovation within its formal structures" (Casey 2000, 228). Thus perdurance allows the past to last only by adjusting it superficially to suit the needs of the present, which keeps it ever meaningful.

Casey also examines socially cohesive meanings that resist the destructive forces of time and the divisive nature of individual will because they are realized through the performance of commemorative ritual (through perdurance): "What in the individual is divisive and diasporadic (thanks to the effects of succession in time) becomes, in and through the perdurance realized by ritual, consolidating. . . . In fact, the commemorating that is accomplished by a memorializing ritual is an especially efficacious remedy against time's dispersive power. Furthermore, it is through perdurance that the past, present, and future dimensions of commemorative ritual are at once affirmed and made compatible with each other" (Casey 2000, 229). Though Casey takes essentially a philosophical rather than a sociological approach to ritual, here he has touched on ritual's essentially social function, that of creating social meaning.

Randall Collins is concerned with commemoration from another angle—the sociology of emotion. He examines temporality and social structure as they are mutually engaged in "interaction rituals." Similar to Casey's lastingness, Collins's theory holds that rituals actively hold together enduring ideas, memories, and traditions through time; this idea is central to Collins's theorization of commemoration. He insists on the centrality of emotion in this commemorative process, explaining that participants in a ritual (especially a regularly repeated ritual) become entrained, sharing collective action and/or focus, which heightens the emotional intensity of the moment (Collins 1998, 21). Collins also stresses the importance of *mediated* events in forming enduring meanings and images. The transnational broadcasting of highly mediated events, such as the sixtieth-anniversary commemoration on Red Square in Moscow, help to affix representative images and songs to specific historical events—and on a very large scale, insofar as such events are widely viewed throughout the former Soviet sphere.

ENDURING NARRATIVES, AND CLASHING CHRONOSOPHIES IN WORLD WAR II COMMEMORATIONS

In Kazakhstan May 9 images and stories about World War II proliferate in various media throughout the holiday. Newspapers run frequent articles of Kazakh war heroes and heroines and print lyrics of Soviet war songs weekly throughout April and May. For a month or more, nearly every television channel runs war movies of a wide variety (favorite Soviet films of World War II, post-Soviet feature films and documentaries about the war in both Kazakh and Russian, and more recent films and television series about the Soviet war in Afghanistan and about Kazakhstani military service in general). War songs of a similarly wide variety can be heard throughout the city in public places, on the radio, and in the frequently televised concerts of music commemorating World War II.

Friends who were children in the 1970s and 1980s in Soviet Kazakhstan and Russia remembered playing intricate war games and reenacting scenes of life at the front in May 9 school plays and concerts. War films, songs, and *intsenarovki* (skits) performed at school—provided children with a plethora of images and information about wartime life, which they integrated into their playtime. These intsenarovki and war games represent narratives of the war, and thus hold an intermediary place between memory (testimony) and history.

On May 9 during the Soviet era, schools invited veterans to attend children's performances, where they were seated in the front rows in places of honor reserved for them. The veterans' presence was an essential part of these reenactments; the children were essentially performing for the veterans, and were conscious of trying to present a realistic portrayal of the war. In some classrooms, the roles were reversed and it was the veterans who "performed" for their young audiences. In some cases veterans spoke about specific war events they had witnessed and at times the teachers spoke emotionally about their memories of the war. Hearing testimony from individuals who witnessed the war effects a kind of transformative experience in which the sharing of heightened emotions in connection with the retelling of war stories helps to connect the past with the present by linking generations in this intensely personal form of commemoration.

Intersections of memory and emotion, an element that Collins describes as key, are central to the veterans' participation in the war commemorations. Several people I spoke with described veterans and teachers weeping as they related their experiences of the war. One woman said that everybody wept on this holiday and that as soon as she stepped outside her door on May 9 she could hear the war songs and see women weeping in the street. In the context of the school commemorations, the skits and songs were powerful catalysts that simultaneously prompted memories and elicited an emotional response on the part of the veterans. In fact, one Kazakhstani friend spoke about how the children would play to the veterans, expecting their tears. The children, she explained, were expressly aware of inducing powerful emotional responses in the veterans.

SOVIET-ERA SCHOOL PERFORMANCES IN KAZAKHSTAN

One acquaintance described her May 9 commemorative school performances, which took place in Almaty from 1984 to 1986, when she was ten to twelve years old. The performances were quite elaborate and took place after months of preparation. The children were divided into performance groups: the choir sang on bleachers set back from the main action of the stage; others performed dances onstage; and still another group acted out skits downstage. All were dressed in soldiers' uniforms sewn specially for May 9. Some intsenarovki were performed to accompany songs and dramatize the lyrics; others took place between musical numbers. The skits she described fit a general pattern that I saw replicated in many May 9 performances, in which the skits or dramatized concerts feature a fixed canon of war songs set in a particular narrative, telling the story of the war: deployment, life at the front, loved ones at home, and finally the announcement of victory. The performances often began with the song "Sviaschennaia Voina" (Sacred War), written on the eve of the declaration of war by Vasilii Lebedev-Kumach, with music by Aleksandr Aleskandrov, the composer of the Soviet national anthem. This song, which became known as the "Anthem of the Defense of the Fatherland," was published on June 24, 1941, in the Soviet newspapers *Izvestiia* and *Krasnaia Zvezda*, and performed two days later in the Belorussky train station in Moscow, one of the major stations for troops deploying to the front. Opening with the words "Stand up, vast country!" it symbolized the beginning of World War II for the Soviet Union. For this reason, my informant explained, it also often opened their school productions, which proceeded in a roughly chronological fashion, outlining the history of the war. At the beginning of the production, the actors were seated on the stage, dressed as soldiers, nurses, and mothers of soldiers. The performers all stood as they began "Sacred War," as if following the directive of the first verse, "Stand up, vast country, / Stand up! To deadly battle / With the Fascists' dark strength, / With the accursed horde." Children dressed as nurses and soldiers were signed up for the war effort and, as the song ended, the new recruits bid tearful farewells and marched off to the front. The veterans cried, my informant said, "as if it were really happening all over again."

This particular dramatization of the "Sacred War" seemed to be a fairly set template, reappearing in virtually identical skits in many concerts I observed. This song lends itself to dramatization. The song text "Vstavai strana ogromnaia" (Stand up, vast country)—speaks to the sheer size of the Soviet territory as well as to the staggering numbers of Soviet casualties (estimated at 24–27 million[3]). The piece is often performed by a large military chorus accompanied by a sizable ensemble or orchestra, with the brass particularly foregrounded. The snare drum punctuates this persistent march in the accompaniment, retelling the Soviet Army's inevitable progress toward the front.

Following "Sacred War," several songs and song excerpts portrayed the experience of life on the front. To the rear of the stage hung a screen onto which scenes from war movies were projected to augment the realism of the scenes onstage. One intsenarovka was a sketch that dramatized the song "Ballad of a Soldier" (*Ballada o Soldate*, music by V. Solov'ev-Sedoi, and words by M. Matusovskii), which paints a picture of a soldier walking in solitude through the fields, singing nostalgically of his home, and prolifically killing his enemies. The first and second verses appear below.

Through the field, along the steep banks,
Past the huts
In a gray military overcoat
Walked the soldier.
Walked the soldier, not knowing obstacles
Walked the soldier, losing his friends,
Often, it happened that,
He walked without rest.
Forward walked the soldier.

He walked through thunderous nights
In the rain and hail.
Songs with his friends from the front
Sang the soldier.
Sang the soldier, swallowing his tears,
Sang the soldier, about Russian birches,
About hazel eyes,
About his father's house,
He sang on the road.

The intsenarovka accompanying the song "Ballad of a Soldier" included several media simultaneously. As the children's choir sang, the actors onstage continued to portray everyday life at the front, while the screen behind them projected a black-and-white video clip of a soldier walking alone across a field. The lyrics and images overlay scenes of solitude—the lone figure on the movie screen—with the violent, chaotic depictions in the lyrics, while the onstage action portrayed troops singing and eating around a campfire. There is a kind of duality to these portrayals that speaks to the essence of war: the violence of the battlefield projected against the nostalgia for home and homeland.

Another such intsenarovka accompanied an excerpt of the song "V Zem-lianke" (In the Dugout). As the choir sang, the action on the stage brought the scene to life and elaborated on its story. Onstage, soldiers were seen sitting around a campfire as nurses treated the wounded and wrapped their heads and limbs in bandages. The song and actions portrayed key tropes of life at the front—the dugout, the cold, the campfire, the accordion, the nearness of death, and the longing for home. Other song excerpts accompanied onstage battle scenes, complete with guns, explosions, and blood. In one skit, a mail carrier ran up with a letter, shouting "Mail!" He then read off names as he distributed letters to the soldiers. At one point he called out a name, "Petrov!" Only silence followed. Again, "Petrov!"—no answer. In response, the soldiers and the mail carrier all took off their hats and observed a moment of silence for the missing soldier. "The veterans always cried at this point," my infor-mant said, "because they remembered this happening." In listening to this description of the intsenarovki I was struck by two things: first, the effort to portray the war scenes realistically, and second, the effort to prompt the vet-erans' actual memories of the war. In this sense, the veterans and their own memories of the war played an active—and interactive—part in the perfor-mance event, their presence a key component of the commemorative ritual.

The performance ended with a final skit, set in 1945 Berlin, in which a radio announcement proclaimed that Soviet troops had gained control of the city. One of the child actors, playing a telegraph operator, ran onstage and shouted to the troops gathered there, "Tovarishchi, Pobeda! POBEDA!!" (Comrades, Victory! VICTORY!!). This crucial point in the story, the moment of victory, was followed by Russian folk dances. The children's dance troupe, having practiced these dances for months, took the stage and performed Russian folk dances to well-known Russian folk songs such as "Kalinka" and "Katiusha." At the end of the performance, the actors presented bouquets of flowers to all the veterans.

The songs and skits that appear in schoolroom performances commem-orating World War II in Kazakhstan serve not only as links in a narrative chain but also as vehicles of emotion that help to establish icons and indec-es of the war and help to link generational experiences and understandings of the war. The giving of flowers, the shedding of tears, the focus on the war reenactments: all these can be thought of as aspects of an interaction ritual. Considering the event as an interaction ritual illuminates its transformative nature. More than a retelling of war stories, it is an event in which both children and veterans are given crucial roles. While the children perform the stories onstage, the veterans' role is primarily to be in attendance, to forge a living connection to these events.

These narratives are aided by war songs that have been popularized and so beloved that their lyrics are all well-known and their imagery has become, in a sense, imagery of the war (along with images from war films, paintings, and posters). These songs, strung together in a musical-dramatic narrative, represent an important symbology of the war, appearing again and again in concerts and televised programs. The staged enactments, which essentially function as war commemorations, are guided in large part by the actions and images described in these song texts.

GENDER, AND EMOTIONAL CHRONOLOGY IN WAR SONGS

Soviet Russian war songs are played throughout the long May 9 holiday and broadcast on television; their lyrics are printed in newspapers. Children from this generation learned a great number of songs for May 9 concerts, and many adults with whom I consulted could still sing a whole repertoire of war songs. These songs, learned in chldhood, seemed to hold an especially potent emotional charge. On May 9, during the Soviet era, the songs were piped through loudspeakers mounted throughout cities, and everyone I interviewed commented on the ubiquity of these war songs in Soviet times.[4] Several people also commented on the intensity of emotion on this day—people would be weeping in the streets and at concerts—stating that this is one of the things that stayed with them and affected them profoundly as children. In fact when I gave a talk on World War II songs and reenactments,[5] there were several scholars in the room who had grown up in the Soviet Union. They confessed to being emotionally, even viscerally, affected by the performances of war songs that I played. One scholar admitted the songs made her hair stand on end.

"THE LITTLE BLUE KERCHIEF" IN TELEVISED AND LIVE CONCERTS

Several Russian and Kazakhstani concerts, as well as a few recent music videos featuring these Soviet war songs, were broadcast on Kazakhstani television as the May 9 holiday approached. The canon of war songs in the concerts tended to be fairly fixed and, like the *intsenarovki*, helped to transmit central tropes of the war, though often in stylistically contrasting portrayals. A Russian concert at the Musical Theater of Svetlana Vezrodnaya in Moscow was a relatively small production, during which performances by Russian *estrada* and pop stars accompanied by the Moscow Philharmonic Orchestra were combined with simply choreographed dances elaborating the song lyrics, much the way that the *intsenarovki* performed in schools. A second concert, also broadcast from Russia, was a more elaborate affair, with collages of war images moving across several screens, and several popular rock bands incorporated into the usual lineup of *estrada* singers. A local Kazakhstani concert, performed in the Republican Palace in Almaty and broadcast on Tang, a mostly Kazakh-language channel, also featured many of the same Soviet staples.

"The Little Blue Kerchief" is a staple of May 9 celebrations. Written in 1940–1942, it has become iconic of the war years and was included in virtually every May 9 concert I observed, including several Russian and Kazakhstani concerts, a music video performed by the Kazakhstani Children's Theater Tangsary (Dawn) on channel Tang, and an informal gathering of Jewish women commemorating Jewish war heroes. It reflects the same loneliness and parting from loved ones as other songs in this vein, such as "My Dear One." The latter is told from the perspective of a woman whose sweetheart has been killed in battle, whereas "The Little Blue Kerchief" (words by Yaakov Galitskii and Mikhail Maksimov; music by Ezhi Petersburskii) takes the perspective of the soldier at the front, thinking about his sweetheart at home.[6] The first and final verses appear below.

> The Little Blue Kerchief
> Fell from hunched shoulders
> You said that you would never forget
> The tender and joyful meetings.
> At night
> We walked with you . . .
> No more nights!
> Where are you, little kerchief,
> My dear, desired, my own?

How many sacred scarves
We carry in our hearts!
The joyful meetings,
The girlish shoulders,
We remember on the battlefield.
For them, our dear ones,
Our beloved and desired ones,
Ratatatats the machine gunner,
For the little blue kerchief,
That was on the shoulders of our loved ones.

The image of the blue kerchief has gained iconic significance somewhat apart from the song itself. In concerts and war commemorations throughout the former Soviet Union, the image of this kerchief—often appearing as a prop in staged skits—represents a soldier and his sweetheart saying goodbye as he is being deployed. For example, the first Moscow concert broadcast from the Vezrodnaya Musical Theater opens with the "Sacred War" and is followed by a verse of "The Little Blue Kerchief." Young soldiers in uniform enter first during the orchestral rendition of "Sacred War"; in the opening measures of "The Little Blue Kerchief," young women in civilian dress enter the stage one by one, searching for their sweethearts. As the song ends, the soldiers, having reunited with their girlfriends for a last embrace, line up for their imminent departure. The girls stand off to the side waving their blue kerchiefs. In these May 9 performances, icons like the blue kerchief appear consistently in strikingly similar scenes, and in this way become a part of the canon of war images that make up the master narrative of World War II.

Along with the visual symbology of the war, the waltz and the accordion appear again and again as sonic references to World War II. The music video performed by the Kazakhstani Children's Theater *Tangsary* on the Tang channel features a version of "The Little Blue Kerchief," in which the waltz is prominent. In this recently produced video, altered to imitate the grainy look of an old black-and-white movie, the setting is a Soviet classroom. The children in school uniforms sit at desks, looking despondent. One student puts on a record and they begin to dance as one of the children sings "The Little Blue Kerchief." This video echoes the nostalgic nature of many of these performances and also underscores the important role of dances, particularly the waltz.

The waltz, as a nostalgic device, represents a way to connect physically, visually, and sonically with the war era. In a Women's Day performance by students of the Women's Pedagogical Institute, female students dressed as soldiers paired off with women in Russian folk costumes and waltzed to the accompaniment of the *garmoshka*. The small button accordion appears in nearly all the performances mentioned above and is prominently featured in other important events such as the gala on Red Square. While the guitar came to be commonly used in later war songs, especially those of the Afghanistan war, the accordion is iconic of World War II songs, particularly dances. Played as an accompaniment to both Russian folk songs and popular tunes of the war era, the button accordion is a potent sonic representation of both Russia and the war era.

THE PANFILOVTSY, *ZA NAMI MOSKVA*, AND THE KAZAKH EXPERIENCE OF WORLD WAR II

Alongside the central narratives of the war such as those in Russian and Kazakhstani concerts and children's skits described above, more focused histories appear in local commemorations of the war. In Kazakhstan, and in Almaty specifically, these locally focused narratives highlight Kazakh participation in the war and are accompanied by a particular set of images, heroes, and veterans' testimony.

Almaty is a particularly important city for the Kazakh commemoration of World War II, as it is home to a park dedicated to the twenty-eight Panfilovtsy referred to hereafter as Panfilov Park. The Panfilovtsy (singular, *panfilovets*) were heroes of Almaty's 316th rifle division almost all of whom, according to Soviet accounts, perished defending Moscow. The division, under the command of General Panfilov, was charged with defending the Volokolmsk Highway, a major thoroughfare leading to Moscow from the west. Completely surrounded, the Kazakhstani division destroyed a large number of German tanks on November 14, 1941, and successfully stopped the Nazis from reaching Moscow. Though the specifics of this battle have been disputed, the story, well-known to every schoolchild and firmly established in film and Kazakhstani history texts, is that very few of the Panfilovtsy survived the battle.

The Panfilovtsy, immortalized in film and song throughout Kazakhstan, remain one of the most important representations of Kazakhstan's participation in the war. A live dramatic performance in Panfilov Park every May 9 in front of the "eternal flame" portrays Soviet Kazakh soldiers facing German soldiers in a miniature battle reenactment. The 1968 film *Za nami Moskva* (Moscow Is behind Us), directed by Mazhit Begalin, follows the story of the Panfilovtsy. Begalin takes as his subject Kazakh participation in World War II. The main character, a Kazakh commander, is the hero of the story, whereas General Panfilov appears as a somewhat less likable character, whose error in sending the Panfilovtsy into this area was essentially their death sentence. In one scene, the Kazakh commander examines a map of the area with fellow officers. He takes out a knife, slices off half of the map, and burns it. In so doing he obliterates the way back and the possibility of retreat. To his assembled comrades he declares that there is "only Moscow" for them now, and they will fight to the death defending it.

The climax of *Moscow Is behind Us* is a battle scene in which the Panfilovtsy are on the edge of a wide, unprotected, snow-covered field that they have to traverse into German-held territory. They lie belly-down in the snow, knowing that many will not survive the crossing. One soldier stands up, yelling "Forward!" and is shot down. After a pause, a young Kazakh soldier stands and is also shot and killed. The leader of the division then gets to his feet, shouts, "Forward!" and all the soldiers follow him. The bloodbath that follows is haunting, as bodies fall one by one onto the white field. These scenes express the central trope of the Panfilovtsy story, which persists in current commemorations: the Panfilovtsy went into battle with the knowledge that there was no road back and they played a crucial role in defending Moscow, the heart of the Soviet Union, from the Nazis. In interviews on Kazakhstani television, small children, ages four and five, recounted the history of the Panfilovtsy. One child explained, "Our veterans defended Moscow, so the Fascists couldn't get any further."

A music video, "Alkissa," performed by the dombra player Mairzhan Ermegiev takes a somewhat different approach to the war. The above films dwell on the violence of war and Kazakh sacrifice, whereas Ermegiev's video depicts the camaraderie among soldiers during wartime. In the video, Ermegiev plays a dombra küi, surrounded by his fellow soldiers, who relax as they sit around a fire and listen. Ermegiev is a virtuoso musician who favors a rollicking, tökpe-style of playing. The fast tempo and major key render it almost joyful, a different kind of heroism, a positive view of the war.

The video emphasizes Soviet camaraderie but also highlights an appreciation of Kazakh culture. They are all Soviet soldiers of various ethnic backgrounds, but they listen appreciatively to the Kazakh küi. At the end of the video the soldier rides home in an old army truck, to a Kazakh aul. He is welcomed home by his old *apa* (Kazakh grandmother) in a white headdress, as other family members run to meet him. It is springtime and the soldier's family has gathered for the celebration; a *dastarkhan*, or Kazakh feast, is laid out on a long row of tables under blooming apple trees. It is a scene that stresses the large Kazakh family common during this era and the importance of family ties. Depicting both wartime camaraderie and Kazakh family life, this production provides a nostalgic view of both Kazakh rural life at this time and a Soviet-style Friendship of the Peoples relationship among various nationalities in Soviet Kazakhstan.

On May 9, the Kazakhstani channel Tang broadcast a lengthy interview, conducted in Kazakh, with the World War II veteran Kaskabay Mukanov. Like Ermegiev's video, this interview presented a mixture of Kazakh and Soviet identities and portrayed the general, shared experience of these years spent as a soldier. At the end of the interview, Mukanov describes his feelings about being a part of the Soviet army. "After Victory, I served in Germany for four years, as a great Russian officer. I am not Russian, but Asian, but ... I was an officer of the victorious Soviet army. This was happiness. What else could I ask of God? It was our victory. Nobody ever said to me, 'This victory is not yours, but the Russians'.' I fought as an equal alongside Russians and Georgians. I consider it my own victory."

Emotional testimony about the war was common in television broadcasts during the May 9 holiday. Veterans spoke of the heroism and hardships of going to battle as well as the emotional ties among soldiers.

JEWISH KAZAKHSTANI COMMEMORATION AND "HIERARCHICAL HEROISM"

Many Kazakhstani and Russian commemorations of World War II reflect a complicated relationship with the "Jewish Problem," as it is called in Soviet wartime and postwar scholarship. The portrayal of universal suffering versus specific Jewish tragedy, a tension between Soviet and Jewish identities on the part of Soviet Jews, the excision of Jewish heroes from Soviet history, and the exclusion of Jewish suffering in the Soviet press and war commemorations all reflect an uneasy relationship between Soviet and Jewish histories. The establishment of the Israeli state immediately following World War II, and the subsequent allowances for Jewish emigration in the 1960s and 1970s only served to further alienate the Jewish population in the perceptions of many Soviets.

Amir Weiner writes about twin institutions of Soviet wartime and post-war commemoration, "hierarchical heroism" and "universal suffering," which he calls the "cornerstones of the Soviet ethnonational ethos of the war" (Weiner 2001, 208). He explains that "whereas the various nations of the Soviet Union were ranked in a pyramid-like order, based on their alleged contribution to the war effort, their suffering was undifferentiated. More so than any other ethnonational community, these aspects of the Soviet ethos were evident with regard to the Jewish community. Jewish participation in the trials of combat service were ignored in public and denied in private . . . the Holocaust was incorporated into the epic suffering of the entire Soviet population, thus ignoring its uniqueness to the Jews" (209).

In all the public events, films, and concerts I observed regarding World War II and the May 9 holiday, I was struck by the complete silence on the subject of the Holocaust. The only time I heard it mentioned was at the Almaty Jewish center, Mitzvah. Instead, concerts stressed common suffering portrayed in individual stories, while war films and television serials tended to follow the stories of whole brigades, stressing heroism and brotherhood within the collective. The historical excision of the Holocaust was particularly glaring in the 2004 epic Russian film *Shtrafbat*, which was shown over several days on the Kazakhstani channel KTK and followed the story of a penal division of the Soviet military that fought at the front. The end of the film shows a list of the numbers of war dead by country, ending with the Soviet Union (six million). Although many of the dead were clearly a result of the Jewish Holocaust, there was no mention of Jewish victims here, or for that matter, anywhere in the eight-hour epic.

The need to fill this historical gap in Soviet history seemed to drive the commemoration of Jewish war heroes at the Mitzvah Jewish center. This event was part of regular meetings at the center, a weekly gathering of elderly women. At this meeting, in honor of May 9, one of the members, a retired history professor, gave a presentation describing the biographies and sacrifices of several Jewish war heroes from Kazakhstan. The presentation and subsequent discussion struck an awkward balance between the themes of universal suffering and an ethnic commemoration of the war, and reflected a marked tension between Jewish and Soviet identification. The discussion included heated debates about the human cost of the war among the Soviet population, the invisibility of Jewish heroes in Soviet reports of the war, and emotional reminiscences of personal tragedies resulting from the war.

At the end of the program, the lecturer attempted to lead the group in singing several romantic and heroic Soviet war songs such as "Katiusha" and "The Little Blue Kerchief." As the retired professor insistently sang all the verses that she knew, some reluctantly joined in but others fidgeted and rolled their eyes. Many in attendance expressed annoyance with the performance of Soviet war songs because the narratives clashed with the express aims of this commemoration. The lecturer, who had taught at the Academy of Sciences, took a distinctly more Soviet approach to this event than the other Mitzvah members assembled on that day. Although many in attendance were willing to consider the larger Soviet picture, to discuss not only Jewish suffering but also the suffering of the Soviet people, this way of commemorating—by singing Russian-Soviet war songs—was rejected in the context of a Jewish memorial event. The singing of war songs in a way emphasized a particular Russian coloring of war, thereby replicating the Soviet historical excision of the Jewish experience. Echoing issues raised by Afghan war vets, this Jewish commemoration challenged the notion of *who belongs* in May 9 commemorations. If public events so often portray the heroism of a Soviet (usually Russian or Kazakh) soldier and the universal suffering of the Soviet population, one might ask, then where does the story of Jewish suffering belong?

Writing about Jewish and Soviet accounts of World War II, Amir Weiner describes a discursive intersection between ethnic particularism and universal suffering. In the event I witnessed this tension seemed to foment dissent, but Weiner describes how postwar memory and wartime suffering helped to encourage Jewish community solidarity (Weiner 2001, 207–8). He contends that such memories may have had a significant influence on the political shape of Soviet-Jewish relations: "Conventional wisdom points to the establishment of the state of Israel and the unfolding cold war as the primary causes for the deterioration in the status of the Jewish community within the Soviet polity. . . . Often glossed over, however, is the centrality of the living memory of the war and the Jewish genocide in shaping the course of Soviet-Jewish relations and providing them with a constant point of reference in the years following the war" (207).

At the Almaty Jewish commemoration I attended, as in Weiner's accounts of Ukraine, the attendees expressed a need to commemorate the specific Jewish experience of the war as a way to offset the public emphasis on pan-Soviet suffering. Indeed, the tension between ethnic particularism and universal suffering was present in many World War II commemorations I witnessed in post-Soviet Kazakhstan, from Kazakh to Jewish to Uighur events.

THE "GOOD" WAR AND THE GREATEST GENERATION

An inscription in Kazakh at the beginning of the music video "Young Kazakh," reflects a generational aspect of World War II portrayals—the heroism of the war generation, and the debt owed them by today's youth and those of the future:

> Рухына болашақ бас иетін,
> Ұмытылас—ерлігін, касіетін!
> The future will bow their heads to your soul,
> Oblivion is bravery and honor!

Such commemorations portray the war as a time of suffering, but also as a kind of golden time, when morality, like films of that era, appeared in black and white. Interviews with participants in Victory Day celebrations often include discussions of grandfathers' participation in the war, and lessons to be learned from the generation of World War II veterans.

The historian David Hoogland Noon probes a parallel generational reverence and indebtedness in American society, in his "Operation Enduring Analogy," which examines the American fascination with World War II, and the war-related analogies that endure in American policy and media. He contends, "Popular memories of war not only claim to preserve some heroic moment of the past, but they often make acute demands upon the living, who must periodically show themselves worthy of the gifts bestowed upon them by the wartime sacrifices of others" (Noon 2004, 342). The sacrifice made by war veterans and the enduring debt owed them by subsequent generations is a very present aspect of commemoration and celebration during May 9 in Kazakhstan. One of the functions of commemorative reenactments is to manifest for younger generations the hardship and loss in veterans' experience of war, to make the past tactile, real, to those who were not there to experience it. In this way, veterans' presence and sometimes their shared memories act as key transformative aspects of these commemorative rituals, triggering a powerful evocation of past events into the present, a coaxed perdurance.

There is a long-standing tradition in Kazakhstan of not only performing skits for veterans to show appreciation but also carrying out good deeds for their benefit on May 9. One acquaintance, Zhazira, relates: "When we were at school—I was twelve or thirteen—they divided us into groups, and we went to help the veterans. We would clean their houses, carry water, and take out the garbage. I was such an 'activist,' I always volunteered! My grandfather fought in the . . . war and was injured—a head injury. I would have to look after him because he would go out and get lost, wandering around the neighborhood."

On May 9 many veterans were invited to children's performances in schools and concert halls and were looked after in their homes by schoolchildren who helped them with everyday tasks. But if young adults described their own grandfathers' participation in the war in an overwhelmingly positive light, the veterans spoke of the younger generations with some ambivalence. One veteran interviewed during a demonstration of Soviet military uniforms and artillery on February 23 (Red Army Day, a former Soviet holiday), said, "This generation can learn something from the workings of the Soviet army." Other veterans also discussed the discipline they learned in the Soviet military, which gave them a rigor and morality that they believed the younger generation lacked. Kaskabay Mukanov, in describing his war experiences and subsequent family life, was asked to compare his generation with today's youth. He answered: "It is hard to talk now about today's youth. The difficulty is because the times are hard. What is the sense of speaking badly about this time? I was invited today to my university as a war veteran. Not one Kazakh could ask me a question" (May 9, 2005, Tang channel broadcast, Kazakhstan). If the transformative power of commemorative rituals is to call forth the past through bodily presence of those who witnessed the event, this process can be complicated by the tangled relationships between generations.

AFGHANISTAN'S UNSUNG WAR HEROES

Hoogland's examination of World War II portrayals as a "good" war in American history stands in direct contrast to the widely unpopular Vietnam War that provoked so much dissent in popular culture over its questionable morality. This discrepancy in the treatment and popular reception of these two wars bears an illuminating comparison to Kazakhstani and Russian portrayals of Soviet participation in the Afghan war. Kazakhstani portrayals of Afghanistan in the media, television, and song, while acknowledging the heroism of soldiers also reflect a fatalism and dismay regarding the futility of the Afghan war, at times portraying the soldiers themselves in a negative light. Whereas Soviet action in World War II is portrayed as unambiguously glorious and heroic in the films and videos discussed above—where we see the war's violence as suffering rather than cruelty—there is a barbarity and moral murkiness in the popular treatments of Afghanistan in Kazakhstani videos and war songs.

"I vot opiat' idem my v gory" (And So, We Go into the Mountains Again) is an Afghanistani war song, which was taught to me by a woman who described it as a "dvorovaia pesnia," a "backyard song" sung in apartment block courtyards—essentially an urban folk song with many different versions. I later learned that this song was recorded, with different lyric variants, by the group Tankist on their 1982 album *Afghanistan*. My informant learned the version below from an Afghan war veteran at her summer camp.

"And So, We Go into the Mountains Again"

And so, we go into the mountains again
We know there is nowhere to hurry to
The *basmachis* will not catch us soon,
The better not to joke with us,
The *basmachis* will not catch us soon,
The better to live on this earth with us a little longer.

A lonely shot rings out,
I quickly drop behind an outcropping.
Ah, thank God, it didn't find its mark,
And the *dushman* [Afghan soldier] didn't get me in his sights.
Ah, thank God it didn't find its mark,
And the *dushman* didn't get me in his sights.

I lie behind the outcropping and see
They are going into the mountains.
In their hands they have English bayonets,
And in their belts, axes.
In their hands they have English bayonets,
And in their belts, axes.

The *basmachi* are so vicious,
You can see it in their eyes.
And we have become just as viscious,
There are no words to describe it.
And we have become just as viscious,
There are no words to describe it.

This song clearly departs from the heroism of the World War II songs, which reflect an unwavering sense of duty, patriotism, and heroism. Here, by contrast, the portrayal is not black and white, of heroes and villains. Rather, there is a fuzzy sense of right and wrong in these verses, a questioning of war ethics that is not present in the World War II songs: "The *basmachi* are so vicious, / you can see it in their eyes. / And we have become just as vicious, / There are no words to describe it."

Although May 9 celebrations are primarily dedicated to veterans of World War II, some commemorations of the Afghan war make their way into televised programs around May 9. Afghanistan veterans take a fringe position in these public celebrations, in which their service is not generally celebrated or acknowledged. One Kazakhstani music video, "Song of the Border Guards," performed by Afghanistan veterans, was broadcast on Tang in early May. The song text (below) makes reference to the May 9 holiday and the experience of veterans celebrating on this day.

"Song of the Border Guards" (original lyrics in Russian)

I will store away my green military cap.
On that day in May I will clean its stars.
I will stay out late (or go out drinking), don't scold me, mother.
On this holiday, I want to remember my [military] service.

It was always hard, raw.
Let's sing about the soul of a soldier:
How it burned in the fire, how it drowned in a tear,
How at night the silence suffocated us.
How it burned in the fire, how it drowned in a tear,
How at night the silence suffocated us.

Let's remember, brother, Afghanistan.
Those heroic guys who stayed behind time.
Let's remember that bitterness in the wine,
Our life at the last border.
Let's remember that bitterness in the wine,
Our life at the last border.

I will store away my green military cap.
On the day in May I will clean its stars.
Zhavnakol' and Hasan, Tegeran and Afghan,
Let the soil there be as featherdown to our guys.

While the author of the song is unknown, the video is specifically about
Kazakhstani soldiers in Afghanistan. As it features Afghanistan veterans,
mostly middle-aged now, there was a striking disconnect between the performers and the narrator, who writes from a youthful perspective. The soldier's appeal to his mother, "Don't scold me mother," emphasizes his youth
and the generation gap they face in discussing the war. Kazakhstani veterans
of the war in Afghanistan, who were interviewed in Almaty's Panfilov Park,
described their struggle to be remembered with the respect and veneration
accorded World War II veterans. Those interviewed during a Kazakhstan
channel broadcast expressed discomfort with the lower status they occupy
as veterans of an unpopular war.

The differences between portrayals of veterans of the Great Patriotic War and Afghanistan war veterans highlight a generational tension. Whereas the former are prized as valuable conveyors of wisdom and morality, the latter are of a generation that has fallen through the cracks in post-Soviet Kazakhstan. As neither the glorified war heroes of World War II nor the new post-Soviet generation, Afghanistan veterans represent a lost generation, a kind of Soviet Generation X.

BROADCASTING MAY 9 FROM MOSCOW

The sixtieth anniversary of Victory Day celebration on Red Square in Moscow on May 9, 2005 was a gala event lasting several hours with many world leaders in attendance. The daylong celebration was broadcast in full throughout Kazakhstan, both live and in multiple subsequent airings. In Kazakhstan viewing this May 9 Red Square commemoration was possibly as important and as common as attending a local commemoration in public squares and parks throughout Kazakhstan. In fact, many people I spoke to preferred watching the Red Square festivities to attending live commemorations in Almaty. Many would get together to watch with family members, spouses, roommates, or friends, as a communal event. In fact, in the weeks and months around May 9, the home viewing of televised war films is frequently experienced as a family-centered event that appeals to both younger and older generations. As at New Year, this family TV watching is an especially common holiday pastime, when families and couples gather to watch annual broadcasts of favorite Soviet films. Community viewership, according to Collins, is a specific kind of interaction ritual, in which the focused action that brings people together in emotional "entrainment" is happening onscreen rather than in the room. Because of this focus and the copresence of family members, this joint viewing acts as a kind of once-removed, mediated commemoration ritual.

The Red Square gala, reminiscent in many ways of Kazakhstani commemorations, outlined a narrative of war drawn from a similar repertoire and imagery as those seen in previously discussed concerts, skits, and music videos. It incorporated localized narratives as well—with skits and footage from films depicting the siege of Leningrad and the battles of Stalingrad, Volgograd, and Sevastopol. The Leningrad *intsenarovka*, in particular, was emotionally striking, a dramatization depicting a line of trucks filled with women and children, wrapped in blankets from the cold, while footage on the screen above shows trucks crossing the frozen Lake Ladoga, some perishing as the trucks break through the ice and disappear into the freezing water.

In the musical/theatrical performances on Red Square, French songs and dances were particularly foregrounded, with the emotional singing of French war-era songs in Édith Piaf cabaret style forming the centerpiece of the celebrations. After the *intsenarovki* depicting a series of battle scenes, similar to the Kazakhstani school performances, as the victory celebration begins soldiers are dancing with young civilian women. They dance to a range of music from 1940s pop tunes, to Russian virtuosic accordion, and then to a Russian folk song, "Valen'ki" performed in a folk style with characteristic whoops and tense high vocals, accompanied by onstage musicians dressed as soldiers (Russian accordion, guitar, balalaika) as well as an offstage orchestra. This Russian dance medley was followed by an Édith Piaf lookalike singing two of her most well-known songs, "Non, rien de rien" and "Ma vie en rose." After this, a female performer in uniform sang the popular Russian folk song, "Katiusha" in Russian, English, and French.

The Moscow commemoration illustrated how war narratives gather meanings with every repetition, in this case, by placing the war story in the context of contemporary political circumstances. France clearly took a prominent place in the Moscow celebration, with Jacques Chirac taking his seat to the right of Putin. The parallels drawn between France and Russia in the performances helped to frame Russia as a European democracy by drawing Russia into the European landscape, while at the same time sidelining American participation, thereby signaling the cooling of Russia's relations with the United States (Wallerstein 2005). Thus, Victory Day celebrations allowed Putin to stake out a new path for Russia—which he had been trying to do for some time—both as an important, though independent, ally of western Europe and as a leader in Eurasia.

The gala finished with a video collage retrospective of the sixty years since World War II. The video, projected onto large screens erected on the staged area of the square, was set to a live performance of Bulat Okudzhava's song "Gorit i kruzhetsia planeta" (The Planet Burns and Spins). The singer, handsome, middle-aged, with a solemn and striking deep bass, gave a dramatic performance as he stood on a tank painted with the words "Za Rodinu!" (For the Motherland!). The song, a popular war ballad written for the film *Belorussian Station*, was accompanied by a surprising video-collage of *postwar* images, including footage of a lunar landing, scenes from various Olympiads, brief clips of Gandhi, and footage from the aftermath of terrorist acts. The combined video and song lyrics seemed to convey that "we" now inhabit one world, its triumph and tragedy now shared; however, the "we" is both assumed and subsumed under political alignments, with globalist sentiment masking Western values and political strategies.

In the commemorative dramatizations, song performances, and imagery I have discussed, although much of the visual and sonic symbolism winds persistently through successive eras and remains surprisingly constant—so that we hear the same songs, see the same blue kerchiefs waved, watch the same scenes of sweethearts parting for war, or soldiers huddled around a campfire playing a button accordion—the framing of the war narrative remains fluid. It is in this flexibility of framing—pulling historical memories through to the present by adapting them to present frames—that such commemorations bear marks of Casey's *perdurance*. Also key to commemoration are the roles of emotion and testimony in commemoration rituals, in which the presence and testimony of veterans helps to elicit an emotional response, which Randall Collins points out as a key ingredient of interaction rituals. These interaction rituals, experienced as a shared event with an emotional focus, in turn produce the enduring symbology of the war.

CHAPTER 7

THE PRECARIOUS PRESENT AND THE CITY OF THE FUTURE

Astana, Islam, and Pilgrimage

You seem to lose a sense of possibility when you follow the paths of happiness.

—Sara Ahmed

Pilgrimage is often framed as a quest, as a removal from the everyday, involving the altering of temporal experience and the sacralization of place, but it can also reflect everyday realities and societal instabilities. Simultaneously mundane and transcendent, shrine pilgrimage can function as a way to integrate Muslim beliefs and practices into contemporary life in Kazakhstan. Often undertaken in times of crisis, pilgrimage may offer an opportunity to imagine a different future, a different self, to effect a transformation or to plead for relief from hardship. Kazakhstan in the twenty-first century represents a particular kind of postsocialist precarity in which religion plays an increasingly important role. As President Nursultan Nazarbaev cautiously approaches his own expression of faith, he simultaneously seeks to position Astana as an exemplary post–9/11 mediator between Christian and Muslim populations and leadership. In this chapter I examine how Kazakhstanis turn to pilgrimage and faith healing to grapple with precarious lives, while the state attempts to form a new moral path forward, balancing an interconfessional citizenry, a secular state, and a culturally Muslim heritage.

Through ethnographies of pilgrimage and faith healing, I consider the exploration of Islam as a way of redefining oneself in a new moral landscape. The postsocialist turn to Islam, the experimentation with different forms of Muslim practice, and the challenging of a variety of Muslim beliefs can be seen as both a response to socioeconomic upheaval and part of a post-Soviet redefinition of the self. The anthropologist Julie McBrien writes about Kyrgyz men and women who are trying new ways to be Muslim, pushing back against Soviet-era biases while still struggling with their influence: "Not only had she confronted the stereotypes of her community, which equated wearing the hijab with extremism and the overturning of Soviet-era notions of gender equality, but she also dealt with an internal struggle of redefinition" (McBrien 2017, 127). In my discussions with urban Kazakh women who practice pilgrimage and faith healing, I saw a similar grappling with what it means to be Muslim, and the trying on of different Muslim personae, in which experimentation with spirituality was complicated by ambivalence about proscriptions regarding proper dress and behavior.

In addition to examining the redefinition of selfhood, many recent studies delve into the question of "right" Islam in post-Soviet Central Asia and consider how Central Asian Islam is being redefined. As the Central Asianist Jeanne Féaux de la Croix writes, "In a region that was cut off from centres of Islamic learning for many decades, the question of 'right Islam' . . . is seen as pressing and urgent" (Feaux de la Croix 2016, 116–17). Works examining Central Asian Islam in the first decades of the twenty-first century have noted a tension between a desire for correctness and orthodoxy and a wish to worship in an unrestricted way. David Montgomery describes an elderly woman in Kyrgyzstan practicing shrine pilgrimage, who "knows that there are other ways to worship in Islam, . . . [but] is less interested in them; she wants to continue to worship the way her ancestors taught her" (Montgomery 2016, 22). Although some scholars see a polarization of views on the question of "right" Islam, others describe open attitudes among Central Asians toward ways of worshipping or practicing Islam. Indeed shrine pilgrimage is often noted as an alternative to other perhaps less accessible forms of mosque-based worship (Feaux de la Croix 2016; Montgomery 2016; Privratsky 2001).

The postsocialist redefinition of Muslim selfhood and the re-formation of nationhood are intertwined. As I discuss in this chapter, leaders like Nazarbaev portray themselves and their mission as governing in morally significant ways. The anthropologist Morgan Liu writes that his interlocutors (Uzbeks in Kyrgyzstan) often steered the discussions toward questions of moral leadership. They described the ideal of the Central Asian leader as a *steward*, whose responsibility is defined by the term *boqmoq*, "meaning to look after the needs of someone or something, such as children, animals, or gardens." Liu continues, "Boqmoq required understanding the character of the times and engaging the complexities of socioeconomic mechanisms" (Liu 2012, 152–53). Such attentive, effective and *moral* governing would "unleash a virtuous cycle of beneficial effects through society" (153). Indeed, Liu notes that his interlocutors' "basic diagnosis of Kyrgyzstan's severe hardships of the 1990s was the *moral* failure of its leadership" (153). In this sense, moral leading and effective leading are connected, or even nearly equivalent.

My study of pilgrimage in Kazakhstan comprised six pilgrimages to more than twenty shrines in several areas, including the Caspian region of western Kazakhstan, Almaty oblast in eastern Kazakhstan, and the sacred pilgrimage to Turkistan in southern Kazakhstan. The shrines were amazingly varied, ranging from the shrines of Sufi saints (*atalar*) in western and southern Kazakhstan to the burial places of legendary musicians who used the qobyz (Kazakh horsehair fiddle) to heal. Pilgrimages in Kazakhstan trace the histories of interconnected belief systems in the region. They also bring to light the concerns of Kazakhstan's citizenry and expose the cracks in the social system. Many of the pilgrims I spoke with were marginalized, on the fringes of Kazakhstani society in one way or another. They were women who had lost their husbands, migrants from Turkmenistan and Uzbekistan, youngish Kazakh women who did not fit the mold of an ideal prospective daughter-in-law, and creative urbanites trying on a new "good Muslim" persona. I saw their stories as representing this stage in early twenty-first-century Kazakhstani history, this era characterized by the struggle to adapt to change.

Victor Turner, in his well-known theorization of liminality, characterizes pilgrimage as "anti-structure," in which participants leave the structure of society to find themselves (Turner 1969). Seen in a different light, however, pilgrimage is embedded in the concerns and demands of daily life; in some cases it is the failure of social institutions that lead pilgrims to seek other means of solving problems. The anthropologist Jill Dubisch, writing on gender and pilgrimage in Greece, contends that pilgrimage is enduring and widespread especially because of "the complex and dynamic character of the ritual of pilgrimage, a ritual that reflects and responds to a variety of both constant and changing beliefs, values, and needs" (Dubisch 1995, 41–42). The flexibility of pilgrimage allows it to function in Kazakhstan as a Muslim religious practice and as an experiment with morality, both of which aid Kazakhstanis in navigating the uncertainties of the twenty-first century.

Seen in a broader context, pilgrimage may be undertaken as a way toward actualizing imagined futures. Vincent Crapanzano's thought-provoking work on imaginative horizons addresses "the way in which we construct, wittingly or unwittingly, horizons that determine what we experience and how we interpret [that] experience" (Crapanzano 2004, 2). Pilgrims I spoke with across Kazakhstan were engaged in acts of faith and imagination: some trying out new kinds of belief, and others hoping for alternative futures. Sara Ahmed, in her work on happiness, consumption, and instability, examines the meaning of happiness and its sense of contingency—the "hap" of happiness: "We may be more used to thinking of happiness as an effect of what you do, as a reward for hard work, rather than as 'simply' what happens to you" (Ahmed 2010). Ahmed's concept of contingent happiness is inherently connected to this struggle with precarity, in that happiness is not necessarily something you can build—for some, it is an endless pursuit. Building happiness, as Ahmed describes it, is a neoliberal project in wealth accumulation; it puts the burden of stability and contentment on individual striving rather than equitable and just governing.

Expanding on Ahmed's reasoning, I suggest that pilgrimage in Kazakhstan is not only a quest for spiritual fulfillment and the addressing of specific needs; it is also an integral part of the capitalist present in Kazakhstan. It reflects precarity on both the individual and state levels, and sheds light on postsocialist Islam. Anna Tsing, in her work on unstable existence in the ruins of late capitalism, advances precarity as a lasting state of late modernity: "Modernization was supposed to fill the world—both communist and capitalist—with jobs, and not just any jobs but 'standard employment' with stable wages and benefits. Such jobs are now quite rare; most people depend on much more irregular livelihoods" (Tsing 2015, 3). Such precarity, Tsing suggests, gives rise to new forms of life and lifeways and requires of survivors an imaginative approach to thriving in the "ruins" of late capitalism. If, according to Tsing, we live in a precarious present, postsocialist societies represent a particular strain of precarity, growing out of the turbulence of the post-Soviet transition and its aftermath as well as the economic downturn of 2008 and the currency devaluations of 2014, 2015, and 2016. Added to the economic precarity that still affects many Kazakhstanis is the ideological

precarity, a precarity of belief, a vulnerability to outside beliefs and new ideologies that characterizes the renewed search for religion in Kazakhstan. In
the midst of this instability, the long-standing Kazakh practice of pilgrimage serves as a stabilizing practice and a way to address their precarious
present. Tsing writes, "To live with precarity requires more than railing at
those who put us here. . . . We might look around to notice this strange new
world, and we might stretch our imagination to grasp its contours" (Tsing
2015, 3). Pilgrimage and faith healing, in addition to providing comfort and
support in difficult times, also allow the envisioning of possible futures and
selves.

Though many Kazakhs are not observant in terms of mosque attendance,
other ways of being Muslim such as fasting during Ramadan, giving alms,
going on pilgrimage, and seeing faith healers are quite common. According
to a Pew Research Center study in 2012, more than a third of Kazakhs (36 percent) sought the services of faith healers in Kazakhstan, whereas only a tenth
attended mosque regularly. A 2016 study of Islam among Kazakh youth puts
participation in Friday prayer among Kazakh-speaking Kazakhs at 21 percent (2.4 times more than their Russian-speaking counterparts) (Kassenova
2018, 118). Nargis Kassenova writes that despite identifying nearly entirely
as culturally Muslim (96.9 percent),[1] "Kazakhstanis remain a fairly secular
society, especially compared with other Muslim countries. This is perhaps
unsurprising given the very low start in terms of religiosity and the strong
position of atheism in Soviet Kazakhstan. As a result of the 70-year-long enforced secularization process, Islam virtually disappeared as an organizing
religious doctrine and survived as rituals or as 'folk Islam'" (Kassenova 2018,
118). Despite the great number of mosques opened in Kazakhstan from 1998
to 2018, mosque attendance has not increased in proportion. Of my interviewees, Kazakhs of different ages on pilgrimage in many different areas of
the country, many (especially women pilgrims) felt that pilgrimage was a
more "comfortable" Muslim practice, whereas mosque attendance remained
unfamiliar for many.

Scholarly attention to Islam in Central Asia has flourished in anthropological and historical studies examining Muslim practices and beliefs as
they relate to issues of gender (Fathi 2006; Peshkova 2014), changing worship practices (Montgomery 2016; Mukhtarova 2009; Roi and Wainer 2009;
Schwab 2012), pre-Islamic belief systems (Dubuisson 2017), secularism (Mc-

Brien 2017), and social and political change (Jones 2017; Louw 2014; Yemelianova 2014). In examining social precarity through wide-ranging and long-term ethnographic fieldwork on pilgrimage and religious healing, I aim to contribute to this multifaceted understanding of Islam in Central Asia.

In writing about Islam in Central Asia, Soviet scholars often used the terms "official" and "unofficial" Islam, a model that was replicated by many scholars of Central Asia during the Soviet era. Other dichotomous descriptions of Islam include "orthodox" and "heterodox," and Ernst Gellner's contested "high" and "low" Islam (Gellner 1996). Although these terms are clearly problematic, artificially dividing Islam into a scripturally based practice and "folk" expressions and practices, I have found that such divisions, particularly the Soviet approach to Islam, have had a lasting effect on local discourse. Thus, although many recent scholars argue that these constructions impose a false structure onto local beliefs and practices, this argument ignores the fact that Muslims in Central Asia are ensconced in transnational scholarly and ideological discourse about Islam. In writing about the concept of orthodoxy among Uighurs in Xinjiang, Paula Schrode holds that "defining 'right' and 'wrong' religious belief or practice is certainly not the concern of scholarship, but it is a central concern of the religious subjects involved. An analysis of religious discourses can hardly do without conceptualizing structures and notions of dogmatic orthodoxy within the respective religious system. . . . The scholarly task is to highlight the social dynamics and power structures at work and not to mask them by tacitly reproducing them" (Schrode 2008, 397–98).

The dichotomies of orthodoxy/heterodoxy and official/unofficial Islam persisted long enough in Central Asia that they have become a part of the ideological landscape. This way of thinking is apparent in the self-designations of healers I studied and in the hierarchically ordered status of different kinds of Muslim practitioners. Talal Asad writes, "Anthropologists like El-Zein, who wish to deny any special significance to orthodoxy, and those like Gellner, who see it as a specific set of doctrines 'at the heart of Islam,' both are missing something vital: that orthodoxy is not a mere body of opinion but a distinctive relationship—a relationship of power. Wherever Muslims have the power to regulate, uphold, require or adjust correct practices, and to condemn, exclude, undermine, or replace incorrect ones, there is the domain of orthodoxy" (Asad 1986, 15).

My aim in noting these contentious discourses is to highlight their problematic use as a scholarly frame of analysis and to recognize their place in local discourse. Schrode advocates studying Islam in its "dogmatic" and "interactive" aspects—that is, looking at ideological, ideational, and discursive factors, while also taking into account the social relations inherent in Muslim belief and practice in Central Asia. Rather than dismissing the concepts of "orthodoxy" or "official" Islam as foreign inventions irrelevant to Central Asia, I seek to clarify how they articulate with local discourse, play into local practices, and affect prestige structures.

TRACING ISLAM IN CENTRAL ASIA

Islam came to Central Asia from the eighth to thirteenth centuries, the timeline and nature of its introduction varying from region to region. The settled oasis cities of Bukhara, Samarkand, and Kokand, in what is now Uzbekistan, and Kashgar and Hotan in today's Xinjiang were exposed to Islam as early as the eighth to tenth centuries, whereas some areas of Kyrgyzstan and Kazakhstan—with the notable exception of Taraz in southern Kazakhstan, which was a Muslim city by the tenth century—did not convert to Islam until the seventeenth or eighteenth century. The local aristocracy in these southern, settled regions, through centuries of contact with Persia, was in closer dialogue with the Muslim world, studying Muslim texts and promoting Islamic arts, sciences, and literature. The areas farther north (Kazakhstan and Kyrgyzstan) were home to mobile pastoralists who lived in pasturelands far from the urban centers in the south and therefore generally experienced less Muslim influence and at a later time. With little access to mosques and madrassas, these northern pastoral regions were exposed to Islam mainly via Sufi clerics. Kassenova explains,

> The Sunni Hanafi school is one of the most prominent schools of traditional Islam in Central Asia. Compared with other schools, it features flexibility, adherence to rational judgment (ra'y), and the wide use of ijma (reliance on a collective, consensual opinion of scholars). Throughout history, it has proved flexible enough to incorporate pre-Islamic popular customs and rights and legitimized some tribal and customary law. The non-Orthodox character of local Islam is also explained by the fact that the conversion of nomads of the Kazakh steppe to Islam at the early stage was mainly carried out by such Sufi mission-

aries as Nakhbandiya, Yassawiya, and Kadiriya . . . in the 12th–16th centuries. (Kassenova 2018, 120)

Indeed, Sufism, particularly Naqshbandi Sufism, has had a strong influence on Islam throughout Central Asia. It is important to recognize, however, that although early urban centers like Bukhara and other oasis cities were strongly influenced linguistically and culturally by Persia, rural areas in the same region (Uzbekistan and Tajikistan) were less so, and retained more Turkic, pre-Islamic practices. Similarly, though the inhabitants of the northern regions (now Kazakhstan) were primarily herders, they had some contact with the Silk Road through trade and were exposed to religious teachings in centers along this historic route.

During the Soviet era Muslim practices were strictly curtailed. In the earliest days of the Soviet Union, an organized anti-Muslim campaign included mosque closings, persecution of Muslim leaders, and *hujum*, the coerced unveiling of Muslim women (Northrop 2004). Despite this, certain loosely organized structures of Muslim community and leadership, like that of the *mahalla*, Muslim neighborhoods—a basic unit of Muslim social structure in some parts of Central Asia (particularly Uzbekistan and Tajikistan)—persisted and were even strengthened by the fact that Soviet institutions like collective farms tended to reinforce these local area designations rather than contradict them. As Kazakhs did not traditionally veil and had many fewer mosques than their southern neighbors, they were not as targeted by these actions. Nevertheless, they were deeply and lastingly affected by anti-Muslim campaigns, particularly the purging of religious practitioners, including mullahs, *shirakshi* (keepers of holy shrines), *emshi* (healers), and *baksy* (shamans). Soviet ideological campaigns were no less ruinous, teaching that on the timeline of social evolution, religion belonged in the unenlightened presocialist past. Religious practices were considered backward, religious leaders regarded as crooked opportunists, and religious beliefs dismissed as empty superstitions of the downtrodden. If this was the Soviet approach regarding Islam, the practices of shamanism and other pre-Islamic belief systems were considered even more backward, and their practitioners blacklisted as charlatans and cheats. This view of religious healers as suspicious, marginal members of society has persisted in Central Asia and continues to affect discourse about faith healing practices in the region.

PILGRIMAGE AND PRECARITY

Unlike mosque attendance, which is relatively low among Kazakhs, the practice of shrine pilgrimage and visiting faith healers is very common, and many Kazakhs, especially women, view the latter as more accessible sacred practices. Although many Kazakhs do not count themselves as observant Muslims, many nevertheless practice pilgrimage and faith healing, either as a regular practice or at some precarious point in their lives. It is often at these points—when financial, legal, marital, or health problems arise—that Kazakhs undertake these culturally Muslim practices. Emshi, or faith healers, in addition to telling the future, will often "prescribe" a new lifestyle, including fasting, giving up alcohol, and undertaking a pilgrimage. Thus the two practices (faith healing and pilgrimage) are often intertwined. Of those I interviewed making pilgrimage and visiting emshi, the majority were women, many in personal states of precarity and change. One was jobless, another was supporting family members in legal battles and financial straits, another was thanking the saints for a successful adoption, and several I met were immigrants from other Central Asian countries. With a long history and widespread use throughout Central Asia, pilgrimage and visits to faith healers continue to be relevant practices in Kazakhstan, particularly during times of economic and social instability.

MIRA, TRANSFORMED

Mira, like many Kazakhs in Almaty, is Muslim culturally but is not observant in most senses of the word. She does not attend mosque or pray at namaz, nor does she abstain from drinking alcohol. She and many other Kazakhs I met quite often engaged the help and services of emshi. Besides being religious healers, emshi are also "seers" and perform many varied services usually aimed at what is known in Kazakh as "opening the road," in other words removing some kind of obstacle to the client's well-being, success, health, or happiness. In seeking the help of several emshi, and in trying pilgrimage as a way to both adjust her lifestyle and resolve problems related to love and money, Mira is not unusual. Her attempt at transformation while on pilgrimage is a way of exploring new approaches to old problems, of questioning life choices, and perhaps also a way of probing an uncertain faith.

FIGURE 7.I. Mira on pilgrimage in Turkistan.

Mira, an Almatyite, works occasionally for the Kazakhstani film industry, when she can find work. She is unmarried at an age where it is mostly
considered too late to be unmarried—a situation caused partly by her lack of
strong family support. In Kazakhstan, where marriage, career, housing, and
social advancement all depend to some extent on family connections, weak
family support can be a great obstacle to success and stability. Mira's mother
died young and her father remarried soon after the funeral, leaving Mira and
her two younger sisters to fend for themselves as teenagers. They depended
on the reluctant charity of their many relatives and occasionally slept in train
stations and bus stations. Their survival depended mostly on Mira's wits until they had traveled the rocky path to young adulthood. By the time I met
Mira in 2004, she had successfully raised her sisters, educated herself, and
built an unsteady career in Almaty's thriving film industry.

Mira saw many emshis in her twenties and thirties. At the time when I
first met her she was seeing a new emshi, a woman in her mid-twenties called
Bayan or Aq-Bayan. The Aq added to her name is a sacralizing prefix meaning "white" or "pure." Mira had heard about Bayan from a friend who raved

about her, and had begun visiting Bayan regularly to alleviate her many problems in health, career, and romance. At one of her visits she happened to mention to the emshi that she was planning a trip with me to southern Kazakhstan. Bayan suggested that Mira go on pilgrimage to the many old, highly venerated sites while we were in the area. Since I was planning a trip to this area to visit the epic singer Abas Abasov, Mira decided to come with me. We would go on pilgrimage together and she also agreed to help me with the task of simultaneous fieldwork and wrangling my three-year-old daughter, Sofie, who accompanied us on the trip.

We began our trip by taking a train to Shymkent, and from there, hired cars to get us to our more remote destinations, Aristanbab, Turkistan, and the shrine of Qorqyt (the latter revered as a musician and shaman who played the qobyz). This is a page of my fieldnotes from that trip:

A wild and sleepless spell in Shymkent, a green, fun-loving city on the Uzbek border where the Soviet hardness blurs into late-night cafes, open leafy courtyards and the endless flow of talk (Kazakh, Uzbek, Turkish, Russian) over green tea with lemon. Cosmopolitan in a totally different way than the cooler, mountainous Almaty, Shymkent is relaxed in a way that you don't see in the north. In June the bazaar overflows with local apricots, cherries and tart summer apples, as well as plentiful fruits and nuts imported from Uzbekistan. Camels are raised here and can be seen wandering the streets of nearby small towns and roaming across the steppe. Camel milk is used to make a fermented yogurt drink and kurt, the delicious salty sour lumps of dried curd that are rumored to have kept Genghis Khan's mighty army alive over vast terrain.

The bright daytime is busy enough, as people go on about the business of making a living, but Shymkent really seems to come alive at night. The city relaxes into the leafy dusk and the back courtyards fill with the smoke of shashlyk searing on woodfires. Smoky grilled skewers of fresh lamb and beef are piled in vast quantities alongside great swaths of greenery—parsley, cilantro, dill, scallion and cucumber. Almaty is almost always still, caught in a windless patch in the mountains, but Shymkent is perched on the steppe, with the mountains distantly visible to the south, and the evening breeze blows through the cafes at night.

We stay with relatives of my friend Mira, who has come with me to help. Her cousin is a highly placed official in Shymkent, and Gulnara, his bitterly sarcastic wife, endures a steady stream of visitors, relatives, colleagues, and general well-wishers. He operates mostly in Russian, Gulnara in Kazakh and this underscores the general impression of familial rift in this prosperous household. On the day we arrive he suddenly receives word of a much awaited promotion. From the moment we arrive there is non-stop celebratory eating and drinking until the wee hours. Sofie stays up until three in the morning like everyone else but wakes with the sun, leaving me to sleepwalk through the bright days, only really coming alive (like everyone else) at 10 at night in time to go out again. Mira's relatives are experts in the best cafes, saunas, nightclubs, and casinos but laughingly tell me they have no idea about museums and music schools.

On the day we are supposed to head north to the ancient city of Turkistan, Mira's friend from Almaty, Sholpan, shows up. She was having family problems and decided to take the 14-hour train ride down from Almaty in order to see a local emshi that Gulnara had told her about. Mira suggests that we visit the emshi on the way to the shrines, so we hire a car and driver and all head out together.

Along this pilgrimage that followed, it emerged that Mira was experimenting with trying out a new Muslim identity—one that adhered more strictly to the ideal of a "good Muslim girl," in her words. Mira was told by her emshi that she should try to alter her habits if she was going to treat this as a pilgrimage, giving up alcohol, smoking, and swearing, and trying to dress more modestly. Mira also had another aim in traveling to southern Kazakhstan. She was romantically involved with a man from this area in southern Kazakhstan, and, hoping to turn this romance into an engagement, had made plans to meet his mother. A rather traditional person, his mother was looking for a proper Kazakh daughter-in-law, and Mira did not look the part. Coming from the film industry, she was used to wearing wild outfits and unusually colorful and dramatic makeup. (Because she had thin eyebrows, she often drew them in—usually blue, red, or green). So, in response to the demands of the pilgrimage and her prospective mother-in-law, Mira decided to transform herself. She stopped drinking and smoking on the trip, wore more subdued prints and colors (which was not easy, choosing from her closet), normalized her makeup a bit, and, at least while at the sacred pilgrimage sites, covered her hair.

FIGURE 7.2. Suyunbai's shrine, with sound waves depicted in the brickwork.

The transformation was short-lived. After things went awry with her potential fiancé, Mira executed a complete reversal, scrapped the idea of becoming a "good Muslim girl," dropped her emshi, and started smoking again.

As Mira's pilgrimage illustrates, pilgrimage and faith healing practices are part of the same ritual complex and tend to be practiced together. Additionally, her reasons for going on pilgrimage and her self-transformation and reversal point toward the flexibility and accessibility of pilgrimage, particularly for young women. Pilgrimage may begin in one form (such as sightseeing or tourism) and with fairly well-outlined goals (seeking health, wealth, or simply entertainment), but it can quickly morph into an experiment with or exploration of faith. Pilgrimage also allows one to try on religious belief, an easy kind of experiment that does not involve mosque-based worship. Especially for women who did not grow up with the tradition, attending mosque can be daunting. Most Kazakh women do not cover their heads, and the rules for modest dress in mosques are worlds away from what most fashionable Kazakhstani women would wear (designer jeans, fitted T-shirts, miniskirts, heels). Attire on pilgrimage is not as strict, loosely requiring head covering and more modest attire, but with quite a wide array of acceptability.

QORQYT'S SHRINE

In Central Asian pilgrimage there is often a physical connection to place—pilgrims tie strips of cloth to branches near the shrines, drink water from nearby wells and springs, and sometimes collect the dusty soil in the most sacred of places, such as Aristambab. Another common aspect of pilgrimage and religious healing in Kazakhstan is sacralization through sound. In musician shrines, connections to sound appear in a few different ways, particularly in the reverence for and depiction of sacred instruments and in the depiction of sound in the actual tombs or shrine buildings.

In emshi practices that I observed, it was largely through the spoken form of the Qur'an that sound took on sacred meaning and transformative power. One emshi I visited several times, Nargulia, used the spoken sounds of Qur'anic verse to "clean" living spaces and turn water into holy water. If a client moved into a new apartment, she might be asked to "clean" the living space of bad spirits. I first met her when she was conducting such a purification. She sat in the kitchen of my friend Aia's house and read the Qur'an for several hours over a large jar of holy water. The reasons for the "cleaning" arose from Aia's precarious family situation. Her husband had recently left her and her young child for another woman, a situation that did not overly upset her—except for the fact that, in the absence of child support laws, her living situation was becoming tenuous and she was worried about paying rent every month. The "cleaning" was conducted to restore order and (particularly financial) stability to Aia's home in the aftermath of the breakup of her marriage. On another visit, I saw Nargulia recite the verses of the Qur'an over a photograph suspended in water. In this way, she explained, she would "cleanse" the man in the picture and in so doing, cure him of alcoholism.

Many of the shrines I visited, both in southern Kazakhstan and on the pilgrimage circuit in Almaty, included sonic or visual depictions of sound at the shrines of musicians. In southern Kazakhstan, one of the most popular shrines is that of the legendary qobyz player Qorqyt, a national hero, who is said to have been a shaman and musician who lived in the ninth century. Funded by the state, the Qorqyt shrine is built high on a hill above an otherwise featureless plain and the main lasting impression of the place is the tremendous wind that blows ceaselessly through the shrine complex. At the center of a circular terrace is an amphitheater for concerts, and to one side stands a tall sculpture of a figure constructed to represent the qobyz in sound and image. Partially embedded within the sculpture is a cluster of pipes that wail when the wind blows through them; according to the shrine's guide these are meant to emulate the melancholy sound of a qobyz. Below this is a small shrine topped with shaman bells to which visitors have attached strips of handkerchiefs. The guide explained that we were to listen to the sound of the "qobyz" and make a wish.

Before the twentieth century the qobyz was the Kazakh shaman's trance-inducing instrument of choice, and many famous qobyz players claim shamans in their family tree. Throughout Central and Inner Asia, the shaman's instrument—whether drum, fiddle, or Jew's harp—represents the shaman's sonic channel to the spirit world. The sound of the instrument is the key medium in inducing trance and opening a gateway to the world of helping spirits, guides, and malevolent entities. In Siberia and other parts of Inner Asia, the instrument is the physical representation of the shaman's helping spirit. Making the instrument is a lengthy and important process, and in some parts of Inner Asia, shamans perform an "enlivening" ceremony calling the spirit into the instrument before it can be used. The qobyz is made from a single piece of wood, skin and horsehair, and, like the Mongolian horsehead fiddle (*morin huur*), it carries animist associations. Several qobyz compositions, such as *Aqqu* (White Swan) and *Qasqyr* (Wolf), use the instrument to imitate animals. Both of my qobyz teachers pointed out that the back of the qobyz itself resembles the body of a swan, its long neck stretching forward in flight. Considering the qobyz's animist associations, the Qorqyt shrine's architects were purposeful in taking advantage of the natural features and acoustics of place (the wind blowing over the open steppe). In resonating when the wind blows, with an eerie low flutelike moan, the sonic sculpture of the qobyz interacts with its natural environment, underscoring the qobyz's animist associations as a conduit to another world.

Qorqyt is a mythical figure, a shaman, composer, and holy man, said to have wandered the world in search of the meaning of life, returning to the Syr Darya region only toward the end of his life. According to legend, he met his end playing the *qobyz* by the banks of the Syr Darya when a giant snake rose up out of the river, swallowed him, qobyz and all, and then disappeared once again into the murky depths. In another version of the story, after traveling around the world and knowing the end was near, Qorqyt sat by the Syr Darya playing continuously day and night, with the knowledge that if he continued to play, he could not die. Finally, exhausted, he stopped playing and died, at which point the giant snake swallowed his body. Central to the Qorqyt legend is his music; figuring prominently in Qorqyt stories, it is his qobyz that represents the channel of both his divine wisdom and healing. With several küis in the present qobyz repertoire attributed to him, he is an important figure in Kazakh music, representing both the "ancient" roots of Kazakh music and its connection to spiritual power.

The Qorqyt museum within the shrine complex features displays that highlight this connection between sound and spirituality. It also includes references to Islam, despite the fact that Qorqyt's lifespan preceded Islam by several centuries. One interesting display is a small dark chamber, lit by black lights, in which a bronze sculpture of a qobyz is suspended from the ceiling. On entering the small space, I recognized an ethereal qobyz piece, attributed to Qorqyt, playing through the sound system. The profusion of images about the chamber represent different aspects of the divine and of ancient cosmology, including a shangyrak (the smoke hole of a Kazakh yurt used by astronomers to read the stars, a symbol of Kazakh cosmology) projected on the ceiling, replicas of local petroglyphs on the walls, and the Muslim eight-pointed star (the *khatim* or *khatim sulayman*, seal of the prophets), projected onto the floor in green light. The mixed collage of animist and Muslim spiritual images seemed an apt representation of Kazakhstan's many-layered spiritual past and perhaps also the present struggle to map out the country's moral future.

MUSICIAN SHRINES ON THE ALMATY PILGRIMAGE

The pilgrimage around Almaty is a smaller, more local affair. The emshi Aq-Bayan served as our guide on this pilgrimage circuit, one in 2004 and another a decade later, in 2014. In 2004 she was very active on the pilgrimage circuit, taking a busload of pilgrims every weekend on this route, which included stops at the shrines of war heroes, musicians, and healers, and Soviet composers. In traveling on this and other various pilgrimages, I found that it was not unusual for musicians—particularly, certain kinds of traditional musicians—to be picked out for special reverence and their graves visited as sacred sites. In the case of epic singers (zhyraular) and poet singers (aqyndar), their elevated status may be related to the importance of orality in Kazakh culture. Reverence for qobyz players has its roots in shamanism and pre-Islamic animist belief, as the qobyz was used in pre-twentieth-century Kazakhstan as a shamanic instrument to appeal to the spirit world in healing illness. Several Kazakh musicians (the epic singers Abbas Abasov and Ulzhan Baibursynova, and the dombra player Sersengaly Zhumazbayev) have articulated to me a similar conception that Kazakh music—particularly the spectacular gifts of memory and improvisation among epic singers and poet singers—comes from the ground on which one is born. Musicians, like saints and healers, carry a spiritual power that ordinary people do not possess, because their roles in Kazakh society have included those of healers, historians, and social critics.

Suyunbay, whose shrine also lies along this pilgrimage route, was an aqyn who accompanied himself on dombra. The architecture of his shrine depicts the physical and sonic aspects of the dombra. The long neck and body of the dombra runs along the interior corners of the shrine, and the brickwork on the walls represents the sound waves from the dombra reaching up to the sky. This explanation was given to us by the shirakshi, the guardian of the shrine, an elderly man who doubles as a kind of tour guide for visitors and pilgrims. Located in the open countryside about an hour's drive from Almaty, Suyunbay's shrine is one of the more impressive roadside shrines in the area. Made of detailed red brick, with a silver dome, the shrine is a beautiful small building, perched on the top of a small rise in the steppe. From the dark interior of the square building, images emerge in the patterning of light cut away from the brick walls. Portrayed in the brickwork are images of a wolf, the symbol of Suyunbay's clan.

Many of those buried at the shrines on this route are members of Nazarbaev's clan. Although the shrines have been marked for nearly a century, they received government funding in the early 2000s to build more substantive gates, sculptures, and small buildings. Suyunbay's shrine is one of those recently renovated. A separate small building contains a plaque stating that this shrine was built at the order of President Nazarbaev in 2000. A black stone, said to have been transported from Mecca, is embedded into the wall. Both the presidential sign-off and the rumored connection with Mecca give Suyunbay's shrine a particular importance and authority in this area. For the shrine keepers, relatives of Suyunbay himself, who depend on revenue

FIGURE 7.3. Toktybai's shrine, 2014.

generated from pilgrims' donations, this special status has financial value. The more pilgrims a shrine can attract, the more revenue the shrine will generate. Visitors often buy charms, cards depicting sacred sites, prayer beads, and whips (used by faith healers), insofar as objects purchased at these sites have special protective power. Rumors and stories about miracles occurring at shrines (and possibly the story about the stone from Mecca) also help to generate attention and attract pilgrims.

Musicians singled out for pilgrimage run a wide gamut, from Soviet composers to the mythical musician Qorqyt. The grave and residence of the famous aqyn Zhambyl has been a tourist destination since the Soviet era and is now part of the pilgrimage circuit outside of Almaty. Along the road leading up to Zhambyl shrine, the musician's likeness is carved into the hillside, underscoring the history of Kazakhs' dependence on the natural world as mobile pastoralists. The image of Zhambyl on the hillside also references his nickname, the "poet of the steppe," and birthplace—the poet singer was named after the nearby Zhambyl mountains. Zhambyl was singled out as a *Soviet* representative of Kazakh culture and promoted by Soviet officials (conversely, other aqynlar were silenced). Built in 1945, this memorial museum still attracts many visitors and pilgrims, despite Zhambyl's awkward reputation as a mouthpiece of the Soviet state. Part shrine, part museum, the site was also Zhambyl's residence and continues to house his family members, who now act as tour guides. A second shrine, that of the Soviet composer Nurgissa Tlendiyev, has since been added on the grounds. At Tlendiyev's shrine, an imprint of his hand in brass is embedded in a block of black granite below his statue. A guide explained to us that a visitor to the shrine, particularly one "undertaking a creative work" of some kind (often a writer, musician, or artist) should place his or her hand on the composer's brass handprint to ensure success. Tlendiyev is widely revered as one of the greatest Kazakh composers.

The same pilgrimage route includes the shrine of Toktybai, a qobyz player. Toktybai was a kind of shaman who used the qobyz to heal, and his resting place is still considered to have healing properties. In 2004 his grave was a simple grassy mound, marked only by a small sign and the image of a qobyz depicted below a Muslim crescent fashioned in the grillwork above the entrance to the makeshift shrine. We were instructed to roll over the ground three times to absorb the healing energies of the sacred site. Now a major pilgrimage site, Toktybai's shrine is protected by a large, colored glass dome and frequented by minibuses carrying tourist and pilgrimage groups. The shirakshi of Toktybai's shrine, his direct descendant, brought us into a separate building where we sat as he gave a *bata* or blessing. I was not allowed to record or take photographs, but he told stories of Toktybai's legendary, almost supernatural powers, and the miraculous feats he achieved through playing his magical qobyz. Finally, he brought out Toktybai's qobyz. Wrapped in a large piece of faded leather, Toktybai's qobyz was very old, of worn, dark wood. It was missing its strings but still held sacred power, although it could not be played. Years ago, the shirakshi said, after Toktybai's death, the qobyz would still sound at night, though no one was playing it.

The sounding of sacred power in the shrines of qobyz players like Toktybai and Qorqyt, and the depiction of musical instruments in the shrines of musicians, epic singers, and composers such as Suyunbay, Zhambyl, and Tlindeev seem to link their legendary powers and talents to the land where they are buried—as if a remainder of their musical power still resides in the dust, the air, and the water near their shrines.

FIGURE 7.4. Mausoleum of Hodja Ahmet Yassaui, Turkistan, Southern Kazakhstan.

A SHRINE TO THE PAST AND THE CITY OF THE FUTURE

In Kazakhstan, many scholars have noted a safeguarding of the secular nature of the state, along with the elevation of Islam as a symbol of national heritage. Shahram Akbarzadeh and others have examined the "nationalization of Islam" in post-Soviet Central Asia. Akbarzadeh discusses how "Islam has been the object of both fear and veneration. Political Islam, that is Islam as a guide for political action, is often stigmatized as 'fundamentalism,' 'Wahabii' and alien to the Central Asian brand of Islam and way of life. The negative portrayal of political Islam is in sharp contrast to the positive image of Islam and Islamic civilization, projected by state officials" (Akbarzadeh 2001, 451).

One focus of the Kazakhstani state's "rediscovery" of Islamic national heritage is the mausoleum of the Sufi poet and philosopher Hodja Ahmet Yassaui, and the surrounding old city. This city, called Turkistan, is one of the most important historic sites in today's Kazakhstan, with an archaeolog-

ical record dating back to the fourth century. Located in southern Kazakhstan, in what is known as the Otrar oasis region, it lies on the edge of the
routes of the historic Silk Road. Yassaui was born in the late eleventh century
and in his lifetime Turkistan became an important city in the region. Yassaui
was buried in the town and a *mazar* (mausoleum) was built within the city
walls in the late fourteenth century, more than two hundred years after his
death, under the orders of Timur (1370–1405), also known as Tamerlane. Although Turkistan flourished well before the name "Kazakh" had emerged as
an ethnic or national designation, it has nevertheless been adopted as part of
Kazakh national heritage.

The city of Turkistan has historical records dating back to the fourth century, but many of the buildings standing today, including the tomb of Hodja
Ahmet Yassaui, were built in the fourteenth–fifteenth centuries during the
city's period of cultural and economic flourishing. Revered for its historical
significance and importance to Islam in Kazakhstan, Turkistan is considered a kind of local equivalent of a hajj and is visited year-round by pilgrims
and tourists from all over the country.[2] Every year the national newspapers
and television stations cover the president's annual pilgrimage to Turkistan.
Turkistan's 1500th anniversary in 2000 was a major national event, marked
by monthlong celebrations and precelebration renovations of the old city. On
a website devoted to the anniversary, Nazarbaev is quoted as saying: "The
celebration of the foundation of Turkestan [Turkistan], now fifteen centuries
old, is a remarkable event not just for the city itself but also for the Republic of
Kazakhstan and all Turkic peoples. Our goal today is to continue the development of Turkestan as an important cultural, spiritual, scientific, and trade
center in Central Asia."[3] In his visits to Turkistan, Nazarbaev uses his own
identity as a Muslim to connect with a national image of Kazakhs as a Muslim people. He moreover applies this identification to "all Turkic peoples,"
thereby linking personal, national, and transnational Muslim identities and
solidarities.

The Kazakhstani diva Roza Rymbaeva was also involved in the anniversary celebrations and produced a music video, "Turkistan," dedicated to the
event. The video is a montage of Kazakh traditions and Muslim practices,
including ritual uses of milk and *kymyss* to mark the beginning of spring,
horseback-riding games, and sheep sacrifice. The lyrics similarly merge Kazakh, Turkic, and Muslim identities:

We are a people with united Turkic roots,
We are a people with a single language.
Turkistan is a supporting pedestal
For the Muslim people,
For the Muslim people of a single creed.
Expansive land, endless land,
Of the Turkic-Kazakh people.

Refrain:
Endless Kazakh land
Turkistan
It became a place
Sacred for Turkic people,
It became the Mecca Turkistan.

The pride of Kazakhs.
The pride of Kazakhs, this city
Built by our ancestors
Amazing city, Turkistan.
The dome of Yassaui Akhmet
Became a monument to our people.

The video "Turkistan" begins with ambient synthesized sounds and the beginnings of a melody, punctuated by the rattle of the hoja's staff as he circumambulates the sacred site. Backed by a bass ostinato and a heavily synthesized pop beat, the melody is rendered by a synthesized metallic sound resembling struck strings (such as a santour, a Persian hammer dulcimer), lending it a vaguely Middle Eastern timbre. As Roza Rymbaeva appears on the screen, her characteristically strong mezzo vocals punch the beat emphatically. Her rippling vibrato and impassioned expression of the song text resonate broadly in every part of her wide range. Rymbaeva's style is most strongly associated with estrada singers—Soviet singers of her age, with dramatic, emotional performance styles and often operatically trained voices. She has remained an icon in Kazakhstan, and her music often mixes newer pop styles with her characteristic vocals. Rymbaeva's powerful mezzo is joined by a mixed chorus that provides a countermelody to her dramatic refrain, as images of Turkistan flash across the screen. On the repeat, a break features calypso-like drum riffs and a synthesized melody approximating the light, treble strum of a dombra. This is followed by a modulation, as Rymbaeva executes the final vocal refrain with drama and flair, stalking across the stage and singing to adoring fans. Her riveting onstage presence is accentuated by the triumphant broad gestures of her arms, as if to take up as much space with her small body as with her huge voice.

Turkistan has become a national symbol giving Kazakhstan a history based on Muslim teachings, poetry, philosophy, and architectural achievement. Both Rymbaeva's lyrics and Nazarbaev's speech at the celebration stress Turkic Muslim culture and history. "We are a people with united Turkic roots, / We are a people with a single language." With this use of the ambiguous "we," "Kazakhs" and "Turkic Muslims" are conflated into one entity, which allows Kazakhstan to claim Turkistan and Yassaui as part of its own history (though neither can be accurately labeled as Kazakh). Nazarbaev and Rymbaeva describe Turkistan in connection with language, architecture and art, science, religion, and economics (trade)—in short, the building blocks of modern cultural formation. On the social evolutionary timeline that underpins much of Soviet and post-Soviet political thought, Turkistan represents the "right" stage of development needed to lay the groundwork for the building of a modern nation. While Kazakh nationalism generally emphasizes the rich historical depth of nomadic culture and verbal arts, Turkistan has been elevated as a national symbol precisely because it (conversely) represents the settled civilization of oasis cities along the Silk Road. Like Bukhara and Samarkand, Turkistan is a physical reminder of Central Asian history, proof in stone, tile, and ink of the presence of science, art, language, and learning.

On a state level then, the state uses shrine pilgrimage as a way to connect with the ancient past and to promote Islamic civilization while at the same time maintaining a secular stance in governing. While Kazakhstanis often practice shrine pilgrimage as a way of experimenting with faith at a time of precarity, the state engages in a curious balancing act with regard to Islam that mirrors this experimental spirit. As people like Mira and Aia explored faith-based yet practical ways of being Muslim in the early years of Kazakhstan's independence, so too Nazarbaev cautiously approached Islam as both a cultural identity for himself and a moral underpinning for the country. In

FIGURE 7.5 Astana, 2014.

particular, he saw Astana's new role as an interfaith, intercultural mediator between East and West. The same precarity that nudged the women I interviewed toward pilgrimage and faith healing also drove the state to seek a moral governing compass and a mediating faith-based role for the new capital. The Congress of Leaders of World and Traditional Religions was a way of establishing Astana in this moral mediating role.

ASTANA, THE MORAL HEART OF EURASIA

Many scholars have written about Nazarbaev's nation-building vision with regard to Kazakhstan's new capital (e.g., Anacker 2004; Buchli 2007; Laszczkowski 2017; Schatz 2004). In addressing this much-studied topic, I want to focus primarily on the concept of Astana from the perspective of *moral governing*. In a meeting of the Congress of World and Traditional Religions in Astana, President Nazarbaev defined Kazakhstan's new role as an intermediary between the Muslim world and the West. During the event, Nazarbaev explained his reasons for founding the congress: "In 2002 when after shocking terrorism on the 11th of September a world has been threatened with [the] danger of [a] notorious 'clash of civilizations,' we proposed an initiative of [a] convocation of Congress. The first forum was held in 2003."[4]

The congress, which is held triennially in Astana, was established to bring together world leaders in dialogue about ways to improve Muslim-Christian relations and in general to look at moral aspects of governing and the creation of a just world. In another speech, given at the ministerial conference Common World: Progress through Diversity, held in Astana on October 17, 2008, Nazarbaev states: "The first objective is to have a frank and constructive discussion of issues of cooperation against the background of globalization of modern cultures and religions, mainly Christianity and Islam. The second objective is to establish a wide-[ranging] political dialogue among nations representing two of the largest cultural communities and civilizations of the modern world, for the sake of the future of our planet."[5]

For Nazarbaev, Kazakhstan, perched culturally and geographically between East and West, represents both a pivot and an example of "interconfessional harmony," with Astana as the new capital built on this ideology. As he stated in a speech at the Third Congress of Leaders of World and Traditional Religions,

> [The city of] Astana, erected at [the intersection] of Asia and Europe, West and East, today is being turned into the centre of interaction of various nations and religions. We are proud of [the nobility of the] people of Kazakhstan, which could preserve interconfessional concord and interethnic friendship. We make our efforts to pass our experience to [the] world community. We stand up against religious oppositions and interethnic conflicts in [a] new millennium at different corners of the world.... Therefore, I consider, that the [Third] Congress of leaders of world and traditional religions will play a significant role in the cause of [the] development of interconfessional concord and interaction of civilizations. (Nazarbayev 2009)

This speech addresses one of Nazarbaev's foundational visions for Astana, as the "heart of Eurasia," which he lays out in his book (*In the Heart of Eurasia*) about the city's history and his plan for its future (Nazarbaev 2005).

When his book was written, Nazarbaev's Eurasianist rhetoric, strategy, and organizational alignment focused largely on political, economic, and military aspects of Eurasianism, based on the geographic and ethnic facets of Eurasianist theory—the union of Turks and Slavs, East and West. The years 2008–18, however, saw an increase in political rhetoric about morality, peace, and other themes of "interconfessional" concern. While still pragmatic in nature, Nazarbaev's speeches have nearly taken on the tone of spiritual leadership. Using Islam as a moral basis, he adds yet another layer to Kazakhstani Eurasianist ideology. Speaking at the Third Congress of World and Traditional Religions, he says, "Today . . . morals should be of primary concern. Without this significant instrument it is impossible to find a way out of the crisis to a higher path of societal development. I am convinced of it. . . . Throughout many centuries the unified people of Kazakhstan, enriched with spiritual heritage of various ethnos and religions, took up such qualities as tolerance, toleration and openness to grasp the new. And we feel our commitment to carry down this cultivated imperative to the entirety of humanity" (Nazarbayev 2009).

Taking "interconfessional harmony" as a theme resembling druzhba narodov (friendship of the peoples), Nazarbaev has woven this moral imperative into Eurasianist strategies for governing and forging transnational alliances. Kazakhstan's active participation in the Organisation of Islamic Cooperation and establishment of the Congress of World and Traditional Religions mark a new direction for Nazarbaev's relationship with the Muslim world. In stressing Muslim heritage and a kind of universal morality he manages to strike a delicate balance. While distancing himself from self-proclaimed Muslim regimes, at the same time he identifies the Muslim cultural heritage of Kazkahstan and stresses the religious tolerance that has allowed multiple religions to flourish there. Further, rather than avoiding spiritual references as he has done in the past, he instead uses them to his strategic advantage in forging an ideology of peaceful coexistence and positing Kazakhstan as an intermediary between the Christian and Muslim worlds.

In the same speech, after quoting the Upanishads, the prophet Muhammad, Jesus Christ, and the Talmud, Nazarbaev explains that "keepers of values and morals at all times were and continue to become spiritual leaders— pastors of various religions. That is why in these difficult times hopes are pinned on religious figures" (Nazarbayev 2009). Proposing that the "clash of civilizations," the economic crisis, and environmental issues are all linked to a crisis in morality and spirituality, Nazarbaev states that his goal is to provide dialogue between Christian and Muslim leaders, in hopes that a moral

FIGURE 7.6. Pilgrimage to Shopan Ata, Mangystau oblast in western Kazakhstan.

solution to these problems will succeed where diplomacy and politics have not. Nazarbaev is describing a state of precarity in the aftermath of 9/11 and the economic instabilities of the mid-2000s, and in a way, the balancing act he accomplishes in the strategic positioning of Kazakhstan is a position of political precarity. As a stabilizing solution, Nazarbaev suggests a new moral compass is needed. In so doing, he replicates at a state level a kind of exploratory Islam, in trying out a new role for Kazakhstan as a majority-Muslim, politically secular, moral leader.

The search for meaning—and solutions—in pilgrimage is about balancing the needs of the present while probing a possible faith and imagining a possible future. In some ways, many Kazakhstanis are still trying on new approaches to faith in the postsocialist present. After the tidal wave of economic and ideological change in 1991, evangelical missionizing and renewed commitment to heritage faiths (Islam and Russian Orthodoxy) significantly changed the spiritual landscape in postsocialist Kazakhstan. In 2018, more than two decades later, the turn to faith continues, as Kazakhstan's state and citizens alike confront religious, moral, or spiritual reframings in the precarious present. In 2004 billboards on the street displayed forward-looking bright young men and women smiling in their new apartments, high above the city, sitting on their brand new sofas, with their perfect children—while behind those billboards, the chaos of the construction site peeked through the cracks in the pretty facade. In 2014 some of those glossy apartment blocks had now been built; others remained construction sites. I have suggested here that Muslim practices such as pilgrimage have helped some Kazakhstanis face the uncertainties caused by political upheaval, social instability, and economic crisis. From this precarious present, who knows what the future holds—happiness, perhaps.

CONCLUSION

STRIKING THE SET

This book has investigated how Kazakhstanis celebrate the year as they experience the passing and marking of time. In such celebrations, the present is often in deep conversation with the past (HadžiMuhamedović 2018, 3). This temporal dialogue can be perceived particularly in holiday commemorations of violence and war as well as in nostalgic portrayals and mythic narratives of nation in national holidays. The weight of the past wields both emotional and political heft that presses on the present ideologically and culturally.

The past also resides in memories of holidays—memories that spur expectation and shape what we anticipate of future commemorations and celebrations. In this sense the marking of holidays imparts a sense of temporal rhythm and anticipation. In following the cycling of seasons and holidays, this book has followed the trauma experienced in commemorating painful events; but it has also observed the pleasure taken in seasonal repetition, in the *expectation* of celebratory events as well as (perhaps even more than) the actual celebration. The stability of the calendrical cycle, I argue, can contribute to a sense of well-being; experienced communally, this temporal stability, repetition, and expectation accord a feeling of belonging. I have written about members of a Korean church in Almaty who have found stability in the reliable community of Sunday mornings and holiday celebrations. I have also described what might be considered a virtual temporal community— viewers who watch the same holiday films every New Year, and whose live celebrations and holiday parties are intertwined with those on the screen (bound together by Soviet-era romance, ideas about the topsy-turvy period of sviatki, and Russian potato salad). In this connection between temporality and well-being, it seems that predictability and communal temporal rhythms contribute to a sense of stability.

Corresponding to this time-based sense of well-being, this book has considered how temporality relates to happiness, particularly recognizing the economic implications in Sara Ahmed's discussion of happiness in which a good citizen obtains the expected points of progress along the path to happiness. Ahmed writes, "For a life to count as a good life, it must take on the direction promised as a social good, which means imagining one's futurity in terms of reaching certain points along a life course" (Ahmed 2011, 164). In Kazakhstan, as in the rest of the Soviet Union and post-Soviet states, the accepted "paths to happiness" changed from the end of the 1980s through the early 2000s. The ethnographic case studies I have written about—especially in regard to Kazakh women trying to navigate the changing expectations in the decades following the transition—help illustrate the economic basis in the ways that people build toward happiness in postsocialist Kazakhstan. I have also been interested in how the state's utopian horizons develop in tandem to its citizens' paths to happiness. As the state changes the script for achieving happiness, it alters the outlook for what is possible—or expected—for its citizens.

Celebration can also mark points of exclusion and conflict. Perhaps this is especially important in places like Kazakhstan that have diverse populations, where fault lines in a community are frequently drawn along ethnic lines. In Kazakhstan, it is also important to note differences between rural Kazakh-speaking Kazakhs and Russian-speaking Kazakhs in Almaty, Astana, and other cities. But as I have shown, these points of weakness in the social fabric can also occur along a temporal axis—as changing habits leave the more traditionally minded behind. This is reflected in generational discrepancies, where memories of childhood celebrations encounter more contemporary ways of celebrating.

So although this book has described how the past lingers in the present, it is also about change. Specifically, I have investigated how a change of regime and economy may correlate with a corresponding change in its citizens' habits, desires, and expectations. In this, I am interested in tracing connections between the state and the self, between governing and the governed. This is the part of the picture that I continue to grapple. It is certainly possible, both in my native United States, now in the third year of Donald Trump's presidency, and in Kazakhstan to see and feel how governing affects those governed; yet it is a struggle to pinpoint exactly how a political leader's ideas and policies are linked to the inner lives and private concerns of the citizenry. I remain very much interested in how political lives are lived in the everyday and how this may shape our interior lives and sense of self. I hope I have begun to construct this connection through the ethnographies and mediated stories presented here.

There is still so much I wish to learn about in Kazakhstan. My next project picks up where this leaves off—examining the politics of belief in Kazakhstan through the sounds and habits of worship. So much has changed since I started this research, as evidenced by the many recent excellent monographs about Islam in Central Asia. The changing practices, habits, and politics surrounding Muslim beliefs and cultural life may turn out to be one of the most dynamic and perhaps surprising aspects of Kazakhstani life in the decades to come.

APPENDIX A

SONGS AND POEMS IN ORIGINAL LANGUAGES

Every effort was made to obtain permissions from the publishers of the songs and poems quoted extensively in this book.

CHAPTER 2

Песня остается с человеком [Pesnia ostaetsia s chelovekom; A Song Remains with You]

Ночью звёзды вдаль плывут по синим рекам,
Утром звёзды гаснут без следа,
Только песня остаётся с человеком,
Песня верный друг твой навсегда.
Через годы, через расстояния,
На любой дороге, в стороне любой
Песне ты не скажешь "до свидания,"
Песня не прощается с тобой!
Наши песни носим в сердце с колыбели,
С песней всюду вместе мы идём,
Сколько песен мы любимым нашим спели,
Сколько мы ещё с тобой споём!
Через годы, через расстояния,
На любой дороге, в стороне любой
Песне ты не скажешь "до свидания,"
Песня не прощается с тобой!

В лютый холод песня нас с тобой согреет,
В жаркий полдень будет как вода,
Тот, кто песни петь и слушать не умеет,

Тот не будет счастлив никогда!

Через годы, через расстояния,

На любой дороге, в стороне любой

Песне ты не скажешь "до свидания,"

Песня не прощается с тобой!

Русские советские песни (1917–1977). Н. Крюков и Я. Шведов. М., «Худож. лит.», 1977 [*Russkie sovetskie pesni* (1917–1977), ed. N. Kriukov and Ia. Shvedov (Moscow: Khudozhestvennaia literatura, 1977)].

CHAPTER 3

"Ёлочка Зелёная" [Elochka zelenaia; Little Green Yule Tree]

Приходит нам праздник

И праздничный город кипит

И каждый купить дом красавицу ёлку спешит.

И тысячи ёлок,

Для тысячи людей,

Приносят веселье но только за несколько дней.

Refrain:

Ёлочка зелёная . . .

И нам на целом свете нет дерева милей.

Ёлочку Зелёную в обиду не дадим.

Ёлочку Зелёную детям сохрани.

Нельзья от нарядной красавицы глаз оторвать.

Часы бьют двенадцать и нужно успеть загадать.

Желание любое исполнит праздничный час.

Нам нравитсья жить и она пусть живёт среди нас.

"В лесу родилась елочка" [V lesu rodilas' elochka; In the Forest a Little Yule Tree Was Born]

В лесу родилась елочка,

В лесу она росла.

Зимой и летом стройная,

Зеленая была.

Метель ей пела песенку:
«Спи, елочка, бай-бай!»
Мороз снежком укутывал:
«Смотри, не замерзай!»

Трусишка зайка серенький
Под ёлочкой скакал.
Порою волк, сердитый волк,
Рысцою пробегал.

Чу! Снег по лесу частому
Под полозом скрипит
Лошадка мохноногая
Торопится, бежит.

Везет лошадка дровенки
На дровнях мужичок
Срубил он нашу ёлочку
Под самый корешок.

И вот она, нарядная,
На праздник к нам пришла,
И много, много радости
Детишкам принесла.

CHAPTER 4

Children's Skit in Televised Nauryz Film

1. Уа, халайық тыңдашы: Мен боламын Жыл басы! Сасып анау сиырын, қапиып екі бұйырым. Сен кімсін менің қасымда? Бар ма түйісін басыңда?

2. Жылдың көзі неме бармақтай, ұрланып барып байқатпай, қуылығыңды асырма, сырымды ішке жасырма. Шықса екі бұйырым, сүті бұлақ сиырмын. Мен боламын жыл басы.

3. Мықты баспын! Алысқанмен алыстым, баршылық барлық бар бардылақты қорғатып. сен қай жақтан жабыстың?

4. Қорқақ емес моянмын, зияны жоқ қоянмын! Қоян жылы қар

қалың,асырап елдің бар малын. Қалың шығар егін шөп,білінер жыл басы деп!

5. Жәндіетердің ішінен ұнаған өзісімен. Жылға лайық Ұлу мен! Құйрығы ұзын шыбалған,сақ болындар -жыланмын!

6. Бұл мен ұлы, шұбар жыланмын. Жүрген жерде ыланмын. Жолыма ешкім тұрмасын! Беріңдер маған жыл басын!

7. Ер қанаты ат деген, біргемін мен адамзатпенен. Мінсе көлік,сүтімді,қымыз деген атпенен,болады адам дәріге. Жетпейсін маған бәрі де.

8. Қойдай қоңыр момын деп, мақтау көрген жылым көп. Қой жылында құт болар,мешін жылы жұт болар. Жыл басы маған құт болар!

9. Мешін деген мешінмін. Мінезіме кесірім мойындама ешкімге. Сайық, мазақ шешімім, бәрінен де пысық, сергекпін. Артықпенен менен кім? Мен боламын жыл басы!

10. Қанатты да тауықпын. Сеземін бәрін қауыптың. Айқайлап таңда аттырған, кеш батса үйге шақырған. Жүрсекте қайда,біз адамға барып қайтамыз. Бізге лайық жыл басы!

11. Суық та да төзіммен, түнде жортқан бөріден, малын қорғап келемін адамзаттың тегінен. Ырыс дейтін ит жылы! Бас боламын тегі мен!

12. Ұмытпандар мені де, демендер жылдан қол үзді. Келсем егер қорсалып, кетесіңдер шошыбақ. Менің де бар керегім! Жыл басы мен көремін!

Comedy Routine in An men Anshi Concert

1: Сержан менің мақтап,баптап,осы сайыстарға дайындап жүрген өзімнің жекеменшік ақыным бар. Қолұстазбын ғой.

2: Сен өзің ақын бола алмай,ақын дайындап жүрсін ба?

1: Сен менің мықты мықты нелерімді білмейсін ғой. Кейін мен саған айтып берем,таныстырам өзімнің шығармашылығымен. Кәзір менің шәкіртім шықсын!

2: Ол қандай ақын?

1: Ой сен байқа! Алдынала ескертіп алайын,ол кішкене нелеу. . . .

2: Нелеу?

1: Ағасы келген кезде,нервный болып кетеді да,шыдай алмайды, содан кейін дұрыс айтыспай қалсан барғой,ағын пағын жүрий санап кетеді.

2: Кімді? Бізді ма?

1: Сені де, ақыныңды да!

2: Сен таяқ жийтін адам тапқан екенсін,менің де ақыным бар! Айтыстырайық!

1: Айтыстырайық!

2: Ақыныңды шақыр.

1: Менің ақыным қайда? Тағы нервы ұстап,бір жаққа кетіп қадған жоқ па?

2: Шақыр!

1: Ол анау мынау шақырымға шықпайды. Құрметті ағайындар,құрметті көрермендер! Менің өзі жеке дайындап жүрген,арқалы ақыным! Спортсмен,ақын,каратист,футболист,боксёрист Дора! Қалайсын? Дайынсын ба? Кішкене еңкейіп істе. Болды,бұл саған тренировка емес. Дискотекада тұрғандай бийлеп кеткен нес? Шақыр!

2: Талай доғалардан байдалған,талай айтыстың бас жүлдесін қанжығасынан байлаған Улан Уде! Біздің ақын бір қалыпта.

1: Мынау ма ақының?

2: Осы кісі.

1: Отырып ал,кім бірінші келеді,сол отырады!

2: Ақырын ойнасаншы ей,ұйықтаған шабытты оятып жібердің ғой. Ақырын ойна!

Дора: Алдартын бұл жамайды ау адам деген. Жалғаннын әр түтібай жалаң деген. Науырыздың бұл тойындай ағайындар сіздерге шын ниетпен сәлем берем! ай ай ай

1: Отыр.

Улан Уде: Мен енді ай айтайын! Халқыма басымды иіп, сәлем берем ай! Содан соң ай жерім менің ай, саған да басымды иіп аяу,сәлем берем ай. Содан соң қарсыласым ай, саған да басымды иіп аяу,сәлем берем. Мен келдім мұн ұядан шекарасы ай. Халқыма жақын барып айу, сәлем берем аяу.

Дора: Біледі моңғол жақтай жатқа халық, қонақты ізипатпен атқаралып. Үкіңіз басыңыздағы ау биік екен, самолёт қағып кетпесін масқара ғып!

Улан Уде: Мен келген оралманмын ай, мұнриядан ай.
Елімді,жерімді аңсап аяу,туған ел топырағына басын ием ай,дәл
мындай бақыт көрмес адам ылғи адам ай. Ел десеу,игіледі ақыл жием
ай! Халқына Қазақстан басымды иемін ай! Алдында ой туған елім ай,
бізде бүгі ай. Елінің керек десен тасын сүйем ай,тасын сүйем ай,сүйем
ай . . . Тас бар ма?

Дора: Тас жоқ!

Улан Уде: Тас жоқ болса,ақындардың басын сүйем ай!

Дора: Қалайша бұл сәлемге ел жиылмас, ағайын қонақ екен енді
Юлдаш! Бұл ұқсап басымды мен ие бермеймін, өйткені біздің бас
нервный бас!

Улан Уде: Үйренген сәлем беру ай,ол жағын өнеріммен дәлелдегем
ай. Бұл саған бас игенім ай аз болып тұрса,мен саған французсша
сәлем берем ай!

-Құдайым кезген тірді кайдан болған, адамым осы ма еді ау арман
қылған? Басым ию керек десен былай тұрсын, мен қазір шыр көбелек
айналдырам ай ай ай! Басын айналдырса, айналдыра берсін, мен
сәлем беріп шығайыншы!

Улан Уде: Әй тоқтай тұр ей! Саған бірге сәлем берем ай. Анасы
барлық сөздің сәлем берем ай, кай жақа ой қашып құтылам деп барады
ай, бәрі бір ұстап алып, сәлем берем ай!

CHAPTER 6

Баллада о солдате [Ballada o soldate; Ballad of a Soldier]

Музыка: В.Соловьев-Седой, Слова: М.Матусовский [Music by V.
Solov'ev-Sedoi; Words by M. Matusovskii]

Полем, вдоль берега крутого
Мимо хат
В серой шинели рядового
Шел солдат.
Шел солдат, преград не зная,
Шел солдат, друзей теряя,
Часто, бывало,
Шел без привала,
Шел вперед солдат.

Шел он ночами грозовыми
В дождь и град.
Песню с друзьями фронтовыми
Пел солдат.
Пел солдат, глотая слезы,
Пел про русские березы,
Про кари очи,
Про дом свой отчий
Пел в пути солдат.

Словно прирос к плечу солдата
Автомат—
Всюду врагов своих заклятых
Бил солдат.
Бил солдат их под Смоленском,
Бил солдат в поселке энском
Пуль не считая,
Глаз не смыкая,
Бил врагов солдат.

Полем, вдоль берега крутого,
Мимо хат.
В серой шинели рядового
Шел солдат.
Шел солдат, слуга Отчизны,
Шел солдат во имя жизни,
Землю спасая,
Мир защищая,
Шел вперед солдат!

"В Землянке" [V zemlianke; In the Dugout]

(Музыка Константин Листов; стихи Алексей Сурков) [Music by Konstantin Listov; poetry by Aleksei Surkov][1]

Бьется в тесной печурке огонь,
На поленьях смола, как слеза.
И поет мне в землянке гармонь
Про улыбку твою и глаза.

Про тебя мне шептали кусты
В белоснежных полях под Москвой,
Я хочу, чтобы слышала ты,
Как тоскует мой голос живой.

Ты сейчас далеко, далеко,
Между нами снега и снега . . .
До тебя мне дойти не легко,
А до смерти—четыре шага

Пой, гармоника, вьюге назло,
Заплутавшее счастье зови!
Мне в холодной землянке тепло
От моей негасимой любви.

"Синий платочек"

There are many versions of this song; the following, which I use in my discussion, is from Нам нельзя без песен. Сост. Ю. Г. Иванов. Муз. редактор С. В. Пьянкова. Смоленск: Русич, 2004. [Nam nel'zia bez pesen, compiled by Iu. G. Ivanov; musical editor S. V. P'iankova (Smolensk: Rusich, 2004).]

"Синий платочек" [Sinii platochek; The Little Blue Kerchief]

(Слова Я. Галицкого и М. Максимова; Музыка Е. Петерсбургского [Words by Ia. Galitskii and M. Maksimov; music by E. Petersburskii])

Синенький скромный платочек
Падал с опущенных плеч.
Ты говорила,
Что не забудешь
Ласковых радостных встреч.
Порой ночной
Мы распрощались с тобой . . .
Нет больше ночек!
Где ты, платочек,
Милый, желанный, родной!

Письма твои получая,
Слышу я голос родной.

И между строчек
Синий платочек
Снова встаёт предо мной.
И мне не раз
Снились в предутренний час
Кудри в платочке,
Синие ночки,
Искорки девичьих глаз.

Помню, как в памятный вечер
Падал платочек твой с плеч,
Как провожала
И обещала
Синий платочек сберечь.
И пусть со мной
Нет сегодня любимой, родной,
Знаю, с любовью
Ты к изголовью
Прячешь платок голубой.

Сколько заветных платочков
Носим мы в сердце с собой!
Радости встречи,
Девичьи плечи
Помним в страде боевой.
За них, родных,
Любимых, желанных таких
Строчит пулеметчик,
За синий платочек,
Что был на плечах дорогих!

"Әлия" [Aliya]

(Music by Seidulla Baiterekov; words by Bakir Tazhibaev)

Қобда, Нева суларын сүйіп өскен
Әсем гүлін құшаққа жиып өскен
Акку құстың бейнебір баласындай
Сұлу сазды, жастықтың күйін кешкен.

Әлия—ару қызы сен халқымның
Әлия—батыр қызы сен халқымның
Ерке құсы сен даламның!

Саған белгі орнаттық мәрмәр тастан
Саған күнде қызыкқан мөлдір аспан
Саған күнде жазылған көркем дастан
Саған күнде құшағын көктем ашқан.

Әлия—ару қызы сен халқымның
Әлия—батыр қызы сен халқымның
Ерке құсы сен даламның!

Шолпан жұлдыз—өзіңсің шоқтай жарық
Көз алмаймыз көркіңнен тоқтай қалып
Туған жердің төсінде мәңгілікке
Тұр ғой сенің жүрегің оттай жанып.

Әлия—ару қызы сен халқымның
Әлия—батыр қызы сен халқымның
Ерке құсы сен даламның!

"И вот опять идём в горы" [I vot opiat' idem v gory; And So, We Go into the Mountains Again]

(author unknown)

И вот опять идём в горы
Мы знаем некуда спешить
Ведь басмачи поймут не скоро,
Что с нами лучше не шутить.
Ведь басмачи поймут не скоро,
Что с нами лучше в мире жить.

Раздался выстрел одиноки
Я быстро за скалу упал.
Ах, слава богу, что не точно
Душман меня на мушку взял.
Ах, слава богу, что не точно

Душман меня на мушку взял.

Лежу я за скалой и вижу
Они спускаются с горы.
В руках английские винтовки,
За поясами топоры.
В руках английские винтовки,
За поясами топоры.

Наглеют прямо на глазах
И стали мы такие злые,
Что не опишешь на словах.
И стали мы такие злые,
Что не опишешь на словах.

И вот опять идём в горы
Мы знаем некуда спешить
Ведь басмачи поймут не скоро,
Что с нами лучше не шутить.
Ведь басмачи поймут не скоро,
Что с нами лучше в мире жить.

"Песня о Пограничниках" or "Зелёная Фурашка"

(author unknown)

Я зелёную фурашку сберегу.
Майский день начищу я на ней звезду.
Буду долго (/пьяным) гулять, не ругай меня, мать,
В этот праздник службу спомнить я хочу.

А она всегда суровая была.
Пусть поёт о том солдатская душа.
Как горела в огне, как тонула в слезе,
Как ночами нас тушила тишина.
Как горела в огне, как тонула в слезе,
Как ночами нас тушила тишина.

Спомним мы с тобой, братишка, про Афган.
Тех парней геройских что остались там.

Пусть напомнить тебе это горечь в вине,

Нашу жизнь на последнем рубеже.

Пусть напомнить тебе это горечь в вине,

Нашу жизнь на последнем рубеже.

Я зелёную фурашку берегу.

Майский день начищу я на ней звезду.

Жавнашколь (Жанкашкой) и Хасан, Тегеран и Афган,

Пусть земля там будет пухом пацанам.

Жавнашколь и Хасан, Тегеран и Афган,

Пусть земля там будет пухом пацанам.

CHAPTER 7

"Түркістан" [Turkestan]

Халықпыз түркі түгі бір

Халықпыз түрі тілі бір

Түркістан тұғыр тірегі

Мұсылман елге

Мұсылман елге діні бір.

Көсілген байтақ жеріміз,

Түркі де қазақ еліміз

Бәріне ортақ түркінің

Түркістан түндік

Түркістан түндік өріміз.

Қайырмасы:

Байтақ қазақ жеріне

Жеке қонған Түркістан,

Аңдары мен бегіне

Мекен болған Түркістан.

Үкіл түркі еліне

Мекке болған Түркістан.

Құндала жатқан мыңдана,

Ерекше жайнап нұрлана,

Түркістан менен тұр дала.

Қазаққа мақтан,
Қазаққа мақтан бұл қала.
Тұрғызып кеткен бабамыз,
Түркістан ғажап қаламыз,
Яссауи,Ахмет күмбезі
Халқымыз мүсіндеп күн көзін.

1. Accessed January 20, 2010, http://ru.wikipedia.org/wiki/Листов,_Константин_Яковлевич.

APPENDIX B

MODIFIED ALA-LC KAZAKH TRANSLITERATION

A a—a

Ә ә—ă

Б б—b

В в—v

Г г—g

Ғ ғ—gh

Д д—d

Е е—e

Ё ё—ë

Ж ж—zh

З з—z

И и—i

Й й—ĭ → i

К к—k

Қ қ—q

Л л—l

М м—m

Н н—n

Ң ң → ng

О о—o

Ө ө → ö¹

П п—p

Р р—r

С с—s

Т т—t

У у—u

Ұ ұ—ū → û

Ү ү —— → ü²

Ф ф—f

Х х—kh

Һ һ → h

Ц ц → ts

Ч ч—ch

Ш ш—sh

Щ щ—shch

Ъ ъ—no transliteration

Ы ы—y

І і—ī → î

Ь ь—'

Э э—ė

Ю ю → iu

Я я → ia

1. For this letter, I use [ö] instead of the ALA-LC's transliteration because it is more universally recognizable as representing this sound.

2. For the same reason as above, I use [ü] for this letter.

GLOSSARY OF TERMS

aitys: A competition between two poet-bards, or *aqynlar*.

aqyn: (Pl. *aqyndar*), a poet-bard who performs solo improvised song, with *dombra* accompaniment.

asatayaq: A shaman's rod, hung with bits of metal.

dombra: A two-stringed, plucked lute with nylon strings.

emshi: Faith healer.

khalyq an: Folk song.

küi: (Pl. *küiler*), an instrumental genre associated with a narrative and with Kazakh philosophy.

oralman: (Pl. *oralmandar*) returnee; refers to Kazakhs from abroad (often from Mongolia and China) who have immigrated to Kazakhstan.

qobyz: A two-stringed horsehair fiddle with skin head.

qongyrau: Bells.

saqpan: Rattles.

shangyraq: Smoke hole of a yurt.

shangqobyz: A Jew's harp.

shirakshi: Shrine keeper.

tuyaq tas: Horse hoofs, played by clapping them together.

sybyzgy: An end-blown flute.

zhetigen: A seven-stringed plucked zither.

zhuz: Umbrella clans

zhyr: Epic song or poem.

zhyrau: (Pl. *zhyraular*), an epic singer.

NOTES

INTRODUCTION

1. The estimated 2015 population of Kazakhstan is 17,544,000 (Encyclopedia Britannica Online, accessed August 3, 2016).

2. Transoxania (Latin, "beyond the Oxus") is the historical name for the region that now comprises most of Uzbekistan, lying between the Amu Darya River and the Syr Darya River.

3. This pass, called the "Jungar Gate," played an important role in early Kazakh history. In the sixteenth century, Kazakh territory extended much farther east into the area across the Tian Shan Mountains in what is now northwest China. In the seventeenth century this eastern territory was lost to the Jungar Mongols in what has come to be known to the Kazakhs as the Great Retreat (Olcott 1995).

4. These three hordes, or "umbrella clans" were the small horde (*kishi zhuz*), middle horde (*orta zhuz*) and large horde (*ulu zhuz*).

5. Clans do not adhere to state borders; many, like Naiman, extend over wide territories in Kyrgyzstan, Uzbekistan, and Kazakhstan. This political and supra/subnational nature of clans has led scholars such as Edward Schatz to contend that shortly after independence clan identity still held more meaning for Kazakhs than national identity (Schatz 2004).

6. The 1891 Steppe Statute stated that all land "in excess of Kazakh needs" was to be handed over to the Ministry of State Properties for redistribution. John Anderson explains that "in practice this soon meant whilst Kazakhs were permitted small amounts of land, much of the best quality land (forty percent was designated 'surplus') was given over to Russian settlers" (Anderson 1997, 15).

7. Forced to settle on limited pastureland, without the possibility of seasonal migration, Kazakh herds starved in massive numbers. A conservative estimate is that 1.5 million Kazakhs died in the resulting famine.

1. SETTING THE SCENE

1. Many of the complaints of this nature were offered by middle-aged and elderly theatergoers, who compared the quality of today's local opera and ballet unfavorably with that of the Soviet era. The complaints of younger Almatyites tended toward what they saw as the irrelevance for today's youth of both European operas and Kazakh operas in the Soviet style, such as *Abay* and *Ablai Khan*. In contrast, *Zheztyrnak* was well attended and well received by younger audience members.

2. "Kazakhstan Minister Gets Musical," BBC, July 9, 2003, http://news.bbc.co.uk/go/pr/fr/-/2/hi/entertainment/3056270.stm.

3. The foundation has many branches; the Aga Khan Trust for Culture, for example, "focuses on the physical, social, cultural and economic revitalisation of communities in the Muslim world," Aga Khan Foundation website, accessed June 29, 2011, https://www.akdn.org/our-agencies/aga-khan-trust-culture.

4. All translations are mine unless otherwise indicated.

5. Tuva is part of the Altai region, which lies at the intersection of Russia, Mongolia, China, and Kazakhstan.

6. Inner Asian animism is a form of nature worship in which the natural world is believed to be inhabited by spirits that, for example, dwell in a stream, rock, tree, or mountain.

7. A Kazakh yurt is a portable dwelling made of wooden accordion-like expandable "ribs" covered with thick felt to create walls. A smoke hole is left open at the center of the roof, where the round crisscrossed wooden center piece (*shangyraq*) functions as a kind of circular cornerstone for the structure.

2. AIRING INDEPENDENCE

Epigraph: Zadie Smith, NPR, November 25, 2016.

1. World War II is known as the Great Patriotic War in Kazakhstan and other post-Soviet spaces.

2. For an excellent encapsulation, see the examination by the media studies scholars Jostein Gripsrud and Hallvard Moe of changes in the meaning of the term "public sphere" as it was adopted in media studies particularly in relation to civil society (Gripsrud and Moe 2010), and the social theorist Kirk Wetters's *Opinion System: Impasses of the Public Sphere from Hobbes to Habermas* (Wetters 2008).

3. The Russian word for prosperity is *blagodenstvie*, which carries implications that the English does not. The Russian word implies that prosperity is a result of good deeds, like a mitzvah. The Golden Man is a Saka statue estimated to be from the third or fourth

century BCE. It was discovered in a burial site at Issyk Kurgan, not far from Almaty, and has been adopted as a national symbol of Kazakhstan. Though Kazakhs are not generally accepted as existing as a named group until the fifteenth or sixteenth century, earlier Turkic civilizations like the Saka are folded into the early Kazakh history; claiming the Golden Man as "Kazakh" serves to strengthen Kazakh nationhood by supplying deeper roots. The snow leopard is native to the region and has been adopted as a national symbol.

4. Dinmukhamed Konaev, whom Kolbin replaced as the first secretary of the Communist Party of the Kazakh SSR, was an ethnic Kazakh.

5. "Anti-Soviet Stirrings, Timeline: Kazakhstan," BBC website, accessed July 1, 2008, https://www.bbc.com/news/world-asia-pacific-15483497.

6. The snow leopard, a symbol of Kazakhstan that appears in many state and local government emblems, is a powerful and rare animal native to the mountainous regions of Central Asia. The warrior figure is a replica of a Sakha warrior (dated to about the third century BCE) found in an archaeological dig fifty kilometers east of Almaty in the rural area of Issyk. The warrior, dubbed the Golden Man, was clothed in a golden peaked hat and a leather tunic completely covered with thousands of arrow-shaped gold ornaments. The warrior, discovered in 1969, was originally thought to be male, but since 1997 scholars have pointed to evidence suggesting the warrior was in fact a woman (Davis-Kimball 1997).

7. Stalin was very influential in the People's Republic of China before the Sino-Soviet split (which began with Khrushchev's denouncement of Stalin in 1956) and his writings on the Soviet nationalities policy were used to form the basis of Chinese policy toward its minority nationalities. The seminal concepts in these writings still persist in Chinese festival performances and minority policies.

8. See Ostrovskii 1997.

9. The son of the poets Anna Akhmatova and Nikolai Gumilev, Lev Gumilev concentrated his early scholarly studies on ancient Turks and geography. His many books on ancient Turkic and Slavic peoples, including *Ancient Turks* (1967) and *Ancient Russia and the Great Steppe* (1989a), constitute a major contribution to this area of Soviet scholarship.

10. Author's translation of the audio recording.

11. The Assembly of Nations is the post-Soviet incarnation of Dom Druzhby (the House of Friendship), the official headquarters of the government-sponsored minority nationalities organizations. All dance troupes and minority performance groups that appear at official functions are organized through the assembly.

12. In particular, see Huyssen 2000; Kligler-Vilenchik, Tsfati, and Meyers 2014; Landsberg 2004; Olick 2003; Tilmans, van Vree, and Winter 2010; and Winter 1995, 2006.

3. SAME TIME NEXT YEAR

1. On a dark January evening, my friend broke out a guitar and played favorites from *The Irony of Fate*. Everyone knew the words.

2. See, e.g., Ahmed 2011; Crapanzano 2004; Dawdy 2010; Halberstam 2015; Jameson 2007; Olma 2007; Tsing 2015.

3. See Kurt Koffka's classic *Principles of Gestalt Psychology* and also Maurice Merleau Ponty's *Phenomenology of Perception*.

4. The Internet Movie Database (www.imdb.com) is a comprehensive database that includes film details as well as commentary by visitors to the website.

5. "Nikogo ne budet v dome" [No One Will Be at Home], in Pasternak (1989 [1931], 404).

6. "Sneg idet" [Snow Is Falling], in Pasternak (1989 [1957], 108–9.

7. The Russian word is an archaic form, meaning something like embrasure, a thick-walled, slanted window opening.

8. Tengri is the god of the animist beliefs prominent in this area before the advent of Islam. Still present in parts of Inner Asia (Kazakhstan, Mongolia, Siberia), Tengri-anism, or animism, is a form of nature worship, which holds that spirits reside in every stream, mountain, rock, and tree. Believers leave offerings at sacred springs and trees, tying pieces of white cloths to branches and stones. In Tuva, "sonic offerings" are given, in the form of throat-singing, which often imitates animals, birds, or even streams situated in these places (Levin 2006).

9. Some groups moved four times, having four basic campgrounds, one each for spring, summer, fall, and winter, but many Kazakhs in the nineteenth century, partially as an adaptation to seminomadic life, had two basic camping places, the summer campground (zhailau), and the winter campground (kistau), moving between them during the spring and fall (Olcott 1995, 90–98).

10. "Aul" is a term that now means "village" or "countryside," but it also refers to a settlement of people, i.e., a unit of people who nomadize and camp together.

11. The author's name rendered in Kazakh is Шәкәрім Құдайбердіұлы and in Russian, Шакарим Кудайбердиев. The title of the song in Kazakh is "Бұл ән бұрынғы әннен өзгерек."

4. AN ARCHAEOLOGY OF NAURYZ

Epigraph: William James, *The Principles of Psychology*, 1890, vol. 1, p. 1406; and Nursultan Nazarbaev, "Qazaqstan Tarihy," July 6, 2018, https://e-history.kz/en/publications/view/4255.

1. See especially scholarship in anthropology (Crapanzano 2004; Dawdy 2010, 2016; Herzfeld 2009; Mankekar 2015), archaeology (Bailey 2007; Olivier 2003, 2013; Witmore

2006), popular culture studies and literary criticism (Jameson 2007; Kaplan 2015; Morris 2012), and queer studies (Ahmed 2011; Halberstam 2011; McCallum and Tuhkanen 2011; Muñoz 2009; Tuhkanen 2007; Villarejo 2014).

2. Both Chagatay Turkic and Persian were in use in the Mughal Empire. Persian was the language of the urban population and the literate elite, whereas Chagatay was more common among rural Turkic peoples of the region as well as Babur's native language. He wrote the *Bāburnāma* in Chagatai Turkic.

3. The Shekty (Шэкты) were a Kazakh tribe of the Lesser Horde (Кiшi Жуз) during the sixteenth century.

4. Traditions of Kazakhtan, Mediaset; translation by the author.

5. Kazakhstan Channel; translation by the author.

6. *Ulu* literally means snail, but many think it is a permutation of the dragon in the Chinese calendar. Another theory holds that this zodiac sign was originally a Wolf, as the Kazakh word for howl (*uluu*) closely resembles this word.

7. Zhut is a late spring freeze, a very dangerous condition for Inner Asian nomads.

8. Kazakhstan Channel; translation by the author.

9. The Camel sometimes appears in place of the Horse in the Kazakh zodiac. Because both camels and horses are riding animals and provide milk products for Central Asian nomads, they are sometimes interchangeable in Central Asian stories.

5. TRAVELING HISTORIES

Epigraph: Colson Whitehead, *The Underground Railroad* (2016).

1. *Prefrontier*, as discussed by Ruben Andersson, involves authorities, aided by technology *anticipating* migrants' crossing (Andersson 2014). *Punctuation* involves different levels of obstruction at borders for different categories of people (Smart and Smart 2008).

2. The Russian acronym is ATsTs.

3. My translation of the original Russian interview.

4. Suchan, now Partizansk, is a town in Primorsky krai, at the foothills of the Sikhote-Alin Mountains. Suchan, at the southern coastal edge of the krai, is nearly the farthest southeast one can get in the Soviet Union. Its Russian name was changed to Partizansk in 1972 during a push to cleanse Chinese toponyms in Outer Manchuria.

5. The numbers of Jews in Kazakhstan rose considerably in the years just before and after the war, increasing from 3,600 in 1936 to 28,000 by 1959 (EAJC).

6. Yiddish had previously had been considered a nonliterary colloquial language, acceptable only for the writing for and by women; Hebrew was the preferred literary language of learned Eastern European Jews.

7. Recorded by the author, with a transcription by Taylor Ackley, 2017.

6. PLAYING AT WAR

Epigraph: Edward S. Casey, *Remembering* (2000 [1987]).

1. For scholarship on memory and commemoration, see: Abramson 1999; Alexander et al. 2004; Benjamin 2003 [1940]; Bodnar 1992; Casanova 1994; Casey 2000 [1987]; Corney 2003; Halbwachs 1992 [1925]; Landsberg 2004, 2009; Mousoutzanis 2013; Olick 2003; Pearce 2009; Ricoeur 2004; Winter 1995, 2006.

2. Casey borrows this from Confucian rituals and philosophy (Casey 2000 [1987], 229).

3. The historian Tony Judt notes the staggering numbers of civilian deaths, which, at roughly sixteen million, is nearly double the number of Soviet military losses (Judt 2005, 18).

4. One war memorial in Almaty's Panfilov Park continues to play its recordings around the clock, all year long.

5. Central Eurasian Studies Society, Bloomington, Indiana, 2011.

6. Several versions of this song have been published. The following version is from the songbook, *Nam nel'zia bez pesen'* (We Cannot Live without Songs) (Ivanov 2004).

7. THE PRECARIOUS PRESENT AND THE CITY OF THE FUTURE

Epigraph: Sara Ahmed, "Happy Futures, Perhaps" (2011).

1. Kassenova cites two polls, in 2014 and 2016, indicating similar numbers. The 2016 poll by the Association of Sociologists and Political Scientists of Kazakhstan (ASiP) shows 97.9 percent of Kazakh language–speaking Kazakhs and 80 percent of Russian language–speaking Kazakhs as Muslims. The 2014 poll by the Friedrich Ebert Foundation shows similar results with 96.9 percent of Kazakhs self-identifying as Muslim.

2. The making of three pilgrimages to Turkistan is considered by many Kazakhstanis to be the equivalent of a hajj to Mecca.

3. Accessed January 12, 2012, http://prosites-kazakhembus.homestead.com/Turkestan.html.

4. Ministerial conference Common World: Progress through Diversity, October 17, 2008, accessed January 12, 2010, http://www.embkazjp.org/additionalpages/special26102008.htm.

5. Ministerial conference Common World, October 17, 2008, accessed January 12, 2010.

REFERENCES

Abramson, Daniel. 1999. "Make History, Not Memory." Special issue, "Constructions of Memory: On Monuments Old and New." *Harvard Design Magazine* 9: 78–83.

Adams, Laura. 2010. *The Spectacular State: Culture and National Identity in Uzbekistan.* Durham, NC: Duke University Press.

Ahmed, Sara. 2010. *The Promise of Happiness.* Durham, NC: Duke University Press.

Ahmed, Sara. 2011. "Happy Futures, Perhaps." In McCallum and Tuhkanen, *Queer Times, Queer Becomings,* 159–82.

Akbarzadeh, Shahram. 2001. Political Islam in Kyrgyzstan and Turkmenistan. *Central Asian Survey* 20, no. 4: 451–65.

Alexander, Jeffrey C, Ron Eyerman, Bernard Giesen, Neil Smelser, and Piotr Sztompka. 2004. *Cultural Trauma and Collective Identity.* Berkeley: University of California Press.

Amanov, Bagdaulet, and Asiya Mukhambetova. 2002. *Kazakhskaia Traditsionnaia Muzyka i XX Vek* [Kazakh Traditional Music and the Twentieth Century]. Almaty: Daik-Press.

Amrekulov, Nurlan, and Nurbulat Masanov. 1994. *Kazakhstan mezhdu proshlym i budushchem* [Kazakhstan between the Past and the Present]. Almaty.

Anacker, Shonin. 2004. "Geographies of Power in Nazarbayev's Astana." *Eurasian Geography and Economics* 45, no. 7: 515–33.

Anash, Duman. 2005. "Dombyranyng kumbiri komputerding tiline kone me?" *Azamat* 1, no. 1, March 17, 2005.

Anderson, John. 1997. *The International Politics of Central Asia.* Manchester: Manchester University Press.

Andersson, Ruben. 2014. "Time and the Migrant Other: European Border Controls and the Temporal Economics of Illegality." *American Anthropologist* 116, no. 4: 795–809.

Asad, Talal. 1986. "The Idea of an Anthropology of Islam." Occasional Paper Series. Washington, DC: Center for Contemporary Arab Studies, Georgetown University.

Bailey, G. N. 2007. Time Perspectives, Palimpsests and the Archaeology of Time. *Journal of Anthropological Archaeology* 26: 198–223.

Ballinger, Pamela. 2012. Borders and the Rhythms of Displacement, Emplacement and Mobility. In *The Blackwell Companion to Border Studies*, edited by Thomas Wilson and Hastings Donnan, 389–404. Oxford: Blackwell.

Bardic Divas: Women's Voices in Central Asia. The Music of Central Asia, vol. 4, 2007. Various artists. Theodore Levin and Joel Gordon, producers. Smithsonian Folkways, SFW40523.

Bassin, Mark. 2016. *The Gumilev Mystique: Biopolitics, Eurasianism, and the Construction of Community in Modern Russia*. Ithaca, NY: Cornell University Press.

Begalin, Mazhit. 1968. *Za nami Moskva* [Moscow Is Behind Us]. Kazakhfilm.

Behar, Ruth, and Lucia M. Suarez. 2008. *The Portable Island: Cubans at Home in the World*. New York: Palgrave Macmillan.

Belasco, Warren. 2006. *Meals to Come: A History of the Future of Food*. California Studies in Food and Culture. Berkeley: University of California Press.

Benjamin, Walter. 2003 [1940]. "On the Concept of History." In *Selected Writings*, vol. 4: 1938–1940. Translated by Harry Zohn. Cambridge, MA: Harvard University Press.

Berger, Harris M. 2010. *Stance: Ideas about Emotion, Style, and Meaning for the Study of Expressive Culture*. Middletown, CT: Wesleyan University Press.

Bloch, Alexia. 2003. *Red Ties and Residential Schools: Indigenous Siberians in a Post-Soviet State*. Philadelphia: University of Pennsylvania Press.

Bodnar, John E. 1992. *Remaking America: Public Memory, Commemoration, and Patriotism in the Twentieth Century*. Princeton, NJ: Princeton University Press.

Born, Georgina. 2010. "For a Relational Musicology: Music and Interdisciplinarity, beyond the Practice Turn." *Journal of the Royal Musical Association* 135, no. 2: 205–43.

Boym, Svetlana. 2001. *The Future of Nostalgia*. New York: Basic Books.

Buchli, V. 2007. "Astana: Materiality and the City." In *Urban Life in Post-Soviet Asia*, edited by C. Alexander, V. Buchli, and C. Humphrey, 40–69. London: University College London Press.

Byman, Caroline Walker. 1987. *Holy Feast and Holy Fast: The Religious Significance of Food to Medieval Women*. Berkeley: University of California Press.

Cameron, Sarah. 2018. *The Hungry Steppe: Famine, Violence, and the Making of Soviet Kazakhstan*. Ithaca, NY: Cornell University Press.

Casanova, José. 1994. *Public Religions in the Modern World*. Chicago: University of Chicago Press.

Casey, Edward S. 2000 [1987]. *Remembering: A Phenomenological Study*, 2nd ed. Bloomington: Indiana University Press.

Chabad of Kazakhstan. http://www.chabad.kz/35373.html.

Claflin, Kyri W., and Peter Scholliers, eds. 2012. *Writing Food History: A Global Perspective*. New York: Berg.

Collins, Randall. 2004. *Interaction Ritual Chains*. Princeton, NJ: Princeton University Press.

Corney, Frederick C. 2003. "Rethinking a Great Event: The October Revolution as Memory Project." In *States of Memory: Continuities, Conflicts, and Transformations in National Retrospection*, ed. Jeffrey K. Olick, 17–42. Durham, NC: Duke University Press.

Crapanzano, Vincent. 2004. *Imaginative Horizons: An Essay in Literary-Philosophical Anthropology*. Chicago: University of Chicago Press.

Cummings, Sally N. 1998. "The Kazakhs: Demographics, Diasporas, and 'Return.'" In *Nations Abroad*, edited by Charles King and Neil J. Melvin, 133–52. Boulder: Westview Press.

Daukeyeva, Saida. 2016. "Gender in Kazakh *Dombyra* Performance." *Ethnomusicology Forum* 25, no. 3: 283–305.

Davis-Kimball, Jeannine. 1997. "Chieftain or Warrior Priestess." *Archaeology*, September 1997: 40–41.

Dawdy, Shannon. 2010. "Clockpunk Anthropology and the Ruins of Modernity." *Current Anthropology* 51, no. 6: 761–93.

Dawdy, Shannon Lee. 2016. *Patina: A Profane Archaeology*. Chicago: University of Chicago Press.

Dayan, Daniel, and Elihu Katz. 1992. *Media Events: The Live Broadcasting of History*. Cambridge, MA: Harvard University Press.

Diener, Alexander. 2009. *One Homeland or Two? The Nationalization and Transnationalization of Mongolia's Kazakhs*. Stanford, CA: Stanford University Press.

Dietz, Barbara, Uwe Lebok, and Pavel Polian. 2002. "The Jewish Emigration from the Former Soviet Union to Germany." *International Migration* 40, no. 2: 29–48.

Do, Tess. 2013. "Food and Crime Fiction: Two Complementary Approaches to the Vietnamese Past in Tran-Nhut's *Les travers du docteur Porc*." *PORTAL: Journal of Multidisciplinary International Studies* 10, no. 2. DOI:10.5130/portal.v10i2.3030.

Donnan, Hastings, Madeleine Hurd, and Carolin Leutloff-Grandits. 2017. *Migrating Borders and Moving Times: Temporality and the Crossing of Borders in Europe*. Manchester: Manchester University Press.

Doss, Erika. 2010. *Memorial Mania: Public Feeling in America*. Chicago: University of Chicago Press.

Drake, Carolyn. 2006. "A Faith Grows in Brooklyn: A Movement Embracing Old-World Orthodox Judaism Is Alive and Thriving in New York City." *National Geographic Magazine*, February 2006.

Dubisch, Jill. 1995. *In a Different Place: Pilgrimage, Gender, and Politics at a Greek Island Shrine*. Princeton, NJ: Princeton University Press.

Dubuisson, Eva-Marie. 2017. *Living Language in Kazakhstan: The Dialogic Emergence of an Ancestral Worldview*. Pittsburgh: University of Pittsburgh Press.

Dugin, Aleksandr. 2004. *Evraziiskaia Missiia Nursultana Nazarbaeva* [Nursultan Nazarbaev's Eurasian Mission]. Moscow: Evraziia.

Egemberdieva, Aida, and G. A. Aïtpaeva. 2009. *Sacred Sites of Ysyk-Köl: Spiritual Power, Pilgrimmage, and Art.* Bishkek: Aigine Cultural Research Center.

Elemanova, Saida. 2001. Kazakhstan: Opera, Orchestral and Chamber Music. In *The New Grove Dictionary of Music and Musicians*, 2nd ed., edited by Stanley Sadie, 431–38. London: Macmillan.

Euro-Asian Jewish Congress (EAJC). "History of the Kazakhstan Jewish Community." Accessed September 9, 2017, http://jewseurasia.org/page270.

Farquhar, Judith. 2002. *Appetites: Food and Sex in Postsocialist China.* Durham, NC: Duke University Press.

Fathi, Habiba, 2006. "Gender, Islam, and Social Change in Uzbekistan." *Central Asian Survey* 25, no. 3: 303–17.

Féaux de la Croix, Jeanne. 2016. *Iconic Places in Central Asia: The Moral Geography of Dams, Pastures and Holy Sites.* Culture and Social Practice Series. Bielefeld: transcript Verlag.

Ferziger, Adam S. 2012. "'Outside the Shul': The American Soviet Jewry Movement and the Rise of Solidarity Orthodoxy, 1964–1986." *Religion and American Culture: A Journal of Interpretation* 22, no. 1: 83–130.

Friedson, Steven M. 2009. *Remains of Ritual: Northern Gods in a Southern Land.* Chicago: University of Chicago Press.

Frolova-Walker, Marina. 1998. "National in Form, Socialist in Content: Musical Nation-Building in the Soviet Republics." *Journal of the American Musicological Society* 4, no. 2: 331–71.

Gaibazzi, Paul. 2015. *Young Men and Rural Permanence in Migrant West Africa.* New York: Berghahn Books.

Gellner, Ernest. 1996. *Conditions of Liberty: Civil Society and Its Rivals.* London: Penguin Books.

Grant, Bruce. 1995. *In the Soviet House of Culture: A Century of Perestroikas.* Princeton, NJ: Princeton University Press.

Gripsrud, J., and H. Moe, eds. 2010. *The Digital Public Sphere: Challenges for Media Policy.* Gothenborg: Nordicom.

Gumilev, L. N. (Lev Nikolaevich). 1967. *Drevnie Tiurki* [Ancient Turks]. Moscow: Nauka.

Gumilev, L. N. (Lev Nikolaevich). 1989a. *Drevniaia Rus' i Velikaia Step'* [Ancient Russia and the Great Steppe]. Moscow: Mysl'.

Gumilev, L. N. (Lev Nikolaevich). 1989b. *Etnogenez i biosfera Zemli* [Ethnogenesis and the Biosphere of Earth]. Leningrad: Izdatel'stvo Leningrada Universiteta.

Habermas, Jürgen. 1989 [1962]. *The Structural Transformation of the Public Sphere: An Inquiry into a Category of Bourgeois Society,* Cambridge: Polity.

HadžiMuhamedović, Safet. 2018. *Waiting for Elijah: Time and Encounter in a Bosnian Landscape*. New York: Berghahn Books.

Halberstam, Judith. 2005. *In a Queer Time and Place: Transgender Bodies, Subcultural Lives*. New York: New York University Press.

Halberstam, Judith. 2011. "Keeping Time with Lesbians on Ecstasy." In McCallum and Tuhkanen, *Queer Times, Queer Becomings*, 333–48.

Halbwachs, Maurice. 1992 [1925]. *On Collective Memory*. Edited and translated by Lewis A. Coser. Chicago: University of Chicago Press.

Harris, Rachel. 2008. *The Making of a Musical Canon in Chinese Central Asia: The Uyghur Twelve Muqam*. Aldershot: Ashgate Press.

Hawkins, Stan. 2016. *Queerness in Pop Music: Aesthetics, Gender Norms, and Temporality*. Routledge Studies in Popular Music. New York: Routledge.

Hayden, Bridget. 2010. "The Hand of God: Capitalism, Inequality, and Moral Geographies in Mississippi after Hurricane Katrina." *Anthropological Quarterly* 83, no. 1: 177–203.

Heidegger, Martin. 1962. *Being and Time*. Translated by John Macquarrie and Edward Robinson. New York: Harper and Row.

Heilman, Samuel C. 2005. "How Did Fundamentalism Manage to Infiltrate Contemporary Orthodoxy?" *Contemporary Jewry* 258: 258–72.

Heilman, Samuel C., and Menachem Friedman. 2010. *The Rebbe: The Life and Afterlife of Menachem Mendel Schneerson*. Princeton, NJ: Princeton University Press.

Herzfeld, Michael. 2009. "Rhythm, Tempo, and Historical Time: Experiencing Temporality in the Neoliberal Age." *Public Archaeology: Archaeological Ethnographies* 8, no. 2–3: 108–23.

Humphrey, Caroline. 1999. "Shamans in the City." *Anthropology Today* 15, no. 3: 3–10.

Humphrey, Caroline. 2002. "'Eurasia': Ideology and the Political Imaginiation in Provincial Russia." In *Postsocialism: Ideals, Ideologies and Practices in Eurasia*, edited by C. M. Hann, 258–76. New York: Routledge.

Humphrey, Caroline, and David Sneath. 1999. *The End of Nomadism? Society, State and the Environment in Inner Asia*. Durham, NC: Duke University Press.

Huxtable, Simon, Sabina Mihelj, Alice Bardan, and Sylwiz Szostak. 2017. "Festive Television in the Socialist World: From Media Events to Media Holidays." *Journal of Popular Television* 67, no. 19: 49–67.

Huyssen, Andreas. 2000. "Present Pasts: Media, Politics, Amnesia." *Public Culture* 12, no. 1: 21–38.

Ivanov, Iu. G., ed. 2004. *Nam nel'zia bez pesen'* [We Cannot Live without Songs]. Smolensk: Rusich.

Jameson, Frederic. 2007. *Archaeologies of the Future: The Desire Called Utopia and Other Science Fictions*. London: Verso.

Jones, Pauline. 2017. *Islam, Society, and Politics in Central Asia.* Pittsburgh: University of Pittsburgh Press.

Judt, Tony. 2005. *Postwar: A History of Europe since 1945.* New York: Penguin Books.

Kammen, Michael G. 2004. *A Time to Every Purpose: The Four Seasons in American Culture.* Chapel Hill: University of North Carolina Press.

Kaplan, E. Ann. 2015. *Climate Trauma: Foreseeing the Future in Dystopian Film and Fiction.* New Brunswick, NJ: Rutgers University Press.

Kassenova, Nargis. 2018. "Kazakhstan: Islamic Revival and Trajectories of State-Society Relations." In *Religion, Conflict, and Stability in the Former Soviet Union*, edited by Katya Migacheva and Bryan Frederick, 115–36. Santa Monica, CA: Rand Corporation.

Kershen, Anne J. 2014. "Food in the British Immigrant Experience." *Crossings: Journal Of Migration and Culture* 5, no. 2–3: 201–11.

Kim, Daniel. 2014. "Twenty-Five Years of Central Asia Mission." InterCP, May 25, 2014. http://www.intercp.org/2014/05/25-years-of-central-asia-mission-part-1/.

Kim, German. 2004. "Koreans in Kazakhstan, Uzbekistan, and Russia." In *Encyclopedia of Diasporas*, edited by Carol R. Ember, Melvin Ember, and Ian A. Skoggard, 985–93. New York: Kluwer Academic/Plenum.

Kim, Sveta. 2015. Personal interview with the author, July 26, 2015. Almaty, Kazakhstan.

Kligler-Vilenchik, Neta, Yariv Tsfati, and Oren Meyers. 2014. "Setting the Collective Memory Agenda: Examining Mainstream Media Influence on Individuals' Perceptions of the Past." *Memory Studies* 7, no. 4: 484–99.

Koen, Benjamin. 2011. *Beyond the Roof of the World: Music, Prayer, and Healing in the Pamir Mountains.* Oxford: Oxford University Press.

Kotkin, Stephen. 2001. *Armageddon Averted: The Soviet Collapse, 1970–2000.* Oxford: Oxford University Press.

Kudaibergenova, Diana. 2016. "'My Silk Road to You': Re-imagining Routes, Roads, and Geography in Contemporary Art of 'Central Asia.'" *Journal of Eurasian Studies* 8: 31–43.

Kudaibergenova, Diana. 2017. "Contemporary Public Art and Nation: Contesting 'Tradition' in Post-Socialist Cultures and Societies." *Central Asian Affairs* 4: 305–30.

Kuzmenko, Inna. 2015. Interview with Lyubov Emolenko. "Stone Figures are the Great Monuments in the Steppe." *National Digital History of Kazakhstan*, January 8, 2015.

Landsberg, Alison. 2004. *Prosthetic Memory: The Transformation of American Remembrance in the Age of Mass Culture.* New York: Columbia University Press.

Landsberg, Alison. 2009. "Memory, Empathy, and the Politics of Identification." *International Journal of Politics, Culture, and Society* 22, no. 2: 221–29.

Laszczkowski, Mateusz, 2016. *"City of the Future": Built Space, Modernity and Urban Change in Astana.* New York: Berghahn Books.

LeBlanc, Ronald D. 1999. "Food, Orality, and Nostalgia for Childhood." *Russian Review* 58: 244–67.

Levin, Theodore. 1996. *The Hundred Thousand Fools of God: Musical Travels in Central Asia (and Queens, New York)*. Bloomington: Indiana University Press.

Levin, Theodore with Valentina Süzükei. 2006. *Where Rivers and Mountains Sing: Sound, Music, and Nomadism in Tuva and Beyond*. Bloomington: Indiana University Press.

Lillis, Joanna. 2019. *Dark Shadows: Inside the Secret World of Kazakhstan*. London: I. B.Tauris.

Liu, Morgan Y. 2012. *Under Solomon's Throne: Uzbek Visions of Renewal in Osh*. Central Eurasia in Context. Pittsburgh: University of Pittsburgh Press.

Louw, Maria Elisabeth. 2014. *Everyday Islam in Post-Soviet Central Asia*. London: Routledge.

Lustiger, Arno. 2003. *Stalin and the Jews: The Red Book: The Tragedy of the Jewish Anti-Fascist Committee and the Soviet Jews*. New York: Enigma Books.

Mankekar, Purnima. 2015. *Unsettling India: Affect, Temporality, Transnationality*. Durham, NC: Duke University Press.

Manuel, Peter. 2012. "The Trajectories of Transplants: Singing Alhā, Birhā, and the Rāmāyan in the Indic Caribbean." *Asian Music* 43, no. 22: 115–54.

McBrien, Julie. 2017. *From Belonging to Belief: Modern Secularisms and the Construction of Religion in Kyrgyzstan*. Pittsburgh: University of Pittsburgh Press.

McCallum, E. L., and Tuhkanen, Mikko, eds. 2011. *Queer Times, Queer Becomings*. Albany: State University of New York Press.

McGraw, Andrew Clay. 2013. *Ombak: Time, Energy, and Homology in the Analysis of Balinese Music*. New York: Oxford University Press.

Merchant, Tanya. 2015. *Women Musicians of Uzbekistan: From Courtyard to Conservatory*. Urbana: University of Illinois Press.

Michaels, Paula. 2003. *Curative Powers: Medicine and Empire in Stalin's Central Asia*. Pittsburgh: University of Pittsburgh Press.

Montgomery, David W. 2016. *Practicing Islam: Knowledge, Experience, and Social Navigation in Kyrgyzstan*. Pittsburgh: University of Pittsburgh Press, 2016.

Morris, Susana M. 2012. "Black Girls Are from the Future: Afrofuturist Feminism in Octavia E. Butler's 'Fledgling.'" *Women's Studies Quarterly* 40, no. 3: 146–66.

Mousoutzanis, Aris. 2013. "Trauma, Memory and Information in American Science Fiction Film and Television, 1980–2010." *Science Fiction Film and Television* 6, no. 3: 327–48.

Muhambetova, Asiya Ibadullaevna. 1995. "The Traditional Musical Culture of Kazakhs in the Social Context of the 20th Century." *World of Music* 37, no. 3: 66–83.

Mukhtarova, G. R. 2009. *Qazaqstandaghy Islam dīnī : qazhylyq (XIX–XX gh. basy): materialdar zhinaghy*. Almaty: Baspalar ÿÏï.

Muñoz, José Esteban. 2009. *Cruising Utopia: The Then and There of Queer Futurity*. New York: New York University Press.

Nazarbaev, Nursultan. 2005. *V serdtse Evraziia* [In the Heart of Eurasia]. Almaty: Atamura.

Nazarbayev [Nazarbaev], Nursultan. 2009. Address at the Third Congress of Leaders of World and Traditional Religions, Palace of Peace and Concord, October 10, 2009. Accessed January 12, 2010, http://www.religions-congress.org/content/view/197/34/lang,english/.

Noon, David Hoogland. 2004. "Operation Enduring Analogy: World War II, the War on Terror, and the Use of Historical Memory." *Rhetoric and Public Affairs* 7, no. 3: 339–64.

Northrop, Douglas. 2004. *Veiled Empire: Gender and Power in Stalinist Central Asia*. Ithaca, NY: Cornell University Press.

Olcott, Martha Brill. 1995. *The Kazakhs*. Studies of Nationalities. Stanford, CA: Stanford University Press.

Olick, Jeffrey, ed. 2003. *States of Memory: Continuities, Conflicts, and Transformations in National Retrospection*. Durham, NC: Duke University Press.

Olivier, Laurent. 2003. "The Past of the Present: Archaeological Memory and Time." *Archaeological Dialogues* 10, no. 2: 204–13.

Olivier, Laurent. 2011. *The Dark Abyss of Time: Memory and Archaeology*. Lanham, MD: Altamira Press.

Olivier, Laurent. 2013. "The Business of Archaeology Is the Present." In *Reclaiming Archaeology: Beyond the Tropes of Modernity*, edited by Alfredo González-Ruibal, 117–29. Abingdon: Routledge.

Olma, Sebastian. 2007. "Physical Bergsonism and the Worldliness of Time." *Theory, Culture and Society* 24, no. 6: 123–37.

Olsen, Bjørnar. 2012. *Archaeology: The Discipline of Things*. Berkeley: University of California Press.

Ostrovskii, Arkadii. 1997. *Pesnia ostaetsia s chelovekom* [A Song Remains with You]. Moscow: Vserossiiskaia gosudarstvennaia televizionnaia i radioveshchatel'naia kompaniia.

Pannier, Bruce. 2006. "Kazakhstan: Zheltoqsan Protest Marked 20 Years Later." Radio Free Europe, Radio Liberty, December 14, 2006.

Parasecoli, Fabio. 2008. *Bite Me: Food in Popular Culture*. Oxford: Berg.

Pasternak, Boris. 1989 [1931]. *Boris Pasternak: sobranie sochinennii v piati tomakh. Tom pervyi: Stikhotvoreniia i poemy 1912–1931* [Boris Pasternak Collected Works in Five Volumes. Volume 1: Poems 1912–1931].

Pasternak, Boris. 1989 [1957]. *Boris Pasternak: sobranie sochinennii v piati tomakh. Tom vtoroi: Stikhotvoreniia 1931–1959* [Boris Pasternak Collected Works in Five Volumes. Volume 2: Poems 1931–1959].

Pearce, Susan C. 2009. "The Polish Solidarity Movement in Retrospect: In Search of a Mnemonic Mirror." *International Journal of Politics, Culture, and Society* 22, no. 2: 159–82.

Peshkova, Svetlana. 2014. *Women, Islam, and Identity: Public Life in Private Spaces in Uzbekistan.* Syracuse, NY: Syracuse University Press.

Pew Research Center. *Religion and Public Life.* The Worlds Muslims: Unity and Diversity, Demographic Study, August 9, 2012. Accessed September 5, 2017, http://www .pewforum.org/2012/08/09/the-worlds-muslims-unity-and-diversity-4-other-be liefs-and-practices/.

Polian, Pavel. 2004. *Against Their Will: The History and Geography of Forced Migrations in the USSR.* New York: Central European University Press.

Porcello, Thomas. 1998. "'Tails Out': Social Phenomenology and the Ethnographic Representation of Technology in Music-Making." *Ethnomusicology* 42, no. 3: 485–510.

Post, Jennifer C. 2007. "'I Take My Dombra and Sing to Remember My Homeland': Identity, Landscape and Music in Kazakh Communities of Western Mongolia." *Ethnomusicology Forum* 1, no. 45: 45–69.

Privratsky, Bruce. 2001. *Muslim Turkistan: Kazak Religion and Collective Memory.* London: Routledge.

Radio Free Europe/Radio Liberty (RFE/RL) Kazakh Service. 2008. Kazakh Police Clash with Protesters on Independence Day. December 16. https://www.rferl.org/a/Ka zakh_Police_Clash_With_Protesters_On_Independence_Day/1360286.html.

Radio Free Europe/Radio Liberty (RFE/RL) Kazakh Service. 2015. Kazakhs Mark Independence Day, Deadly Protest Anniversaries. December 16. https://www.rferl .org/a/kazakhstan-anniversaries-independence-day/27431299.html.

Radio Free Europe/Radio Liberty (RFE/RL) Kazakh Service. 2018. Activists, Journalists Detained as Kazakhstan Marks Anniversary of Independence. December 16. https://www.rferl.org/a/activists-journalists-detained-as-kazakhstan-marks-anni versary-of-independence/29658974.html.Rancier, Megan. 2014. "The Musical Instrument as National Archive: A Case Study of the Kazakh Qyl-qobyz." *Ethnomusicology* 58, no. 3: 379–404.

Rapport, Evan. 2014. *Greeted with Smiles: Bukharian Jewish Music and Musicians in New York.* New York: Oxford University Press.

Ricoeur, Paul. 2004. *Memory, History, Forgetting.* Translated by Kathleen Blamey and David Pellauer. Chicago: University of Chicago Press.

Robinson, Gregory J. 2013. "Remembering the Borderlands: Traditional Music and the Post-Frontier in Aisén, Chile." *Ethnomusicology* 57, no. 3: 455–84.

Roi, Yaacov, and Alon Wainer. 2009. "Muslim Identity and Islamic Practice in Post-Soviet Central Asia." *Central Asian Survey* 28, no. 3: 303–22.

Rorlich, Azade-Ayşe. 2000. Kazakh Intellectuals, Identity and Collective Memory:

Echoes of Recent Debates. *Cahiers d'études sur la Méditerranée orientale et le mode turco-iraniaen* 29, no. 1: 261–70.

Rouby, Catherine. 2015. *Olfaction, Taste, and Cognition.* Cambridge: Cambridge University Press.

Ryan, W. F. 1999. *The Bathhouse at Midnight: An Historical Survey of Magic and Divination in Russia.* Magic in History. University Park: Pennsylvania State University Press.

Sanadjian, Manuchehr. 1995. "Temporality of 'Home' and Spatiality of Market in Exile: Iranians in Germany." *New German Critique* 64: 3–36.

Sarbasova, Kumysai. 2004. "O chem poet Ulytau?" [What Does Ulytau Sing About?]. *Stolichnaya Zhizn'* [Life in the Capital] , November 18, 2004.

Savage, Roger W. H. 2009. "Being, Transcendence, and the Ontology of Music." *World of Music* 52, no. 2: 5–20.

Schatz, Edward. 2004. *Modern Clan Politics: The Power of "Blood" in Kazakhstan and Beyond.* Jackson School Publications in International Studies. Seattle: University of Washington Press.

Schrode, Paula. 2008. "The Dynamics of Orthodoxy and Heterodoxy in Uyghur Religious Practice." *Die Welt des Islams* 48: 394–433.

Schwab, Wendell. 2012. "Traditions and Texts: How Two Young Women Learned to Interpret the Qur'an and Hadiths in Kazakhstan." *Contemporary Islam: Dynamics of Muslim Life* 6, no. 2: 173–97.

Shannon, Jonathan H. 2007. "Performing Al-Andalus, Remembering Al-Andalus: Mediterranean Soundings from Mashriq to Maghrib." *Journal of American Folklore* 120, no. 477: 308–34.

Shannon, Jonathan Holt. 2015. *Performing Al-Andalus: Music and Nostalgia across the Mediterranean.* Public Cultures of the Middle East and North Africa. Bloomington: Indiana University Press.

Shirane, Haruo. 2012. *Japan and the Culture of the Four Seasons: Nature, Literature, and the Arts.* New York: Columbia University Press.

Simeti, Mary Taylor. 1986. *On Persephone's Island: A Sicilian Journal.* New York: Vintage Books.

Slominski, Tes. 2015. "Doin' Time with Meg and Cris, Thirty Years Later: The Queer Temporality of Pseudonostalgia." *Women and Music: A Journal of Gender and Culture* 19, no. 1: 86–94.

Smart, Alan, and Josephine Smart. 2008. "Time-space Punctuation: Hong Kong's Border Regime and Limts on Mobility." *Pacific Affairs* 81, no. 2: 175–93.

Smith, Anthony. 2013. "'The Land and Its People': Reflections on Artistic Identification in an Age of Nations and Nationalism." *Nations and Nationalism* 19, no. 2, 87–106.

Smith, Zadie. Interviewed by Terry Gross, NPR, November 25, 2016.

soviet chick from Latvia. "excellent!" September 21, 2005. IMDB. Accessed October 28, 2008, http://www.imdb.com/user/ur7245446/comments.

spaceblossom from Ukraine. Perfect encapsulation of the Russian spirit, May 16, 2005. IMDB. Accessed October 28, 2008, http://www.imdb.com/user/ur3754133/comments.

Stoler, Ann Laura. 2016. *Duress: Imperial Durabilities in Our Times.* Durham, NC: Duke University Press.

Stone, Ruth M. 2008. *Theory for Ethnomusicology.* Upper Saddle River, NJ: Pearson.

Stone, Ruth M. 2010 [1982]. *Let the Inside Be Sweet: The Interpretation of Music Event among the Kpelle of Liberia.* Bloomington, IN: Trickster Press.

Sultanova, Razia. 2014. *From Shamanism to Sufism: Women, Islam and Culture in Central Asia.* London: I. B. Taurus, 2014.

Svanberg, Ingvar, ed. 1999. *Contemporary Kazaks: Cultural and Social Perspectives.* New York: St. Martin's Press.

Tilmans, Karin, Frank van Vree, and Jay Winter. 2010. *Performing the Past: Memory, History, and Identity in Modern Europe.* Amsterdam: Amsterdam University Press.

Tosic, Jelena. 2017. "Travelling Genealogies: Tracing Relatedness and Diversity in the Albanian-Montenegrin Borderland." In Donnan, Hurd, and Leutloff-Grandits, *Migrating Borders*, 80–101.

trionon0o7. "Superb," February, 17, 2006. IMDB. Accessed November 18, 2019, https://m.imdb.com/user/ur9394109/reviews?ref_=m_ur.

Tsing, Ann Lowenhaupt. 2015. *The Mushroom at the End of the World: On the Possibility of Life in Capitalist Ruins.* Princeton, NJ: Princeton University Press.

Tuhkanen, Mikko. 2007. "'Out of Joint': Passing, Haunting, and the Time of Slavery in Hagar's Daughter." *American Literature* 79, no. 2: 335–61.

Turner, Victor. 1974. "Liminal to Liminoid, in Play, Flow, and Ritual: An Essay in Comparative Symbology." *Rice Institute Pamphlet—Rice University Studies* 60, no. 3: 53–92.

Turner, Victor Witter. 1969. *The Ritual Process: Structure and Anti-structure.* Chicago: Aldine.

UNESCO World Heritage. Accessed March 24, 2014, http://whc.unesco.org/en/list/1145.

Viejo-Rose, Dacia. 2011. "Memorial Functions: Intent, Impact and the Right to Remember." *Memory Studies* 4, no. 4: 465–80.

Villarejo, Amy. 2014. *Ethereal Queer: Television, Historicity, Desire.* Durham, NC: Duke University Press.

Vishnevsky, A., and Z. Zayonchkovskaya. 1994. "Emigration from the Former Soviet Union: The Fourth Wave." In *European Migration in the Late Twentieth Century: Historical Patterns, Actual Trends and Social Implications*, edited by Heinz Fassmann and Rainer Münz, 239–59. Hants: Edward Elgar.

Wallerstein, Immanuel. 2005. "Putin's Diplomatic Triumph." Commentary no. 161, Fernand Braudel Center, May 15, 2005. Accessed December 20, 2018, https://www.binghamton.edu/fbc/commentaries.

Watkins, Lee. 2009. "Minstrelsy and Mimesis in the South China Sea: Filipino Migrant Musicians, Chinese Hosts, and the Disciplining of Relations in Hong Kong." *Asian Music* 40, no. 2: 72–99.

Weiner, Amir. 2001. *Making Sense of War: The Second World War and the Fate of the Bolshevik Revolution*. Princeton, NJ: Princeton University Press.

Werner, Cynthia, and Holly Barcus. 2015. "The Unequal Burdens of Repatriation: A Gendered View of the Transnational Migration of Mongolia's Kazakh Population." *American Anthropologist* 117, no. 2: 257–71.

Wetters, Kirk. 2008. *Opinion System: Impasses of the Public Sphere from Hobbes to Habermas*. New York: Fordham University Press.

Whitehead, Colson. 2016. *The Underground Railroad*. New York: Doubleday.

Winter, Jay. 1995. *Sites of Memory, Sites of Mourning: The Great War in European Cultural History*. Cambridge: Cambridge University Press.

Winter, Jay. 2006. *Remembering War: The Great War between Memory and History in the Twentieth Century*. New Haven, CT: Yale University Press.

Witmore, Christopher. 2006. "Vision, Media, Noise and the Percolation of Time: Symmetrical Approaches to the Mediation of the Material World." *Journal of Material Culture* 11: 267–92.

Wong, Chuen-Fung. 2012. "Reinventing the Central Asian Rawap in Modern China: Musical Stereotypes, Minority Modernity, and Uyghur Instrumental Music." *Asian Music* 43, no. 1: 34–63.

Wong, Ketty. 2012. *Whose National Music? Identity, Mestizaje, and Migration in Ecuador*. Studies in Latin American and Caribbean Music. Philadelphia: Temple University Press.

Yemelianova, Galina M. 2014. "Islam, National Identity and Politics in Contemporary Kazakhstan." *Asian Ethnicity* 15, no. 3: 286–301.

Zardykhan, Zharmukhamed. 2004. "Russians in Kazakhstan and Demographic Change: Imperial Legacy and the Kazakh Way of Nation Building." *Asian Ethnicity* 5, no. 1: 61–79.

Zerubavel, Eviatar. 1981. *Hidden Rhythms: Schedules and Calendars in Social Life*. Berkeley: University of California Press.

Zerubavel, Eviatar. 2003. *Time Maps: Collective Memory and the Social Shape of the Past*. Chicago: University of Chicago Press.

Zhanaidarov, Orynbai. 2003. *Mening elim Kazakstan: balalargha arnalghan entsiklopediia* [My Nation Kazakhstan: A Children's Encyclopedia]. Almaty: Balausa Baspasy.

Zhanguttin, B. 2016. "Evacuation of the Soviet population in Kazakhstan (1941–1942). *New History Bulletin* 14: 73–84.

Zheng, Su. 2010. *Claiming Diaspora: Music, Transnationalism, and Cultural Politics in Asian/Chinese America.* American Musicspheres. Oxford: Oxford University Press.

Zhumakhanov, T., T. Shabai, B. Zhumataev, and L. I. Tetenko. 2004. *Drevnii Kazakhstan: detskaia entsiklopediia Kazakhstana* [Ancient Kazakhstan: Children's Encyclopedia of Kazakhstan]. Almaty: Aruna.

INDEX

Note: Page numbers in *italics* refer to figures.